LIFE OF JESUS RESEARCH
AN ANNOTATED BIBLIOGRAPHY

NEW TESTAMENT TOOLS
AND STUDIES

EDITED BY

BRUCE M. METZGER, Ph.D., D.D., L.H.D., D.Theol., D.Litt.

Professor of New Testament Language and Literature, Emeritus
Princeton Theological Seminary
and
Corresponding Fellow of the British Academy

VOLUME XIII

LIFE OF JESUS RESEARCH
AN ANNOTATED BIBLIOGRAPHY

BY

CRAIG A. EVANS, Ph.D.

Chairman, Department of Biblical Studies
Trinity Western University
Langley, British Columbia

E.J. BRILL
LEIDEN • NEW YORK • KØBENHAVN • KÖLN
1989

For Lee Martin McDonald
Mentor, Colleague, and Friend

Library of Congress Cataloging-in-Publication Data

Evans, Craig A.
    Life of Jesus research: an annotated bibliography/by Craig A.
Evans.
    p.   cm. — (New Testament tools and studies, ISSN 00778842;
v.   12)
    Includes bibliographical references.
    ISBN 9004091807
    1. Jesus Christ—Biography—Bibliography. 2. Jesus Christ—
Biography—History and criticism. I. Title. II. Series.
Z8455.E94   1989
    [BT301.9]
    016.2329'01—dc20   89-35243
                                                                              CIP

ISSN   0077-8842
ISBN   90 04 09180 7

PRINTED IN THE NETHERLANDS BY E. J. BRILL

CONTENTS

PREFACE

It is often in the class room that the idea for a book comes to mind. After years of preparing for my students bibliographies on various aspects of the life of Jesus, it occurred to me that my colleagues and their students might also find these bibliographies useful. Soon the opportunity to make these available arose when I was asked to prepare an annotated bibliography for another series. No sooner was the first draft complete when the series was cancelled. (It has since, I understand, been resurrected.) I showed the manuscript to Professor Bruce M. Metzger and he graciously accepted it for inclusion in his series, New Testament Tools and Studies. To him I owe my thanks. My thanks are also due to President Thomas W. Gillespie, who invited me to spend my sabbatical leave at Princeton Theological Seminary as a Visting Fellow, to the Rev. Sandra Hughes Boyd, Public Services Librarian at Speer Library, whose cheerful and expert assistance enabled me to exploit my time of study to its fullest, and to Mr. Richard A. Wiebe, Reference Librarian at Trinity Western University, for preparing the indexes in his usual competent and expeditious manner. Finally, I wish to take the opportunity to express my appreciation for my long-time friend and mentor, Dr. Lee Martin McDonald, to whom this volume is appropriately dedicated, who first aroused my interest in research in the gospels and in the intriguing problem of the historical Jesus.

Trinity Western University   C. A. Evans
Langley, British Columbia
April, 1989

ABBREVIATIONS

ABRL	Anchor Bible Reference Library
ANQ	*Andover Newton Quarterly*
ANRW	W. Haase and E. Temporini, eds., *Aufsteig und Niedergang der römischen Welt* II (Berlin: de Gruyter, 1979-87)
ANTJ	Arbeiten zum Neuen Testament und Judentum
ASNU	Acta seminarii neotestamentici upsaliensis
ATD	Acta Theologica Danica
ATLA	American Theological Library Association Bibliography Series
ATR	*Anglican Theological Review*
AusBR	*Australian Biblical Review*
BBB	Bonner biblische Beiträge
BEvT	Beiträge zur evangelischen Theologie
BFCT	Beiträge zur Förderung christlicher Theologie
BG	Berlin Gnostic Codex
Bib	*Biblica*
BibT	*Biblical Theology*
Bij	*Bijdragen*
BJRL	*Bulletin of the John Rylands University Library of Manchester*
BO	*Bibliotheca Orientalis*
BR	*Biblical Research*
BSac	*Bibliotheca Sacra*
BTB	*Biblical Theology Bulletin*
BTS	*Bible et Terre Sainte*
BWANT	Beiträge zur Wissenschaft vom Alten und Neuen Testament
BZ	*Biblische Zeitschrift*
BZNW	Beihefte zur Zeitschrift für die neutestamentliche Wissenschaft
C	*Catholica*
CBQ	*Catholic Biblical Quarterly*
CBQMS	Catholic Biblical Quarterly Monograph Series
CH	Calwer Hefte
ChrCent	*Christian Century*
ChrCris	*Christianity and Crisis: A Christian Journal of Opinion*
CJT	*Canadian Journal of Theology*
col(s).	column(s)
ComVia	*Communio Viatorum*
ConcorJ	*Concordia Journal*
CQR	*Church Quarterly Review*

Crit	*Criterion*
CSR	*Christian Scholars Review*
CTM	*Concordia Theological Monthly*
Dial	*Dialog*
DLZ	*Deutsche Literaturzeitung*
DRev	*Downside Review*
DrewG	*Drew Gateway*
DTT	*Dansk teologisk tidsskrift*
ed(s).	edition, editor(s), or edited
EgliseTh	*Église et Théologie*
EK	*Evangelische Kommentare*
Encount	*Encounter*
EpworthRev	*Epworth Review*
EstBíb	*Estudios Bíblicos*
ET	English translation
ETR	*Études théologiques et religieuses*
EvFo	Evangelisches Forum
EvQ	*Evangelical Quarterly*
EvT	*Evangelische Theologie*
ExpTim	*Expository Times*
FBBS	Facet Books, Biblical Series
FF	*Forschungen und Fortschritte*
Forum	*Forum: Foundations and Facets*
FRLANT	Forschungen zur Religion und Literatur des Alten und Neuen Testaments
FSÖT	Forschungen zur systematischen und ökumenischen Theologie
FT	French Translation
FZPT	*Freiburger Zeitschrift für Philosophie und Theologie*
GA	Gesammelte Aufsätze
GNS	Good News Studies
Greg	*Gregorianum*
GT	German translation
HBD	*Harper's Bible Dictionary*
HBT	*Horizons in Biblical Theology*
HeyJ	*Heythrop Journal*
HibJ	*Hibbert Journal*
HTR	*Harvard Theological Review*
HUCA	*Hebrew Union College Annual*
IBR	Institute for Biblical Research
IBS	*Irish Biblical Studies*
IDB	*Interpreter's Dictionary of the Bible*
IJPR	*International Journal for Philosophy of Religion*

IJT	*Indian Journal of Theology*
Interp	*Interpretation*
IRT	Issues in Religion and Theology
ITQ	*Irish Theological Quarterly*
JAAR	*Journal of the American Academy of Religion*
JBL	*Journal of Biblical Literature*
JBR	*Journal of Bible and Religion*
JC	Judaica et Christiana
JETS	*Journal of the Evangelical Theological Society*
JHS	*Journal of Historical Studies*
JJS	*Journal of Jewish Studies*
JR	*Journal of Religion*
JSNT	*Journal for the Study of the New Testament*
JSNTSup	Journal for the Study of the New Testament, Supplement Series
JTC	*Journal for Theology and the Church*
JTS	*Journal of Theological Studies*
Jud	*Judaica: Beiträge zum Verständnis des jüdischen Schiksals in Vergangenheit und Gegenwart*
KD	*Kerygma und Dogma*
KiZ	*Kirchen in der Zeit*
LCL	Loeb Classical Library
LQ	*Lutheran Quarterly*
LTK	*Lexikon für Theologie und Kirche*
LumVie	*Lumière et Vie*
McCQ	*McCormick Quarterly*
ModCh	*The Modern Churchman*
ModTh	*Modern Theology*
MPTh	*Monatsschrift für Pastoraltheologie*
MS(S).	manuscript(s)
MTZ	*Münchener theologische Zeitschrift*
NBlack	*New Blackfriars*
NHL	Nag Hammadi Library
NHS	Nag Hammadi Studies
NovT	*Novum Testamentum*
n.p.	no publisher (cited)
NRT	*Nouvelle Revue Théologique*
n.s.	new series
NTM	New Testament Message
NTS	*New Testament Studies*
NTTij	*Nederlands Theologisch Tijdschrift*
NTTS	New Testament Tools and Studies
Numen	*Numen: International Review for the History of Religions*

NZST	*Neue Zeitschrift für systematische Theologie und Religionsphilosophie*
PerRelSt	*Perspectives in Religious Studies*
PIBA	*Proceedings of the Irish Biblical Association*
PrincSB	*Princeton Seminary Bulletin*
PSTJ	*Perkins School of Theology Journal*
QD	Quaestiones Disputatae
RB	*Revue biblique*
RCB	*Revista de Cultura Biblica*
Ref	*Reformatio*
RelS	*Religious Studies*
repr.	reprint(ed)
RestQ	*Restoration Quarterly*
rev.	revised
RevExp	*Review and Expositor*
RGG	*Religion in Geschichte und Gegenwart*
RHPR	*Revue d'histoire et de philosophie religieuses*
RL	*Religion in Life*
RR	*Review of Religion*
RSB	*Religious Studies Bulletin*
RSPT	*Revue des sciences philosophiques et théologiques*
RSR	*Recherches de science religieuse*
RSRev	*Religious Studies Review*
RTR	*The Reformed Theological Review*
SB	Stuttgarter Bibelstudien
SBB	Stuttgarter Biblische Beiträge
SBET	*Scottish Bulletin of Evangelical Theology*
SBLSemPap	*Society of Biblical Literature Seminar Papers*
SBT	Studies in Biblical Theology
Scr	*Scripture*
SE	*Studia Evangelica*
SEÅ	*Svensk exegetisk årsbok*
SHT	Studies in Historical Theology
SIJB	Schriften des Institutum Judaicum in Berlin
SJT	*Scottish Journal of Theology*
SNT	Studien zum Neuen Testament
SNTSMS	Society for New Testament Studies Monograph Series
SPB	Studia postbiblica
SR	*Studies in Religion/Sciences religieuses*
ST	*Studia Theologica*
SVTQ	*Saint Vladimir's Theological Quarterly*
SWJT	*Southwest Journal of Theology*

TBR	Theological and Biblical Resources
TEv	*Theologia Evangelica*
TF	*Theologische Forschung*
Th	*Theology*
ThB	*Theologische Beiträge*
ThEx	Theologische Existenz heute
ThLife	*Theology and Life*
TLZ	*Theologische Literaturzeitung*
TQ	*Theologische Quartalschrift*
TRev	*Theologische Revue*
TrinJ	*Trinity Journal*
TRu	*Theologische Rundschau*
TS	*Theological Studies*
TSF	Theological Students Fellowship
TSK	*Theologische Studien und Kritiken*
TTij	*Theologisch Tijdschrift*
TToday	*Theology Today*
TTZ	*Trierer Theologische Zeitschrift*
TU	Texte und Untersuchungen
TynBul	*Tyndale Bulletin*
TZ	*Theologische Zeitschrift*
UnSanc	*Una Sancta*
USQR	*Union Seminary Quarterly Review*
WMANT	Wissenschaftliche Monographien zum Alten und Neuen Testament
WUNT	Wissenschaftliche Untersuchungen zum Neuen Testament
VC	*Vigiliae Christianae*
VF	*Verkündigung und Forschung*
ZKT	*Zeitschrift für katholische Theologie*
ZNW	*Zeitschrift für die neutestamentliche Wissenschaft*
ZRGG	*Zeitschrift für Religions- und Geistesgeschichte*
ZTK	*Zeitschrift für Theologie und Kirche*
ZZ	*Zeichen der Zeit*

Introduction

Life of Jesus Research: An Annotated Bibliography provides bibliography that concentrates on the most significant scholarship concerned with the problem of the historical Jesus and special topics. Every attempt has been made to provide complete bibliographical information, i.e., original language and edition, translations, if any, into other major languages, and most recent edition. Brief notes or comments are included with most of the bibliographic items. All major sections and subsections are introduced. These introductions are intended primarily for the beginning student, for it is assumed that the veteran scholar needs no such introduction. The book also includes excerpts from the most important extra-biblical sources that make reference to Jesus. An Index to Modern Authors that is keyed to the bibliographical items enables the reader to locate the works of a given scholar with ease.

The volume is divided into three major sections. The first section cites bibliographies and surveys of research. The second section provides the bibliography concerned with the scholarly quest of the historical Jesus. Although many of these items are concerned with various topics (e.g., Jesus' parables), they are cited here because they make a significant contribution to historical Jesus scholarship. The third section is broken down into several subsections which cover various special topics (e.g., demythologization, criteria of authenticity, etc.). Most of these studies are written with the question of the historical Jesus very much in mind.

In its original form the bibliography was complete only to the end of 1987. A delay in publication, however, has allowed for the inclusion of a few items that appeared in 1988.

BIBLIOGRAPHIES AND SURVEYS OF RESEARCH

A. *Introduction*

The items cited in this section are particularly valuable for their bibliographies and surveys of the scholarly problem of the historical Jesus, though many of the studies cited in Sections 2 and 3 also provide helpful bibliographical material. Other reports of research will be will found in Section 2. The Indices below are cited in alphabetical order, but the other items are in chronological order.

B. *Indices*

1   P.-E. Langevin, ed., *Bibliographie Biblique I: 1930-70; II: 1930-1975; III: 1930-1983* (3 vols.; Quebec: Les Presses de l'Université Laval, 1972, 1978, 1985).

2   B. M. Metzger, *Index to Periodical Literature on Christ and the Gospels* (NTTS 6; Leiden: Brill, 1966). See pp. 40-51, 188-191.

3   *New Testament Abstracts* 1 (1956) — present.

4   P. Nober, *Elenchus Bibliographicus Biblicus* (Rome: Pontifical Biblical Institute, 1968 — present).

5   *Religion Index One* 13 (1977) — present; formerly called *Index to Religious Periodical Literature* 1-12 (1949-76).

6   *Religion Index Two* 1 (1970) — present.

C. *Books*

7   A. Schweitzer, *Von Reimarus zu Wrede: Eine Geschichte des Leben-Jesu-Forschung* (Tübingen: Mohr, 1906; 2nd ed.: *Die Geschichte der Leben-*

Jesu-Forschung, 1913); ET: *The Quest of the Historical Jesus: A Critical Study of its Progress from Reimarus to Wrede* (London: A & C Black, 1910; with Introduction by J. M. Robinson; New York: Macmillan, 1968). Outstanding survey of nineteenth-century quest. See comments in Section 2.

8   C. C. McCown, *The Search for the Real Jesus: A Century of Historical Study* (New York: Scribner's, 1940). Discusses D. F. Strauss, Hegelianism, F. C. Baur, historiography, A. Harnack, A. Schweitzer.

9   J. G. H. Hoffmann, *Les Vies de Jésus et le Jésus de l'histoire: Étude de la valeur historique des Vies de Jésus de langue français, non catholiques, d'Ernest Renan à Charles Guignebert* (ASNU 17; Lund: Gleerups; Copenhagen: Munksgaard; Paris: Messageries evangéliques, 1947). Critical survey of the works of E. Renan, J. Bovon, A. Loisy, M. Goguel, and other French scholars.

10   H. K. McArthur, *The Quest through the Centuries: The Search for the Historical Jesus* (Philadelphia: Fortress, 1966). A survey of life of Jesus study.

11   N. Perrin, *Rediscovering the Teaching of Jesus* (New York: Harper & Row, 1967; 2nd ed., 1976). See pp. 249-66 for several brief, but very helpful, annotated bibliographies.

12   H. Zahrnt, "Die Wiederentdeckung des historischen Jesus," in Zahrnt, *Die Sache mit Gott. Die protestantische Theologie im 20. Jahrhundert* (Munich: Piper, 1966) 326-81; ET: "The Rediscovery of the Historical Jesus," in Zahrnt, *The Question of God: Protestant Theology in the Twentieth Century* (New York: Harcourt, Brace & World, 1969) 253-94. An excellent survey of the new quest.

13   G. Aulén, *Jesus i nutida historisk forskning* (2nd ed., Stockholm: Verbum, 1974); ET: *Jesus in Contemporary Historical Research* (Philadelphia: Fortress, 1976). Good critical survey and bibliography; observes an increasing tendency among scholars to view gospels as containing reliable historical material.

14   D. E. Aune, *Jesus and the Synoptic Gospels* (TSF-IBR Bibliographic Study Guides; Madison: TSF, 1980). Annotated bibliography is provided; see pp. 1-4, 42-48.

15 D. L. Pals, *The Victorian "Lives" of Jesus* (Trinity University Monograph Series in Religion; San Antonio: Trinity University, 1982). As counterpart to Schweitzer's German focus (see 7) Pals surveys the British quest of the historical Jesus.

16 W. B. Tatum, *In Quest of Jesus: A Guidebook* (Atlanta: John Knox, 1982). Provides a good introductory survey and basic bibliography; pays close attention to the crucial issues.

17 C. Brown, *Jesus in European Protestant Thought, 1778-1860* (SHT 1; Durham: Labyrinth, 1985). Critical survey and bibliography; assessment in many ways quite different from that of Schweitzer's (see 7).

18 D. J. Harrington, *The New Testament: A Bibliography* (TBR 2; Wilmington: Glazier, 1985). See pp. 81-89.

19 W. S. Kissinger, *The Lives of Jesus: A History and Bibliography* (New York: Garland, 1985). Helpful introductory survey of the scholarly quest; bibliography of lives of Jesus, however, is cluttered with hundreds of unscholarly contributions.

20 W. G. Kümmel, *Dreissig Jahre Jesusforschung (1950-80)* (BBB 60; ed. H. Merklein; Bonn: Hanstein, 1985). Collection of bibliographical articles originally published in *TRu* 31 (1965-66) 15-46, 289-315; 40 (1975) 289-336; 41 (1976) 197-258, 295-363; 43 (1978) 105-61, 233-65; 45 (1980) 40-84, 293-337; 46 (1981) 317-63; 47 (1982) 136-65, 348-83. One of the most valuable resources for research on the historical Jesus.

21 E. G. Lawler, *David Friedrich Strauss and His Critics: The Life of Jesus Debate in Early Nineteenth-Century German Journals* (New York: Lang, 1986). An invaluable aid to research on the nineteenth-century quest.

22 J. H. Charlesworth, *Jesus Within Judaism* (ABRL; Garden City: Doubleday, 1988). Provides annotated bibliography of recent scholarship. See comments in Section 2.

D. *Articles*

23 P. Feine, "Die Aufgabe der heutigen Jesusforschung," *Studien und Kritiken zur Theologie* (TSK 103; Gotha: Leopold Klotz, 1931) 161-78. Reviews and assesses some of the most important historical Jesus research to date.

24   D. T. Rowlingson, "The Continuing Quest of the Historical Jesus," in E.
      P. Booth, ed., *New Testament Studies: Critical Essays in New Testament
      Study* (New York and Nashville: Abingdon-Cokesbury, 1942) 42-69.
      Reviews recent form and source critical work, and several recent books on
      Jesus (1918-40).

25   S. Ben-Chorin, "Das Jesusbild im modernen Judentum," *ZRGG* 5 (1953)
      231-57. A survey of recent Jewish studies in the historical Jesus, including
      those by H.-J. Schoeps, J. Klausner, R. Eisler, C. G. Montefiore, and oth-
      ers.

26   P. Biehl, "Zur Frage nach dem historischen Jesus," *TRu* 24 (1957) 54-76.
      Examines the views of R. Bultmann, H. Diem, E. Heitsch, E. Käsemann,
      N. Dahl, and E. Fuchs.

27   H. Conzelmann, "Jesus Christus," *RGG* 3 (3rd ed., 1959) cols. 619-53;
      ET: *Jesus* (Philadelphia: Fortress, 1973). Excellent introduction and
      bibliography.

28   H. K. McArthur, "Basic Issues: A Survey of Recent Gospel Research,"
      Interp 18 (1964) 39-55.

29   H. C. Kee, "The Historical Jesus: A Survey of Literature (1959-65),"
      DrewG 36 (1965-66) 44-49.

30   J. H. Elliott, "The Historical Jesus, the Kerygmatic Christ, and the
      Eschatological Community," *CTM* 37 (1966) 470-91.

31   H. Conzelmann, "Ergebnisse wissenschaftlich-theologischer Forschung?
      Neue Taschenbücher über Jesus," *Evangelischer Erzieher* 23 (1971) 254-62.

32   P. Grech, "Recent Developments in the Jesus of History Controversy,"
      BTB 1 (1971) 190-213.

33   W. Horbury, "Passion Narratives and Historical Criticism," *Th* 75 (1972)
      58-71.

34   J. Roloff, "Auf der Suche nach einem neuen Jesusbild: Tendenzen und
      Aspekte der gegenwärtigen Diskussion," *TLZ* 98 (1973) cols. 561-72.

35   J. Reumann, "'Lives of Jesus' During the Great Quest for the Historical Jesus," *IJT* 23 (1974) 33-59.

36   L. S. Wai, "The Problem of the Historical Jesus," *ThLife* 3 (1980) 53-67.

37   J. P. Galvin, "Schillebeeckx: Retracing the Story of Jesus: Theology as Narrative," *Worldview* 24 (1981) 10-12.

38   E. Stauffer, "Jesus, Geschichte und Verkündigung," *ANRW* 25/1 (1982) 3-130. See comments in Section 2.

39   P. W. Hollenbach, "Recent Historical Jesus Studies and the Social Sciences," *SBLSemPap* 22 (1983) 61-78.

40   I. W. Batdorf, "Interpreting Jesus since Bultmann: Selected Paradigms and Their Hermeneutic Matrix," *SBLSemPap* 23 (1984) 187-215.

41   H. Koester, "Überlieferung und Geschichte der frühchristlichen Evangelien-literatur," *ANRW* 25/2 (1984) 1463-1542.

42   J. H. Charlesworth, "Research on the Historical Jesus," *PIBA* 9 (1985) 19-37. Reviews and discusses work from 1980 to 1984.

43   H. L. Stein-Schneider, "À la recherche du Judas historique: une enquête exégétique à la lumière des textes de l'ancien testament et des *logia*," *ETR* 60 (1985) 403-23.

44   J. H. Charlesworth, "From Barren Mazes to Gentle Rappings: The Emergence of Jesus Research," *PrincSB* 7 (1986) 221-30. Survey with annotated bibliography; see *Jesus Within Judaism* (22).

45   J. R. Michaels, "Off on a New Quest for the Historical Jesus," *Books and Religion* 14 (1986) 3-4. Surveys recent work.

46   C. A. Evans, "Jesus of Nazareth: Who Do Scholars Say that He Is?" *Crux* 23/4 (1987) 15-19. Review article of recent contributions by G. Vermes, B. F. Meyer, A. E. Harvey, E. P. Sanders, and others.

47   E. W. Stegemann, "Aspekte neuerer Jesusforschung," *Der Evangelische Erzieher* 39 (1987) 10-17. Reviews recent trends.

48   C. A. Evans, "The Historical Jesus and Christian Faith: A Critical
      Assessment of a Scholarly Problem," *CSR* 18 (1988) 48-63. Survey and
      bibliography.

49   W. G. Kümmel, "Jesusforschung seit 1981," *TRu* 53 (1988) 229-49. Up-
      dates and continues work noted above (20).

GENERAL DISCUSSION

A. *Introduction*

The beginning of the life of Jesus research is traced back to the posthumous publication of seven writings of Hermann Samuel Reimarus, particularly fragment 7 entitled, *Von dem Zwecke Jesu und seiner Jünger* ["On the Aim of Jesus and His Disciples"], published in 1778 (see 51). Reimarus believed that Jesus had not anticipated his death, but had hoped to become Israel's earthly Messiah. After the crucifixion, his disciples reformulated Jesus' teachings and proclaimed his resurrection and return. This critical assessment of the gospel story of Jesus inaugurated the scholarly quest of the historical Jesus.

The nineteenth-century "Old Quest" of the historical Jesus represents the first major phase of this scholarly quest. In his *Das Leben Jesu, kritisch bearbeitet* ["The Life of Jesus Critically Examined"] (1835-36, see 58) David Friedrich Strauss argued that the gospels do not present us with history, whether embellished with supernatural elements (so the liberals), or not (so the conservatives), but present us with myth. Liberal and conservative scholars alike opposed this radical skepticism, and searched for what was then regarded as "historical" material. For a short time the Gospel of John was viewed as the best source, since it lacked some of the miraculous features of the synoptics (e.g., virgin birth, demon exorcisms), which many scholars viewed as mythological. But Ferdinand Christian Baur's *Kritische Untersuchungen über die kanonischen Evangelien* ["Critical Studies on the Canonical Gospels"] (Tübingen: L. F. Fues, 1847), which concluded that John was written late in the second century, brought an end to this thinking. It was then concluded that the historical Jesus would have to be found in the synoptic gospels after all. In his *Die synoptischen Evangelien: Ihr Ursprung und geschichtlicher Charakter* ["The Synoptic Gospels: Their Origin and Historical Character"] (1863, see 61) Heinrich Julius Holtzmann showed that Mark was written first, and that Matthew and Luke used it and another source of sayings (eventually called "Q" for the German word *Quelle*, "source"). Mark and Q became the sources from which a historical Jesus might be reconstructed. Most scholars assumed that these sources were relatively free from mythological embellishment.

With the appearance of certain publications at the turn of the century, it became evident that the old quest had not been successful. Martin Kähler's *Der sogenannte historische Jesus und der geschichtliche, biblische Christus* ["The So-Called Historical Jesus and the Historic, Biblical Christ"] (1892, see 65) argued that the historical Jesus of the nineteenth-century quest bore little resemblance to, or had little significance for, the Christ of faith. That same year Johannes Weiss published *Die Predigt Jesu vom Reiche Gottes* ["The Preaching of Jesus concerning the Kingdom of God"] (see 66), in which he argued that Jesus was not a social reformer, but an apocalyptic prophet who summoned people to repent because judgment was near. In 1901 William Wrede published *Das Messiasgeheimnis in den Evangelien* ["The Messianic Secret in the Gospels"] (see 68), in which he argued that far from being a simple historical account, Mark's gospel was a theologically-oriented document comparable to John's gospel. Finally, the appearance of Albert Schweitzer's *Von Reimarus zu Wrede* ["From Reimarus to Wrede"] (1906, see 71), in which he concluded that Jesus had died a deluded apocalyptic fanatic, led many scholars and theologians to believe that the quest of the historical Jesus was impossible (so the form critics) and perhaps even illegitimate (so many neo-orthodox theologians). Speaking as a form critic Rudolf Bultmann once stated that "we can now know almost nothing concerning the life and personality of Jesus" (*Jesus and the Word*, 1926, p. 8, see 77) The popular neo-orthodox theologian Emil Brunner claimed that "the Christian faith does not arise out of the picture of the historical Jesus" and that "the Jesus of history is not the same as the Christ of faith" (*The Mediator* [London: Lutterworth, 1934; Philadelphia: Westminster, 1957] p. 159). Moreover, the recognition, thanks largely to Schweitzer, that the lives of Jesus of the old quest reflected the issues and emphases of each generation of scholars (the major error of the old quest) led many to suppose that the objectivity necessary for a truly fair portrait of Jesus simply could not be had. Therefore, in many circles the scholarly quest was abandoned.

When in 1953 Ernst Käsemann read his paper, "Das Problem des historischen Jesus" ["The Problem of the Historical Jesus"] (see 111), a new quest of the historical Jesus was inaugurated among Bultmannian scholars. Käsemann argued that a new quest, one that was careful to avoid the errors of the old quest, was historically possible and theologically necessary. A link between the Christ of faith and the Jesus of history was necessary, if Christianity were to avoid lapsing into a form of docetic gnosticism. While Käsemann emphasized the recovery of certain authentic sayings of Jesus, Ernst Fuchs (see 121) argued for the presence of certain authentic actions or attitudes. Other Bultmannians to participate in the new quest included Hans Conzelmann, Erich Dinkler, Herbert Braun, Gerhard Ebeling, and James M. Robinson (see bibliography). The new quest is part of what is sometimes referred to as the "post-Bultmannian" movement.

In the 1960's and 70's life of Jesus research was continued, but often the emphasis was placed on Jesus as a social or political figure, rather than as one relevant for faith (as the emphasis had been during the new quest). For example, Jesus became the champion of the poor and the oppressed and as such is sometimes the inspiration for liberation theologies. Although the legitimacy of some of this work cannot be denied, one cannot help but wonder if the basic error of the old quest is recurring. Some of the studies that appeared in the 70's and 80's, however, seem to represent a return to a quest not governed by theological or political agendas. The emphasis now is on seeing Jesus against the background of first-century Palestinian Judaism. Among these are the works of C. H. Dodd (1970), John Bowker (1973), Geza Vermes (1974, 1984), A. E. Harvey (1982), Gerald Sloyan (1983), Marcus Borg (1984, 1987), E. P. Sanders (1985), and J. H. Charlesworth (1988). Unlike the "new quest," which had emphasized discontinuity between Jesus and his contemporaries, the more recent studies tend to emphasize continuity. These studies may very well usher in a new phase in the life of Jesus research.

B. *Bibliography*

1768-1900

50   J. J. Hess, *Geschichte der drei letzen Lebensjahre Jesu* (3 vols.; Leipzig and Zurich: Weidmann, 1768-72). Accepts most miracles as historical; doubts existence of demons; accepts essential historicity of the gospel narratives.

51   H. S. Reimarus, *Von dem Zwecke Jesu und seiner Jünger: Noch ein Fragment des Wolfenbüttelschen Ungenannten* (Fragment 7; G. E. Lessing, ed.; Braunschweig: [n.p.], 1778); ET: *Fragments from Reimarus consisting of Brief Critical Remarks on the Object of Jesus and His Disciples* (C. Voysey, ed.; London: Williams and Norgate, 1879; new ed.: *Reimarus: Fragments* (C. H. Talbert, ed.; Philadelphia: Fortress, 1970). The first critical attempt to distinguish a historical Jesus from the Jesus presented in the gospels and assumed to lie behind christology; part of a larger unpublished MS. entitled, *Apologie oder Schutzschrift für die vernünftigen Verehre Gottes.*

52   J. S. Semler, *Beantwortung der Fragmente eines Ungenannten insbesondere vom Zwecke Jesu und seiner Jünger* (Halle: Erziehungsinstituts, 1779; 2nd. ed., 1780). A critical response to H. S. Reimarus (51).

53   K. Bahrdt, *Ausführung des Plans und Zwecks Jesu* (4 vols.; Berlin: [n.p.], 1784-93). In response to Reimarus (51), an early attempt to grapple with the problem of myth in the gospels.

54   J. G. Herder, *Vom Erlöser der Menschen. Nach unsern drei ersten Evangelien* (Riga: Hartknoch, 1796). Offers a symbolic interpretation of the miracles in the synoptic gospels.

55   J. G. Herder, *Von Gottes Sohn, der Welt Heiland. Nach Johannes Evangelium* (Riga: Hartknoch, 1797). Offers a symbolic interpretation of the miracles in the fourth gospel.

56   K. Venturini, *Natürliche Geschichte des grossen Propheten von Nazareth* (3 vols.; Bethlehem: [n.p.], 1800-02). An attempt to produce a non-supernatural account of the historical Jesus.

57   H. E. G. Paulus, *Das Leben Jesu, als Grundlage einer reinen Geschichte des Urchristentums* (2 vols.; Heidelberg: Winter, 1828). Believes that a historical, non-supernatural Jesus can be recovered from the gospels.

58   D. F. Strauss, *Das Leben Jesu, kritisch bearbeitet* (2 Vols.; Tübingen: C. F. Osiander, 1835-36; repr. in 1984; 3rd ed., 1838-39); FT: *Vie de Jésus, un examen critique de son histoire* (2 vols.; Paris: Librairie de Ladrange, 1839-40); ET: *The Life of Jesus, critically examined* (3 vols.; London: Chapman, 1846; Philadelphia: Fortress, 1972; Lives of Jesus Series; London: SCM, 1973). Responding to the rationalist approaches of J. G. Herder (54,55) and H. E. G. Paulus (57), the gospel portrait of Jesus is viewed as mythological, with little of the Jesus of history recoverable.

59   J. E. Kuhn, *Das Leben Jesu, wissenschaftlich bearbeitet* (Mainz: Florian Kupferberg, 1838). An early Roman Catholic response to Strauss; argues that the gospels are historical, but not in ordinary sense of history, for the gospels give us "sacred history."

60   D. F. Strauss, *Hermann Samuel Reimarus und seine Schutzschrift für die vernünftigen Verehrer Gottes* (Leipzig: F. A. Brockhaus, 1862). Criticizes Reimarus's conspiracy theory (see 51) as naive and unconvincing.

61   H. J. Holtzmann, *Die synoptischen Evangelien: Ihr Ursprung und geschichtlicher Charakter* (Leipzig: Engelmann, 1863). Although chiefly concerned with the origin and relationship of the Synoptic gospels, there is a chapter on the historical Jesus entitled, "Lebensbild Jesu nach der Quelle A [i.e., Mark]" (pp. 468-96). In this chapter Holtzmann responds to Strauss and the scholarship from the 1830's to the 1860's. Holtzmann also offers his own sketch of the historical Jesus based upon Mark.

62 E. Renan, *La Vie de Jésus* (Paris: Michel Lévy Frères, 1863); ET: *The Life of Jesus* (New York: Random, 1955). The first major French work on the quest.

63 D. F. Strauss, *Das Leben Jesu für das deutsche Volk* (Leipzig: F. A. Brockhaus, 1864); ET: *A New Life of Jesus* (London and Edinburgh: Williams and Norgate, 1865). Less radical than earlier work, more in line with the contemporary liberal viewpoint. See 3rd ed. of *Das Leben Jesu kritisch bearbeitet* (58).

64 D. F. Strauss, *Der Christus des Glaubens und der Jesus der Geschichte: Eine Kritik des schleiermacher'schen Lebens Jesu* (Berlin: Franz Duncker, 1865); ET: *The Christ of Faith and the Jesus of History: A Critique of Schleiermacher's Life of Jesus* (Philadelphia: Fortress, 1977). Strauss faults Schleiermacher for failing to approach the subject free from presuppositions and for thinking that a fully human Jesus could nevertheless "stand above the whole of humanity."

65 M. Kähler, *Der sogenannte historische Jesus und der geschichtliche, biblische Christus* (Leipzig: A. Deichert, 1892; 2nd ed., 1896); ET: *The So-Called Historical Jesus and the Historic, Biblical Christ* (Philadelphia: Fortress, 1964). Called into question the relevance of the so-called "historical Jesus" for Christian faith, noted wide gap between the critical reconstruction of the historical Jesus of the nineteenth-century quest and the theological confession of the church, and concluded that the gospels simply do not offer the information necessary for the biography that so many have attempted to write.

66 J. Weiss, *Die Predigt Jesu vom Reiche Gottes* (Göttingen: Vandenhoeck & Ruprecht, 1892; 2nd ed., 1900; 3rd ed. edited by F. Hahn, with introduction by R. Bultmann, 1964); ET: *Jesus' Proclamation of the Kingdom of God* (Chico: Scholars, 1985). Argues that Jesus' preaching was apocalyptic, not social.

67 A. Harnack, *Das Wesen des Christentums* (Leipzig: Hinrichs, 1900); ET: *What is Christianity?* (London: Williams and Norgate, 1900); also trans. in French, Italian, Japanese, Dutch, Norwegian, Danish, Swedish, and Russian. Concluded that Jesus' teaching emphasized (1) the Kingdom of God and its coming, (2) God the Father and the infinite value of the human soul, and (3) higher righteousness and the love commandment.

1901-1940

68 W. Wrede, *Das Messiasgeheimnis in den Evangelien. Zugleich ein Beitrag zum Verständnis des Markusevangeliums* (Göttingen: Vandenhoeck & Ruprecht, 1901); ET: *The Messianic Secret* (Cambridge and London: James Clarke, 1971). Regards the messianic elements in Mark (and the other gospels) as read into the gospel by the post-Easter Church. Jesus was a teacher, a teller of parables, a healer, and an exorcist. He was popular with the people, viewed the Law in such a way that he felt that it was appropriate to associate with sinners. This leads to Pharisaic opposition and, when in Jerusalem, to the death of Jesus. Jesus was not condemned for claiming to be the Messiah.

69 A. Loisy, *L'Évangile et l'Eglise* (Paris: Picard, 1902); ET: *The Gospel and the Church* (London: Isbister, 1903; Philadelphia: Fortress, 1978). Argues that Harnack (67) has stripped the historical Jesus of the essentials.

70 H. Weinel, *Jesus im neunzehnten Jahrhundert* (Tübingen: Mohr [Siebeck], 1904). Contrary to Strauss (58), believed that the gospels are essentially historical and that the historical Jesus is sufficient for Christian faith.

71 A. Schweitzer, *Von Reimarus zu Wrede: Eine Geschichte des Leben-Jesu-Forschung* (Tübingen: Mohr [Siebeck], 1906); ET: *The Quest of the Historical Jesus: A Critical Study of its Progress from Reimarus to Wrede* (London: A & C Black, 1910; with Introduction by James M. Robinson; New York: Macmillan, 1968; rev. ed.: *Die Geschichte der Leben-Jesu-Forschung*, 1913; 6th ed., 1951). Masterful survey of nineteenth-century quest; proposes that Jesus be understood in terms of "thorough-going" eschatology.

72 E. Troeltsch, *Die Bedeutung der Geschichtlichkeit Jesu für den Glauben* (Tübingen: Mohr [Siebeck], 1911). Concluded that although the historicity of Jesus is important for Christian faith, Christian faith cannot be based upon the ever-changing results of critical-historical inquiry; regarded the "Christ-myth" theory of A. Drews (611) absurd.

73 S. J. Case, *The Historicity of Jesus* (Chicago: University of Chicago, 1912; 2nd ed., 1928). Responding to the "Christ-myth" theory, argues that Jesus was a pious teacher who taught that God was loving, forgiving, and inclusive.

74   G. H. Dalman, *Jesus-Jeschua* (Leipzig: Hinrich, 1922; 2nd ed., 1929); ET:
       Jesus-Jeshua (New York and London: Macmillan, 1929). Excellent for
       Semitic background.

75   J. Klausner, *Yeshu ha-Notzri* [Hebrew] (2 vols.; Jerusalem: Stybel, 1922);
       ET: *Jesus of Nazareth: His Life, Times, and Teaching* (London and New
       York: Macmillan, 1925; 3rd ed., 1952); FT: *Jésus de Nazareth* (Paris:
       Payot, 1933). One of the first serious attempts to understand Jesus against
       a Jewish background; concludes that "Jesus was convinced of his mes-
       siahship; of this there is no doubt; were it not so he would have been
       nothing more than a deceiver and imposter—and such men do not make
       history" (p. 342).

76   M. Goguel, *La Vie de Jésus* (Paris: Payot, 1925); ET: *The Life of Jesus*
       (London: Unwin, 1926; New York: Macmillan, 1933); repr. as *Jesus and
       the Origins of Christianity* (2 vols.; New York: Harper Torchbooks, 1960,
       with introduction by C. L. Mitton). Argues that Jesus broke with John the
       Baptist over the question of repentance and grace, that Jesus' preaching of
       the Kingdom was not apocalyptic, and that Jesus ministered in Jerusalem
       about six months (instead of one week).

77   R. Bultmann, *Jesus* (Berlin: Deutsche Bibliothek, 1926); ET: *Jesus and the
       Word* (New York: Scribner's, 1934, 1958); FT: *Jésus. Mythologie et
       Démythologisation* (Paris: Seuil, 1968). Bultmann's classic statement of
       Jesus' relationship to the Christian message; very skeptical of the historical
       content of the gospels: "I think that we can now know almost nothing
       concerning the life and personality of Jesus" (p. 8).

78   S. J. Case, *Jesus: A New Biography* (Chicago: University of Chicago,
       1927). Sees Jesus as a prophet of reform, gospels as products of the faith of
       the early Christian communities.

79   P. Feine, *Jesus* (Gütersloh: Bertelsmann, 1930). A comprehensive study of
       the historical sources and the various aspects of Jesus' person and ministry,
       with three chapters devoted to Jesus' proclamation of the Kingdom.

80   J. Mackinnon, *The Historic Jesus* (London: Longmans, 1931). Concludes
       that at his baptism, after much time of introspection, Jesus came to realize
       that he was the Messiah, but did not anticipate his rejection and death.

81   F.-M. Braun, *Où en est le problèm de Jésus?* (Paris: Gabalda, 1932). Criti-
       cally assesses the assumptions and conclusions of the life of Jesus research.

82   F. C. Burkitt, *Jesus Christ: an Historical Outline* (London and Glasgow:
        Blackie & Son, 1932). Accepts the essential historicity of Mark, believed
        largely to derive from Peter's "reminiscences," and examines problems
        arising from virtually every topic.

83   H. J. Cadbury, *The Peril of Modernizing Jesus* (New York: Macmillan,
        1937). Warns against reading modern ideas into the historical Jesus. To
        avoid this error it is necessary to (1) recognize our own prejudices, (2) learn
        the mentality of Jesus' times, and (3) study the gospels critically.

84   M. Dibelius, *Jesus* (Berlin: de Gruyter, 1939; 2nd ed., 1949); ET: *Jesus*
        (Philadelphia: Westminster, 1949; repr. 1963). Jesus' ministry is a sign of
        the presence of the Kingdom of God; the crucifixion is evidence that Jesus
        understood himself as the Messiah.

85   G. Ogg, *The Chronology of the Public Ministry of Jesus* (Cambridge:
        University Press, 1940; New York: Gordon Press, 1980). Argues for three-
        year public ministry and crucifixion in 33 CE.

                                    1941-1950

86   C. J. Cadoux, *The Historic Mission of Jesus: A Constructive Reexamina-
        tion of the eschatological Teaching in the Synoptic Gospels* (London: Lut-
        terworth; New York: Harper & Row, 1941). Concludes that Jesus did not
        expect to have his messianic credentials rejected, but hoped to avert the
        threatened clash between Israel and Rome.

87   J. W. Bowman, *The Intention of Jesus* (Philadelphia: Westminster, 1945).
        Concludes that Jesus, a "Messiah of the remnant," was a prophet calling
        people to return to God and be delivered from impending judgment and that
        he went to Jerusalem expecting to die.

88   W. G. Kümmel, *Verheissung und Erfüllung: Untersuchungen zur eschatol-
        ogischen Verkündigung Jesu* (Basel: Majer, 1945; 2nd ed., Zürich: Zwingli,
        1953); ET: *Promise and Fulfilment* (SBT 23; London: SCM, 1957).
        Argues that Jesus expected to appear as the Son of Man, but did not expect
        a long interim or the founding of the church.

89   W. Manson, *Jesus the Messiah* (Philadelphia: Westminster, 1946); GT: *Bist Du der da kommen soll?* (Zollikon-Zürich: Evangelischer Verlag, 1952). Argues that Jesus saw himself as Israel's Messiah, who proclaimed the fulfillment of Israel's eschatological hopes.

90   F.-M. Braun, *Jesus: Histoire et Critique* (Tournai: Casterman, 1947). Defends the essential historicity of the gospels, providing chapters devoted to the sources, background, Jesus' proclamation of the Kingdom, and the significance of the twelve.

91   H. J. Cadbury, *Jesus: What Manner of Man?* (New York: Macmillan, 1947; London: SPCK, 1962). Intended as a more positive sequel to *The Peril of Modernizing Jesus* (83), examines the novel features in Jesus' teaching and ministry.

92   G. S. Duncan, *Jesus, Son of Man* (London: Nisbet, 1947). Optimistic of recovering the historical Jesus, argues that Jesus understood himself and his message very differently from popular messianic expectation, although Jesus may have accepted the title "Messiah."

93   J. W. Bowman, "The Quest of the Historical Jesus," *Interp* 3 (1949) 184-93. Review of A. Schweitzer's *The Quest of the Historical Jesus* (71). Offers what he regards the critical review that Schweitzer deserved, but never received; claims that Schweitzer exaggerated the apocalyptic element in Jesus' teaching and psychologized beyond the limits of history.

94   M. S. Enslin, "Light from the Quest," *HTR* 42 (1949) 19-34. Argues that Jesus preached the Kingdom and the end of the world, but when these things did not materialize, the tradition came to view the disciples, not Jesus, as mistaken, a perspective from which Mark was written. Concludes: "We shall never see [Jesus] as he was" (p. 32).

95   J. McIntyre, "Christ and History," *RTR* 8 (1949) 9-42. Reviews the problem of the relation of Christian faith to historical evidence.

96   J. T. Noonan, "Renan's Life of Jesus: A Re-examination," *CBQ* 11 (1949) 26-39. A critical assessment of E. Renan's *La Vie de Jésus* (62).

97   H. Clavier, "Figure historique de Jésus," *RHPR* 30 (1950) 41-50. Review article of G. S. Duncan, *Jesus, Son of Man* (92).

1951-1955

98   D. T. Rowlingson, "On the Neglect of the Jesus of History," *RL* 20 (1951)
      541-52. Argues that the quest of the historical Jesus is not hopeless, but is
      necessary to the vitality of the Christian faith.

99   E. Fuchs, "Jesu Selbstzeugnis nach Mt 5," *ZTK* 51 (1952) 14-34; repr. in
      Fuchs, *Zur Frage nach dem historischen Jesus* (GA 2; Tübingen: Mohr
      [Siebeck], 1960) 100-25. Argues that Jesus' manner of teaching, as seen in
      Matthew 5, is an important aspect of Jesus' self-testimony.

100   E. Käsemann, "Zum Thema der Nichtobjektivierbarkeit," *EvT* 12 (1952/53)
      455-66; repr. in Käsemann, *Exegetische Versuche und Besinnungen* (vol. 1;
      Göttingen: Vandenhoeck & Ruprecht, 1960) 224-36; ET: "Is the Gospel
      Objective?" in Käsemann, *Essays on New Testament Themes* (SBT 41;
      London: SCM, 1964) 48-62. Argues that critical scholarship is incapable
      of objectifying the gospel or the historical Jesus; nothing can guarantee
      faith.

101   N. A. Dahl, "Problemet den historiske Jesus," in Dahl, *Rett laere og kjet-
      terske meninger* (Oslo: Land og Kirke, 1953) 156-202; expanded and pre-
      sented in German: "Der historische Jesus als geschichtswissenschaftliches
      und theologisches Problem," *KD* 1 (1955) 104-32; ET: "The Problem of
      the Historical Jesus," in C. E. Braaten and R. A. Harrisville, eds., *Kerygma
      and History: A Symposium on the Theology of Rudolf Bultmann*
      (Nashville: Abingdon, 1962) 138-71; repr. in Dahl, *The Crucified Messiah
      and Other Essays* (Minneapolis: Augsburg, 1974) 48-89, 173-74. Finds
      link between historical Jesus and Christ of faith, for the former anticipated
      his death and attempted to interpret its significance.

102   R. C. Johnson, "The Jesus of History and the Christian Faith," *TToday* 10
      (1953) 170-84. Discusses the theological and philosophical problems that
      attend the historical Jesus quest, argues that the "Christ" of Christian faith
      is Jesus; there can be no dichotomy.

103   R. Ludwig, "Zwischen Licht und Schatten. Randgestalten der Geschichte
      Jesu in der neueren Literatur," *EvT* 13 (1953/54) 277-81. Reviews some of
      the recent discussion of various figures in the gospel stories, such as
      Nicodemus, Pilate, Mary, Simon of Cyrene, and Barabbas.

104 T. W. Manson, *The Servant-Messiah: A Study of the Public Ministry of Jesus* (Cambridge: University Press, 1953). Argues that the crisis that Jesus faced was avoiding being recognized as a militaristic Messiah; Kingdom was realized in his ministry of love and service.

105 C. L. Mitton, "Goguel's 'Life of Jesus'," *ExpTim* 65 (1953/54) 259-63. Assessment of M. Goguel's *La Vie de Jésus* (76).

106 O. Piper, "Das Problem des Lebens Jesu seit Schweitzer," in W. Foerster, ed., *Verbum Dei Manet in Aeternum* (O. Schmitz Festschrift; Witten: Luther, 1953) 73-93. Reviews the problems and attempted solutions proposed in the aftermath of A. Schweitzer's *Von Reimarus zu Wrede* (71).

107 P. E. Davies, "The Tradition of Jesus at the Point of Origin," *JBR* 22 (1954) 94-98. Arguing against R. Bultmann and others, claims that the gospels are historically trustworthy, concluding that faith "does not obscure historical fact" (p. 97).

108 E. Dinkler, "Jesu Wort vom Kreuztragen" in W. Eltester, ed., *Neutestamentliche Studien für Rudolf Bultmann* (BZNW 21; Berlin: Töpelmann, 1954) 110-29. Examines some of Jesus' sayings about discipleship and others concerned with rejection, death, and denying oneself.

109 H. Engelland, "Gewissheit um Jesus von Nazareth," *TLZ* 79 (1954) cols. 65-74. Explores the implications that 1 Cor 15:3-8 has for the"certainty" concerning Jesus, concluding that "the present Christ and Jesus of Nazareth are one" (col. 74).

110 R. H. Fuller, *The Mission and Achievement of Jesus* (SBT 12; London: SCM, 1954). Argues that Jesus not only announced the Kingdom of God, but intended to establish it through his death as the Lord's Servant, and that the Kingdom has dawned, but has not arrived.

111 E. Käsemann, "Das Problem des historischen Jesus," *ZTK* 51 (1954) 125-53; repr. in Käsemann, *Exegetische Versuche und Besinnungen* (vol. 1; Göttingen: Vandenhoeck & Ruprecht, 1960) 187-214; ET: "The Problem of the Historical Jesus," in Käsemann, *Essays on New Testament Themes* (SBT 41; London: SCM, 1964) 15-47. The classic paper that was read in 1953 at the gathering of "old Marburgers" and is credited with launching the new quest; expressed dissatisfaction with R. Bultmann's position and offered a "corrective."

112   T. W. Manson, "The Life of Jesus: Some Tendencies in Present-day
       Research," in W. D. Davies and D. Daube, eds., *The Background of the
       New Testament and Its Eschatology* (C. H. Dodd Festschrift; Cambridge:
       University Press, 1954) 211-21. Discusses the implications of form criti-
       cism and C. H. Dodd's "realized eschatology" (818) and concludes that the
       quest of the historical Jesus is healthy and necessary.

113   W. N. Pittinger, "The Problem of the Historical Jesus," *ATR* 36 (1954)
       89-93. Argues that an assessment of the historical Jesus should rest on the
       whole testimony of the gospels, recognizing that some units of tradition
       may not be historical.

114   M. Stallmann, "Die biblische Geschichte im Unterricht," *ZTK* 51 (1954)
       216-50. Discusses the problem of biblical history, demythologization, and
       the historical Jesus.

115   S. G. F. Brandon, "The Historical Element in Primitive Christianity,"
       Numen 2 (1955) 156-67. Concludes that much of the earliest so-called
       "historical" elements in early Christian traditions about Jesus had at an
       early date been lifted out of their original historical context and had been
       made into symbol and myth.

116   W. E. Bundy, *Jesus and the First Three Gospels* (Cambridge: Harvard Uni-
       versity, 1955). A massive study, analyzing the synoptic gospels as sources;
       considers hundreds of units of tradition; does not think that Jesus regarded
       himself as Messiah.

117   F. Lieb, "Geschichte und Heilsgeschichte in der Theologie Rudolf Bult-
       manns," *EvT* 15 (1955) 507-22; repr. in Lieb, *Sophia und Historie: Auf-
       sätze zur östlichen und westlichen Geistes- und Theologiegeschichte* (M.
       Rohkrämer, ed.; Zürich: EVZ, 1962) 321-39; "Die Geschichte Jesu Christi
       in Kerygma und Historie. Ein Beitrag zum Gespräch mit Rudolf Bult-
       mann," in E. Wolf, et al., eds., *Antwort* (K. Barth Festschrift; Zollikon-
       Zürich: Evangelischer Verlag, 1956) 582-95; repr. in Lieb, *Sophia und
       Historie*, 340-55. In these two chapters Lieb assesses R. Bultmann's
       understanding of history and kerygma.

118   O. Michel, "Der 'historische Jesus' und das theologische Gewissheitsprob-
       lem," *EvT* 15 (1955) 349-63. Assesses the problem of the historical Jesus
       and certainty in light of the objections raised by M. Kähler (65).

119   V. Taylor, *The Life and Ministry of Jesus* (Nashville: Abingdon, 1955, 1968). Rejecting the skepticism of the times, believes that the gospels, especially Mark, provide a fairly accurate account of Jesus' ministry. Like M. Goguel (76), believes that Jesus ministered in Jerusalem several months, and not only a week or so.

1956-1960

120   G. Bornkamm, *Jesus von Nazareth* (Urban-Bücher 19; Stuttgart: Kohlhammer, 1956; 11th ed., 1977); ET: *Jesus of Nazareth* (New York: Harper & Row, 1960); translated into Japanese (1961), Danish (1963), Dutch (1963), Italian (1968), French (1973), Spanish (1975), and Portugese (1976); chap. 1, "Glaube und Geschichte in den Evangelien," repr. in G. Otto, ed., *Glauben heute* (Stundenbücher Sonderband 48; Hamburg: Furche, 1965) 96-112; Chap. 1, "Faith and History in the Gospels," and chap. 3, "Jesus of Nazareth," repr. in H. K. McArthur, *In Search of the Historical Jesus* (New York: Scribner's, 1969) 41-53 and 164-73, respectively. Classic statement from the "post-Bultmannian" perspective. See review article by L. E. Keck, *JR* 49 (1969) 1-17.

121   E. Fuchs, "Die Frage nach dem historischen Jesus," *ZTK* 53 (1956) 210-29; repr. in Fuchs, *Zur Frage nach dem historischen Jesus* (GA 2; Tübingen: Mohr [Siebeck], 1960) 143-67; ET: "The Quest of the Historical Jesus," in Fuchs, *Studies of the Historical Jesus* (SBT 42: London: SCM, 1964) 11-31. Christology is to be found in Jesus' attitude and conduct toward sinners, faith in Jesus is to repeat Jesus' decision to have faith.

122   W. Grundmann, *Die Geschichte Jesu Christi* (Berlin: Evangelische Verlagsanstalt, 1956; 2nd ed., 1959). A massive study, systematically investigates the events in the life and ministry of Jesus; covers all of Jesus' teaching; regards the gospels as essentially reliable.

123   E. Heitsch, "Die Aporie des historischen Jesus als Problem theologischer Hermeneutik," *ZTK* 53 (1956) 192-210. Criticizes R. Bultmann; argues that the historical aspect of Jesus has been neglected.

124   H. Braun, "Der Sinn der neutestamentlichen Christologie," *ZTK* 54 (1957) 341-77; ET: "The Meaning of New Testament Christology," *JTC* 5 (1968) 89-127. Argues that although there is little historical Jesus material that

appears in Paul and the Johannine writings, there is essential agreement in these diverse traditions.

125   H. Conzelmann, "Gegenwart und Zukunft in der synoptischen Tradition," *ZTK* 54 (1957) 277-96; ET: "Present and Future in the Synoptic Tradition," *JTC* 5 (1968) 26-44. Examines Son of Man sayings and Jesus' preaching of the Kingdom and the way these subjects are worked out in the synoptic gospels; finds traces of concern with the past (Jesus' death and resurrection), present (fulfillment in Jesus experienced by community), and future (the parousia).

126   H. Diem, *Der irdische Jesus und der Christus des Glaubens* (Sammlung gemeinverständlicher Vorträge und Schriften aus dem Gebiet der Theologie und Religionsgeschichte 215; Tübingen: Mohr [Siebeck], 1957); repr. in H. Ristow and K. Matthiae, eds., *Der historische Jesus und der kerygmatische Christus* (182, pp. 219-32); ET: "The Earthly Jesus and the Christ of Faith," in C. E. Braaten and R. A. Harrisville, eds., *Kerygma and History* (Nashville: Abingdon, 1962) 197-211. Criticizes R. Bultmann arguing that historical involves more than only what can be verified.

127   E. Fuchs, "Glaube und Geschichte im Blick auf die Frage nach dem historischen Jesus," *ZTK* 54 (1957) 117-56; repr. in Fuchs, *Zur Frage nach dem historischen Jesus* (GA 2; Tübingen: Mohr [Siebeck], 1960) 168-218. Review of Bornkamm's *Jesus von Nazareth* (120).

128   E. Käsemann, "Neutestamentliche Fragen von heute," *ZTK* 54 (1957) 1-21; repr. in Käsemann, *Exegetische Versuche und Besinnungen* (2nd ed.; vol. 2; Göttingen: Vandenhoeck & Ruprecht, 1965) 10-31; ET: "New Testament Questions Today," in Käsemann, *New Testament Questions Today* (London: SCM; Philadelphia: Fortress, 1969) 1-22. Affirms that post-Bultmannians are "compelled to enquire as to what the significance of the historical Jesus for faith may be" (p. 12).

129   F. Mussner, "Der historische Jesus und der Christus des Glaubens," *BZ* 1 (1957) 224-52; repr. in H. Vorgrimler, ed., *Exegese und Dogmatik* (Mainz: Matthias-Grünewald, 1962) 153-88. Argues that a picture of the historical Jesus, one that is relevant for faith, can be recovered from the gospels, despite their kerygmatic orientation.

130   R. W. Odom, "An Analytical Approach to the Study of Jesus," *JBR* 25 (1957) 199-202. Suggests that it would be helpful to ask what specific

form or content of each of the major roles (rabbi, prophet, Messiah) makes up the major components in Jesus' teachings.

131 J. E. Olford, "History, Theology, and Faith," *TToday* 14 (1957) 15-28. Asserts that Christian faith should never be reduced to belief in historical facts, for "theological statements are not reducible to historical statements" (p. 28); yet the Christian faith must be capable of making statements about history.

132 J. M. Robinson, "The Historical Jesus and the Church's Kerygma," *RL* 26 (1957) 40-49. Examines the problem of the lack of continuity between the Jesus of history and the Christ of Christian dogma; deals with some of the difficulties inherent in the most commonly accepted criteria for determining the authenticity of the tradition.

133 E. Stauffer, *Jesus: Gestalt und Geschichte* (Bern: Francke, 1957); ET: *Jesus and His Story* (London: SCM; New York: Knopf, 1960). Marshalls background materials as evidence of the historical reliability of the gospels; defends the historicity of virtually all gospel details (see 146).

134 P. Althaus, *Das sogenannte Kerygma und der historische Jesus: Zur Kritik der heutigen Kerygma-Theologie* (BFCT 48; Gütersloh: Bertelsmann, 1958); ET: *The So-Called Kerygma and the Historical Jesus* (Edinburgh and London: Oliver and Boyd, 1959). A critical assessment of Bultmann's demythologizing approach.

135 E. Barnikol, *Das Leben Jesu der Heilsgeschichte* (Halle: Niemeyer, 1958). Massive study; examines some 158 pericopae (mostly from Mark and Q); dates the synoptics very late (105 CE for Mark; 119 CE for Matthew; 125 CE for Luke); regards "high christology" as inauthentic tradition; views Jesus as prophet and teacher.

136 G. Ebeling, "Jesus und Glaube," *ZTK* 55 (1958) 64-110; repr. in Ebeling, *Wort und Glaube* (vol. 1; Tübingen: Mohr [Siebeck], 1962) 203-54; ET: "Jesus and Faith," in Ebeling, *Word and Faith* (Philadelphia: Fortress, 1963) 201-46. Asserts that Jesus is not object of faith, but its source and ground, and that the task of christology is to explain what is meant by the statement, "I believe in Jesus." Concludes that the historical Jesus illustrates faith and that Christian faith must have a basis in the historical Jesus.

137   E. Fuchs, "Jesus und der Glaube," *ZTK* 55 (1958) 170-85; repr. in Fuchs,
       Zur Frage nach dem historischen Jesus (GA 2; Tübingen: Mohr [Siebeck],
       1960) 238-57; ET: "Jesus and Faith," in Fuchs, *Studies of the Historical
       Jesus* (SBT 42; London: SCM, 1964) 48-64. Considers the question of
       how the faith of Jesus becomes faith *in* Jesus; concludes that in taking
       Jesus' faith upon oneself, one believes *in* Jesus (i.e., in Jesus' understand-
       ing of faith in God).

138   J. Jeremias, "The Present Position in the Controversy Concerning the
       Problem of the Historical Jesus," *ExpTim* 69 (1958) 333-39 [trans. of
       essay that had appeared in *Wissenschaftliche Zeitschrift der Universität
       Greifswald* 6 (1956-57)]; rev. and repr. as Jeremias, *The Problem of the
       Historical Jesus* (FBBS 13; Philadelphia: Fortress, 1964; 2nd ed., 1969);
       rev.: "Der gegenwärtigen Stand der Debatte um das Problem des
       historischen Jesus," in H. Ristow and K. Matthiae, eds., *Der historische
       Jesus und der kerygmatische Christus* (182, pp. 12-25); expanded as
       Jeremias, *Das Problem des historischen Jesus* (T. Schlatter, ed.; CH 32;
       Stuttgart: Calwer, 1960; 5th ed., 1966). Concise presentation of the
       problems and proposals of the new quest; argues that the quest of the
       historical Jesus is the most important task of New Testament scholarship.

139   D. E. Nineham, "Eyewitness Testimony and the Gospel Tradition," *JTS* 9
       (1958) 13-25, 243-57. Attempts to develop method for assessing presence
       of eyewitness testimony in the gospel tradition, concluding that eyewitness
       testimony had little to do with the composition of the gospels. See also
       Nineham, *JTS* 11 (1960) 253-64.

140   B. Rigaux, "L'historicité de Jésus devant l'exégèse récente," *RB* 65 (1958)
       481-522. Argues that R. Bultmann's following has defected, his influence
       has waned, and that the gospels do give us a reliable picture of the histori-
       cal Jesus.

141   J. T. Ross, "Source Analysis for Study of the Life of Christ," *JBR* 26
       (1958) 314-17. An attempt to isolate the historical tradition common to the
       gospels.

142   J. M. Robinson, "The Quest of the Historical Jesus Today," *TToday* 15
       (1958) 183-97. Explanation and defense of the new quest (see 156).

143   J. Schneider, *Die Frage nach dem historischen Jesus in der neutesta-
       mentlichen Forschung der Gegenwart* (Aufsätze und Vorträge sur Theologie
       und Religionswissenschaft 5; Berlin: Evangelische Verlagsanstalt, 1958).

Critical assessment of the new quest, in which it is concluded that the new research should result in a history of Jesus.

144 H.-J. Schoeps, "Protestantische Neuerscheinungen zur Erkenntnis Jesu Christi," *ZRGG* 10 (1958) 160-65. Reviews the works of major scholars (O. Cullmann, E. Stauffer, and H. Braun) concerned with christology and historical Jesus.

145 H. Schürmann, "Die Sprache des Christus. Sprachliche Beobachtungen an den synoptischen Herrenworten," *BZ* 2 (1958) 54-84. Tries to show how dominical tradition can in some instances be regarded as "sayings of Christ" (by observing authority and dignity).

146 E. Stauffer, "Neue Wege der Jesusforschung" in *Gottes ist der Orient* (O. Eissfeldt Festschrift; Berlin: Evangelische Verlagsanstalt, 1959) 161-86. Assessment of major trends in the new quest.

147 V. Taylor, *The Person of Christ in New Testament Teaching* (London: Macmillan, 1958); FT: *La personne du Christ dans le Noveau Testament* (Lectio Divina 57; Paris: Cerf, 1969). Attempts to show how New Testament christology developed from the person and ministry of the historical Jesus (as seen especially in Mark).

148 S. G. F. Brandon, "Recent Study of the Sources for the Life of Jesus," *ModCh* 2 (1959) 160-69. Calls for a new assessment of Jesus' relationship to the social and political factors of his day; links Jesus to Palestinian zealotry.

149 L. Cerfaux, "La vie de Jésus devant l'histoire," *Euntes Docete* 12 (1959) 131-40; repr. in Cerfaux, *Recueil Lucien Cerfaux: Études d'exégèse et d'histoire religieuse de Monseigneur Cerfaux* (vol. 3; Gembloux: Duculot, 1962) 161-82. Argues that scholars can recover the historical Jesus.

150 H. Conzelmann, "Jesus Christus," *RGG* 3 (3rd ed., 1959) cols. 619-53; ET: *Jesus* (Philadelphia: Fortress, 1973). Classic assessment of historical Jesus scholarship, good bibliography.

151 H. Conzelmann, "Zur Methode der Leben-Jesu-Forschung," *ZTK* 56 (1959) 2-13. Repr. in Conzelmann, *Theologie als Schriftauslegung* (BEvT 65; Munich: Kaiser, 1974) 18-29; ET: "The Method of the Life of Jesus Research," in C. E. Braaten and R. A. Harrisville, eds., *The Historical Jesus and the Kerygmatic Christ: Essays on the New Quest of the*

Historical Jesus (Nashville: Abingdon, 1964) 54-68. Defends the necessity of the quest of the historical Jesus; identifies several areas where important gains have been made.

152   G. Ebeling, "Die Frage nach dem historischen Jesus und das Problem der Christologie," *ZTK* 56 (1959) 14-30; repr. in Ebeling, *Wort und Glaube* (Tübingen: Mohr [Siebeck], 1960) 300-318; ET: "The Question of the Historical Jesus and the Problem of Christology," in Ebeling, *Word and Faith* (Philadelphia: Fortress, 1963) 288-304. Emphasizes continuity between Jesus of history and Christ of faith; Jesus is basis, not object, of faith.

153   F. C. Grant, "Jesus of History," *USQR* 14/3 (1959) 1-16. Concludes that "we still believe it is possible to trace the general outlines of the life and the career, the teaching and the personality of Jesus of Nazareth" (p. 4).

154   B. Noack, "Om Stauffers Jesubog," *DTT* 22 (1959) 16-35. A critical review of E. Stauffer's research and arguments (see 133,146).

155   L. Randellini, "Possiamo ricostruire una biografia di Gesù?" *BO* 1 (1959) 82-88. Concludes that a biography of Jesus is not possible, but gospels do provide us with much information about Jesus' ministry and self-under-standing.

156   J. M. Robinson, *A New Quest of the Historical Jesus* (SBT 25; London: SCM, 1959; Missoula: Scholars, 1979); repr. *A New Quest of the Historical Jesus and Other Essays* (Philadelphia: Fortress, 1983); GT: *Kerygma und historischer Jesus* (Zürich and Stuttgart: Zwingli, 1960; 2nd ed., 1967); FT: *Le kérygme de l'Église et le Jésus de l'histoire* (Geneva: Labor et Fides, 1961). An assessment of the post-Bultmannian new quest of the historical Jesus. Robinson argues that the new quest is both histori-cally possible and theologically legitimate.

157   R. Schnackenburg, "Jesusforschung und Christusglaube," *C* 13 (1959) 13 (1959) 1-17. Reviews R. Bultmann's position and those of his critics (e.g., P. Althaus and G. Bornkamm), and concludes that the gospel portrait is essentially historical.

158   J. A. Ubieta, "El Kerygma apostólico y los Evangelicos," *EstBíb* 18 (1959) 21-61. Concludes that Mark is closest to apostolic kerygma, but it nevertheless offers important historical data.

159   A. Wikgren, "Biography and Christology in the Gospels," *SE* 1 [=TU 73] (1959) 115-25. Argues that the gospels evince an interest in biographical detail that does not likely derive from christology only, but from historical Jesus.

160   H. Anderson, "The Historical Jesus and the Origins of Christianity," *SJT* 13 (1960) 113-36. Cites reasons why the historical Jesus has become less important to the proclamation of the church.

161   P. Althaus, "Der gegenwärtige Stand der Frage nach dem historische Jesus," *DLZ* 81 (1960) 1133-34. Summarizes the new quest.

162   A. Barr, "More Quests of the Historical Jesus," *SJT* 13 (1960) 394-409. Reviews new quest scholarship.

163   H.-W. Bartsch, *Das historische Problem des Lebens Jesu* (ThEx 78; Munich: Kaiser, 1960); ET: "The Historical Problem of the Life of Jesus," in C. E. Braaten and R. A. Harrisville, *The Historical Jesus and the Kerygmatic Christ* (Nashville: Abingdon, 1964) 106-41. A brief statement of what can be known of the historical Jesus, including an analysis of Mark 1:15, which is viewed as an early Christian summary of Jesus' preaching.

164   M. Berg, "Die Frage nach dem historischen Jesus und die evangelische Unterweisung," in H. Heeger, ed., *Glauben und Erziehen, Pädagogen und Theologen im Gesprach* (G. Bohne Festschrift; Neumünster: Ihloff, 1960) 215-26. Deals with the problem of teaching the critical aspects of historical Jesus research in a Lutheran context.

165   R. Bultmann, *Das Verhältnis der urchristlichen Christusbotschaft zum historischen Jesus* (Heidelberg: Winter, 1960; 3rd ed., 1962); ET: "The Primitive Christian Kerygma and the Historical Jesus," in C. E. Braaten and R. A. Harrisville, eds., *The Historical Jesus and the Kerygmatic Christ* (Nashville: Abingdon, 1964) 15-42. Bultmann's response to the new quest advocates, in which he clarifies in what sense there is continuity between the historical Jesus and the kerygma and how much relevant data can be obtained beyond the "that" of Jesus' existence.

166   W. D. Davies, "A Quest to be Resumed in New Testament Studies," *USQR* 15 (1960) 83-98. Because the gospels proclaim the Jesus of history, even though obviously reflecting the early church's kerygma, the quest for the historical Jesus is an essential component of Christian theology. Concludes that the quest is therefore imperative.

167   W. R. Farmer and N. Perrin, "The Kerygmatic Theology and the Question
       of the Historical Jesus," *RL* 29 (1960) 86-97. A discussion of the
       contributions of R. Bultmann (77,165), E. Käsemann (111), G. Bornkamm
       (120), E. Fuchs (121), and Bultmann's response to his pupils.

168   E. Fuchs, "Die Theologie des Neuen Testaments und der historische Jesus,"
       ZTK 57 (1960) 296-301; repr. in Fuchs, *Zur Frage nach dem historischen
       Jesus* (GA 2; Tübingen: Mohr [Siebeck], 1960) 377-404; ET: "The Theo-
       logy of the New Testament and the Historical Jesus," in Fuchs, *Studies of
       the Historical Jesus* (SBT 42; London: SCM, 1964) 167-90. Raises several
       questions for further discussion of the problem of the historical Jesus.

169   E. Fuchs, *Zur Frage nach dem historischen Jesus* (GA 2; Tübingen: Mohr
       [Siebeck], 1960); ET of selections in Fuchs, *Studies of the Historical Jesus*
       (SBT 42; London: SCM, 1964). Collection of several articles, some of
       which are cited elsewhere.

170   G. Haufe, "Zur Methode einer 'Leben-Jesu'-Darstellung," *FF* 34 (1960)
       377-78. Criticizes the assumptions and logic of the old quest.

171   G. Koch, "Dominus praedicans Christus — id est Jesum praedicatum,"
       ZTK 57 (1960) 238-73. Argues that the Christian kerygma is based in
       Jesus' preaching; the resurrection is God's response to Jesus' faith and the
       ground of faith for the Christian.

172   W. G. Kümmel, "Diakritik zwischen Jesus von Nazareth und dem Chris-
       tusbild der Urkirche," in F. Hauss and E. Roth, eds., *Ein Leben für die
       Kirche* (J. Bauer Festschrift; Jarlsruhe: Thoma, 1960) 54-67; repr. in
       Kümmel, *Heilsgeschehen und Geschichte* (Marburg Theologische Studien
       3; E. Grässer, O. Merk, and A. Fritz, eds.; Marburg: Elwert, 1965) 382-
       391. Examines the assumptions and methods of the leading scholars who
       distinguish the Jesus of history from the Christ of faith.

173   W. G. Kümmel, "Kerygma, Selfhood, or Historical Fact," *Encount* 21
       (1960) 232-34. A review of James M. Robinson's *A New Quest of the
       Historical Jesus* (156).

174   R. Marlé, "Bemerkungen zur Theologie des Wortes bei Bultmann," *C* 14
       (1960) 23-34. Argues that R. Bultmann's position does not do justice to
       the Jewish and Old Testament background against which Jesus must be
       viewed.

175   R. Marlé, "The Problem of the Historical Jesus," *HeyJ* 1 (1960) 229-32.
      See also Marlé, "Der Christus des Glauben und der historische Jesus," in H.
      Ristow and K. Matthiae, eds., *Der historische Jesus und der kerygmatische
      Christus* (182, pp. 26-38). Comments on the new quest, views its
      development as good, although thinks that it is unnecessarily too cautious.

176   W. Marxsen, *Anfangsprobleme der Christologie* (Gütersloh: Mohn, 1960);
      ET: *The Beginnings of Christology: A Study in Its Problems* (FBBS 22;
      Philadelphia: Fortress, 1969; 2nd ed., 1979). Searches for the link between
      the Jesus of history and the church's christology; concludes that the mes-
      sage of the historical Jesus is a constituent part of the post-Easter kerygma.

177   J. L. Moreau, "The Historic Value of the Gospel Materials: Epitome and
      Prospect," *BR* 5 (1960) 22-43. Concludes that the form critics were essen-
      tially correct, the christological material reflects the beliefs of the early
      church, not the historical Jesus.

178   F. Mussner, "Der 'historische' Jesus," *TTZ* 69 (1960) 321-37; repr. in K.
      Schubert, ed., *Der historische Jesus und der Christus unseres Glaubens*
      (Wien: Herder, 1962) 103-28. Argues that the gospel witness is historically
      accurate, and that its witness should be presupposed by Christian faith.

179   D. E. Nineham, "Eyewitness Testimony and the Gospel Tradition," *JTS* 11
      (1960) 253-64. Argues that eyewitness testimony has little to do with bio-
      graphical information about Jesus. See also Nineham, *JTS* 9 (1958) 13-25,
      243-57.

180   H. Ott, *Die Frage nach dem historischen Jesus und die Ontologie der
      Geschichte* (Theologischen Studien 62; Zürich: EVZ, 1960); ET: "The
      Historical Jesus and the Ontology of History," in C. E. Braaten and R. A.
      Harrisville, eds., *The Historical Jesus and the Kerygmatic Christ*
      (Nashville: Abingdon, 1964) 142-71. Assesses the philosophical problems
      inherent in historical research and how these problems relate to historical
      Jesus research; argues that facts cannot be separated from their
      interpretation.

181   W. Pannenberg, "Jesu Geschichte und unsere Geschichte," *Radius* 6 (1960)
      18-27; ET: "Jesus' History and Our History," *PerRelSt* 1 (1974) 134-42.
      Argues that "Christian faith depends wholly upon the historical events of
      nearly two thousand years ago and on the meaning inherent with their con-
      text. It has no truth independent of this" (pp. 134-35).

182 H. Ristow and K. Matthiae, eds., *Der historische Jesus und der kerygmatische Christus: Beiträge zum Christusverständnis in Forschung und Verkündigung* (Berlin: Evangelische Verlaganstalt, 1960). Very important collection of studies, some of which include: J. Jeremias, "Der gegenwärtigen Stand der Debatte um das Problem des historischen Jesus" (pp. 12-25), R. Marlé, "Der Christus des Glaubens und der historische Jesus" (pp. 26-38), W. G. Kümmel, "Das Problem des geschichtlichen Jesus in der gegenwärtigen Forschungslage" (pp. 39-53), E. Heitsch, "Jesus aus Nazareth als Christus" (pp. 62-86), H. Conzelmann, "Jesus von Nazareth und der Glaube an den Auferstandenen" (pp. 188-99), B. Reicke, "Der Fleischgewordene. Zur Diskussion über den 'historischen' Jesus und den kerygmatischen Christus" (pp. 208-18), H. Diem, "Der irdische Jesus und der Christus des Glaubens" (pp. 219-32), R. Bultmann, "Das Verhältnis des urchristlichen Christuskerygmas zum historischen Jesus" (pp. 233-35), O. Cullmann, "Unzeitgemässe Bemerkungen zum 'historischen Jesus' der Bultmann-Schule" (pp. 266-80), G. Bornkamm, "Glaube und Geschichte in der Evangelien" (pp. 281-88), and E. Fuchs, "Die Verkündigung Jesu. Der Spruch von den Raben" (385-88).

183 H. Simonsen, "Den historiske Jesus og menighedens Kristuskerygma," *DTT* 23 (1960) 193-208. Surveys the assumptions and methods of various modern approaches: liberalism, dialectical theology, form criticism, demythologization, kerygmatic theology.

184 J. J. Vincent, "Discipleship and Synoptic Studies," *TZ* 16 (1960) 456-69. Argues that the believer's response is the link between the Jesus of history of the Christ of faith.

185 A. Vögtle, "Jesus Christus," *LTK* 5 (2nd ed., 1960) cols. 922-32. Reviews the essential facts of the life of Jesus, his ministry, teaching, and self-understanding.

186 H. Zahrnt, *Es begann mit Jesus von Nazareth: Die Frage nach dem historischen Jesus* (Gütersloh: Mohn, 1960); ET: *The Historical Jesus* (New York: Harper & Row, 1963). Very helpful survey of the life of Jesus research, especially with regard to the new quest.

1961-1965

187   A. E. Barnett, "Jesus as Theologian," in A. Wikgren, ed., *Early Christian Origins* (H. R. Willoughby Festschrift; Chicago: Quadrangle, 1961) 16-23. Argues that the gospels' oral traditions reflect, but not originate Jesus' historical career and message. Central to Jesus' theology was his faith in the providence of God.

188   D. M. Beck, "The Never-Ending Quest for the Historical Jesus," *JBR* 29 (1961) 227-31. Review of G. Bornkamm's *Jesus von Nazareth* (120). Calls for clarification of what Bornkamm means by "messianic."

189   E. C. Blackman, "Jesus Christ Yesterday: The Historical Basis of the Christian Faith," *CJT* 7 (1961) 118-27. Calls for reconstruction of picture of the historical Jesus; reaffirms the essential historicity of the gospels.

190   G. Bornkamm, "Die Bedeutung des historischen Jesus für den Glauben," *KiZ* 16 (1961) 3-8; expanded in F. Hahn, W. Lohff, and G. Bornkamm, *Die Frage nach dem historischen Jesus* (EvFo 2; Göttingen: Vandenhoeck & Ruprecht, 1962) 57-71; ET: "The Significance of the Historical Jesus for Faith," in Hahn, Lohff, and Bornkamm, *What Can We Know about Jesus?* (Philadelphia: Fortress, 1969) 69-86; overlaps with earlier study in H. Ristow and K. Matthiae, eds., *Der historische Jesus und der kerygmatische Christus* (182, pp. 281-88).

191   O. Cullmann, "Out of Season Remarks on the 'Historical Jesus' of the Bultmann School," *USQR* 16 (1961) 131-48; Germ. ed.: "Unzeitgemässe Bemerkungen zum 'historischen Jesus' der Bultmann-Schule," in H. Ristow and K. Matthiae, eds., *Der historische Jesus und der kerygmatische Christus* (182, pp. 266-80). Argues that the existentialist approach to hermeneutics of R. Bultmann and pupils hinders the efforts of the new quest, a quest which is otherwise appropriate and necessary.

192   G. Delling, "Geprägte Jesustradition im Urchristentum," *ComVia* 4 (1961) 59-71. Argues that the dominical tradition is rooted in the teaching of the historical Jesus and his messianic self-understanding, a tradition which was viewed as sacred and worthy of preservation by Jesus' disciples.

193   O. A. Dilschneider, "Die Geistvergessenheit der Theologie. Epilog zur Diskussion über den historischen Jesus und den kerygmatischen Christus,"

TLZ 86 (1961) cols. 255-66. Emphasizes the important role of the Holy Spirit who is at work in the preacher of the kerygma.

194   J. W. Duddington, "The Historic Jesus," *ATR* 43 (1961) 168-78. Urges the pupils of R. Bultmann to move further and to follow O. Cullmann's position that christology is ultimately based on the life of Jesus.

195   M. S. Enslin, *The Prophet from Nazareth* (New York: McGraw-Hill, 1961). Argues that Jesus viewed himself as only a prophet, but later the church deified him (see further discussion in 217 below).

196   P. Fannon, "Can We Know Jesus?" *Scr* 13 (1961) 44-51. Argues that the gospels are historically reliable and so make the reconstruction of a life of Jesus possible.

197   E. Fuchs, "Muss man an Jesus glauben, wenn man an Gott glauben will?" *ZTK* 58 (1961) 45-67; repr. in Fuchs, *Glaube and Erfahrung: Zum christologischen Problem im Neuen Testament* (GA 3; Tübingen: Mohr [Siebeck], 1971) 249-79; ET: "Must One Believe in Jesus if He Wants to Believe in God?" *JTC* 1 (1965) 147-68. Argues that one need not believe in Jesus to believe in God, but one is invited to believe in Jesus, for it was in him, in the historical Jesus and in the resurrected Christ, that God has spoken to humankind.

198   E. Fuchs, "Das Neue Testament und das hermeneutische Problem," *ZTK* 58 (1961) 198-226. Explores the new quest's relationship to the old quest; argues that the gospels are concerned with the historical Jesus.

199   H. Gerdes, "Die durch Martin Kählers Kampf gegen den 'historischen Jesus' ausgelöste Krise in der evangelischen Theologie und ihre Überwindung," *NZST* 3 (1961) 175-202. Examines the implications of M. Kähler's views (65) concerning the historical Jesus of the nineteenth century and how biblical scholars and theologians have approached the problem.

200   R. M. Grant, *The Earliest Lives of Jesus* (New York: Harper & Row, 1961). Assessment of interest in historical Jesus among early fathers.

201   P. C. Hodgson, "The Son of Man and the Problem of Historical Knowledge," *JR* 41 (1961) 91-108. Assesses the problems of the Son of Man sayings, considers the view of the leading contributors to the discussion, and concludes that faith and historical scholarship must be allied, not separated.

202   W. G. Kümmel, "Das Problem des historischen Jesus in der gegenwärtigen Diskussion," *Deutsches Pfarrerblatt* 61 (1961) 573-78; repr. in Kümmel, *Heilsgeschehen und Geschichte* (Marburg Theologische Studien 3; E. Grässer, O. Merk, and A. Fritz, eds.; Marburg: Elwert, 1965) 417-56. Reviews recent discussion.

203   R. Leaney, "Jesus and History and Faith," *CQR* 162 (1961) 408-14. A review article of G. Bornkamm's *Jesus von Nazareth* (120).

204   J. D. McCaughey, "The Question of the Historical Jesus," *RTR* 20 (1961) 1-12. Reviews history of debate, theological problems, concluding that final proof is impossible; gospel story must be approached in faith.

205   W. Marxsen, "Was Sollen wir Predigen: Homiletische Erwägungen zur gegenwärtigen Diskussion über den historischen Jesus," *KiZ* 16 (1961) 284-292; repr. in Marxsen, *Exeget als Theologe: Vorträge zum Neuen Testament* (Gütersloh: Mohn, 1968) 139-59. Offers insights into the pastoral implications of the scholarly discussion.

206   W. Matthias, "Der historische Jesus und der irdische Jesus," *TLZ* 86 (1961) cols. 571-74. Review article of H. Diem, *Der irdische Jesus und der Christus des Glaubens* (126), probing the distinction between "historical" and "earthly."

207   D. T. Rowlingson, "Jesus in History and in Faith," *JBR* 29 (1961) 35-38. Applauds the new quest, thinks results have significance for the layman.

208   P. J. Achtemeier, "Is the New Quest Docetic?" *TToday* 19 (1962) 355-68. Argues that advocates of new quest define faith in terms of what is proclaimed, rather than in terms of revelatory events, thus tending toward docetism (contrary to Paul). The quest should focus on the revelatory facts.

209   H. Anderson, "Existential Hermeneutics: Features of the New Quest," *Interp* 16 (1962) 131-55. Compares T. W. Manson, *The Teaching of Jesus* (799), with G. Bornkamm, *Jesus von Nazareth* (120).

210   H.-W. Bartsch, "Der historische Jesus als dogmatisches Problem," *TF* 26 (1962) 193-209. Argues that pursuing the kerygma, as opposed to the historical Jesus, does not resolve the problem inherent in the kerygma itself. The historical Jesus is an integral part of the kerygma.

211   D. L. Bell, "The New Quest of the Historical Jesus—a Critique," *ATR* 44 (1962) 414-20. Criticizes J. M. Robinson (see 156) and other new quest advocates, arguing that the kerygma has been misunderstood.

212   W. D. Davies, "Comment on Christology," *TToday* 19 (1962) 422-27. Responding to O. Piper, *TToday* 19 (1962) 324-40), asks if Jesus is not proper object of research.

213   E. C. Blackman, "Jesus Christ Yesterday: Further Notes on the Historicity of the Kerygma," *CJT* 8 (1962) 116-25. See also Blackman, *CJT* 7 (1961) 118-27. Concludes that the historical Jesus is essential to any theology that claims to be Christian.

214   G. Bornkamm, "Geschichte und Glaube im Neuen Testament. Ein Beitrag zur Frage 'historishen' Begründung theologischer Aussagen," *EvT* 22 (1962) 1-15; repr. in Bornkamm, *Geschichte und Glaube* (vol. 1; GA 3; BEvT 48; Munich: Kaiser, 1968) 9-24. Argues that the evangelists present Jesus through the Spirit and in light of Easter faith, but it is a presentation grounded on the historical Jesus himself.

215   S. G. F. Brandon, "Further Quest for the Historical Jesus," *ModCh* 5 (1962) 212-20. After criticizing E. Stauffer (133) and J. M. Robinson (156), argues that a quest for the historical Jesus should begin with why the Romans crucified Jesus.

216   D. L. Deegan, "Albrecht Ritschl on the Historical Jesus," *SJT* 15 (1962) 133-50. Argues that new quest advocates disregard important advances of the old quest, such as that of Ritschl who had clarified the significance of Jesus, but had not attempted to find a historical Jesus behind the gospels.

217   M. S. Enslin, "The Meaning of the Historical Jesus for Faith," *JBR* 30 (1962) 219-33. Argues that historical Jesus can be known and that he was a prophet who announced the fulfillment of God's promises to Israel, a message that survived his death and led to the formation of christology.

218   H. Gollwitzer, "The Jesus of History and Faith in Christ," *Th* 65 (1962) 90-94. Christian faith cannot be independent of history; Jesus is historic, not symbolic.

219   F. C. Grant, "Jesus Christ," *IDB* 2 (1962) cols. 869-96. Reviews sources, background, birth, relation to the Baptist, mission and message, miracles, death, and resurrection.

220 F. Hahn, W. Lohff, and G. Bornkamm, *Die Frage nach dem historischen Jesus* (EvFo 2; Göttingen: Vandenhoeck & Ruprecht, 1962): Hahn, "Die Frage nach dem historischen Jesus und die Eigenart der uns zur Verfügung stehenden Quellen" (pp. 7-40), Lohff, "Die Bedeutung der philosophische Frage nach Jesus für den Glauben" (pp. 41-56), and Bornkamm, "Die Bedeutung des historischen Jesus für den Glauben" (pp. 57-71); ET: *What Can We Know about Jesus?* (Philadelphia: Fortress, 1969): Hahn, "The Quest of the Historical Jesus and the Special Character of the Sources Available to Us" (pp. 9-48), Lohff, "The Significance for Faith of the Philosophical Quest for Jesus" (pp. 49-68), and Bornkamm, "The Significance of the Historical Jesus for Faith" (pp. 69-88).

221 V. A. Harvey and S. M. Ogden, "Wie neu ist die 'Neue Frage nach dem historischen Jesus'?" *ZTK* 59 (1962) 46-87; ET: "How New is the 'New Quest of the Historical Jesus'?" in C. E. Braaten and R. A. Harrisville, eds., *The Historical Jesus and the Kerygmatic Christ* (Nashville: Abingdon, 1964)197-242. Claim that J. M. Robinson has misunderstood R. Bultmann and the main lines of difference between him and his pupils who have called for a new quest. See Robinson's reply in *A New Quest of the Historical Jesus* (156) p. 6.

222 L. Hejdánek and P. Pokorny, "Jesus, Glaube, Christologie," *TZ* 18 (1962) 268-82. Argue that something from the gospels can be learned of Jesus' personal faith, something that is especially relevant for Christian faith today.

223 J. Jervell, *Den historiske Jesus* (Oslo: Land og Kirke, 1962); ET: *The Continuing Search for the Historical Jesus* (Minneapolis: Augsburg, 1965). Concludes that Jesus "claimed to represent God in an exclusive and decisive way" (p. 78). New edition released under the title of *Historiens Jesus* (1978).

224 H.-D. Knigge, "Glaube und historischer Jesus," *UnSanc* 17 (1962) 6-23. Reviews question of faith and the historical Jesus from Reimarus to new quest; concludes that faith in kerygma today links believer to the faith of Jesus in the past.

225 J. Knox, *Church and the reality of Christ* (New York Harper & Row, 1962). Examines the relevance of the historical Jesus for the Christian church.

226   W. Kreck, "Die Frage nach dem historischen Jesus als dogmatisches Prob-
       lem," *EvT* 22 (1962) 460-78. Assesses the views of J. Jeremias, E. Fuchs,
       and H. Braun, and concludes that whereas the historical Jesus is important
       theologically, it makes no significant contribution to faith.

227   W. Lillie, "'Jesus of History' in 1961," *SJT* 15 (1962) 151-63. Argues that
       the historical Jesus can be recovered and is very relevant for Christian faith.

228   G. Lindeskog, "Christuskerygma und Jesustradition," *NovT* 5 (1962) 144-
       56. Argues that a history of Jesus cannot be recovered that is distinct from
       the christological confession of the early community.

229   E. Lohse, "Die Frage nach dem historischen Jesus in der gegenwärtigen
       neutestamentlichen Forschung," *TLZ* 87 (1962) cols. 161-74. Reviews and
       sharpens the issues raised by the advocates of the new quest.

230   T. W. Manson, "The Life of Jesus: A Study of the Available Materials," in
       Manson, *Studies in the Gospels and Epistles* (M. Black, ed.; Philadelphia:
       Westminster, 1962) 13-27. Assesses the nature of the materials from which
       one can recover the historical Jesus; sees Mark as providing the framework
       of Jesus' teaching and Q the details of his teaching. Since Mark and Q are
       independent and complement one another, we may conclude that they are
       historically reliable.

231   W. Marxsen, "Zur Frage nach dem historischen Jesus," *TLZ* 87 (1962)
       cols. 575-80. Argues that the gospels do not tell us who Jesus *was*, but
       who Jesus *is*. The story of Jesus cannot verify the kerygma, but it does
       make it relevant.

232   F. Neugebauer, "Geistsprüche und Jesuslogien. Erwägungen zu der von der
       formgeschichtlichen Betrachtungsweise R. Bultmanns angenommenen
       grundsätzlichen Möglichkeit einer Identität von prophetischen
       Geistsprüchen mit Logien des irdischen Jesus," *ZNW* 53 (1962) 218-28.
       Criticizes Bultmann's application of form criticism, especially his
       assumption that sayings of the early community became confused with the
       sayings of Jesus.

233   S. Ogden, "Bultmann and the 'New Quest,'" *JBR* 30 (1962) 209-18.
       Reviews R. Bultmann's criticisms of the new quest.

234   O. Piper, "Christology and History," *TToday* 19 (1962) 324-40. Reviews
       the various theological approaches of several schools of thought.

235   B. Reicke, "Incarnation and Exaltation: The Historic Jesus and Kerygmatic
        Christ," *Interp* 16 (1962) 156-68. Appeared earlier as "Der Fleischgeword-
        ene. Zur Diskussion über den 'historischen' Jesus und der kerygmatischen
        Christus," in H. Ristow and K. Matthiae, eds., *Der historische Jesus und
        der kerygmatische Christus* (182, pp. 208-18). Argues that the historical
        element cannot be separated from the kerygmatic and that the gospels, our
        only sources, portray the historical Jesus in kerygmatic terms.

236   J. M. Robinson, "The Recent Debate on the 'New Quest,'" *JBR* 30 (1962)
        198-208. Argues that the new quest is trying to find historical material that
        is significant for the Christ of faith, something R. Bultmann thought was
        impossible and irrelevant.

237   W. Schmithals, "Paulus und der historische Jesus," *ZNW* 53 (1962) 145-
        60. Argues that Paul's negligible view of the historical Jesus, shared by
        many of the early fathers, assumed the importance of the event (*das Dass*)
        and not the content (*das Was*) of the Jesus of history.

238   J. Schneider, "Der Beitrag der Urgemeinde zur Jesusüberlieferung im Lichte
        der neuesten Forschung," *TLZ* 87 (1962) cols. 401-12. Criticizes R.
        Bultmann at several points, concludes that gospels contain more
        historically reliable tradition than has been allowed, and that the critic's
        disposition toward authenticity of material is to a great extent conditioned
        by his assumptions about Jesus' messianic self-consciousness.

239   K. Schubert, ed., *Der historische Jesus und der Christus unseres Glaubens:
        Eine katholische Auseinandersetzung mit den Folgen der Entmythologis-
        ierungstheorie* (Vienna and Freiburg: Herder, 1962). A collection of Roman
        Catholic studies concerned with the new quest.

240   L. H. Silberman, "Survey of Current Theological Literature: The New
        Quest for the Historical Jesus," *Judaism* 11 (1962) 260-67. Optimistic
        about new quest, but warns its advocates not to lift Jesus out of his Jewish
        context.

241   C. W. F. Smith, "Is Jesus Dispensable?" *ATR* 44 (1962) 263-80. Con-
        cludes that the historical Jesus is indispensable to christology.

242   W. Trilling, "Jesusüberlieferung und apostolische Vollmacht," *TTZ* 71
        (1962) 352-68. Argues that the gospels do not offer brute facts, but seek to
        interpret the divine mystery at work in Jesus.

243   W. Bradley, "The Theological Quest of the Historical Jesus," *JR* 43 (1963) 35-48. Concludes that a historical Jesus cannot be recovered apart from the theological interpretation that has colored and shaped the tradition.

244   A. R. Dulles, *Apologetics and the Biblical Christ* (Westminster: Newman, 1963). Argues that although the gospels are admittedly confessional documents, they do not indulge in fanciful fabrication.

245   R. M. Grant, "The Problem of the Life of Jesus," in Grant, *Historical Introduction to the New Testament* (New York: Harper & Row; London: Collins, 1963) 284-377. A helpful introduction to the life of Jesus research, especially the new quest.

246   F. Herzog, "Possibilities and Limits of the New Quest," *JR* 43 (1963) 218-33. Assesses the results of the new quest, concludes that the new quest is scarcely an advance beyond the old quest, for a new dogma (existentialism) has replaced the older ones of liberal theology.

247   W. Kreck, "Die Christologie Gogartens und ihre Weiterführung in der heutigen Frage nach dem historischen Jesus," *EvT* 23 (1963) 169-97. Compares Gogarten's christology to that of R. Bultmann and his pupils.

248   X. Léon-Dufour, *Les Évangiles et l'histoire de Jésus* (Paris: Éditions de Seuil, 1963); ET: *The Gospels and the Jesus of History* (New York and Tournai: Desclée, 1968; Garden City: Doubleday, 1970). Argues that Jewish principles of teaching and memorization make it likely that the gospel tradition is reliable (so H. Riesenfeld and B. Gerhardsson), especially since Jesus' disciples would have regarded Jesus' teaching as *sacra traditio*.

249   U. Luck, "Himmlisches und irdisches Geschehen im Hebräerbrief: Ein Beitrage zum Problem des historischen Jesus im Urchristentum," *NovT* 6 (1963) 192-215. Shows the significance of Hebrews' presentation of Jesus in both heavenly and earthly terms, as the one who has suffered and has been exalted.

250   J. D. Plenter, "De Betekinis can de historische Jezus voor het kerygma," *NTTij* 18 (1963) 94-123. Review article of R. Bultmann, *Das Verhältnis der urchristlichen Christusbotschaft zum historischen Jesus* (165), and W. Marxsen, *NTS* 8 (1962) 204-14.

251 D. T. Rowlingson, "The Focal Point of Faith: Jesus or Tradition?" *JBR* 31 (1963) 17-22. Argues that Jesus is the object of faith and the tradition is the means to that end; therefore, historical research is essential.

252 G. Schneider, "Die Evangelien im Urteil der neueren Forschung und unsere biblische Katechese," *TTZ* 72 (1963) 349-62. Surveys recent contributions and developments in form criticism, demythologization, background studies, and redaction criticism.

253 G. Schreiner, "De historische Jezus en de kerygmatische Christus," *Bij* 24 (1963) 241-79. Discusses several of the contributions in H. Ristow and K. Matthiae, eds., *Der historische Jesus und der kerygmatische Christus* (182); surveys and evaluates the trends of the last ten years.

254 G. F. Snyder, "The Historical Jesus in the Letters of Ignatius of Antioch," *BR* 8 (1963) 3-12. Argues that Ignatius has little interest in the historical Jesus and that for Ignatius the life of Jesus is wrapped up in the life of the church.

255 H. E. W. Turner, *Historicity and the Gospels* (London: Mowbray, 1963). Argues that historical material can be extracted from the gospels, material that is relevant to Christian faith in Jesus; searches for authenticity criteria. See the review of C. Tennent, *ExpTim* 75 (1963) 95.

256 A. N. Wilder, "The New Quest for the Historical Jesus," *ChrCris* 22 (1963) 245-48. A positive assessment of the new quest; states: "The new quest extrapolates backward from the faith of the first reporters to the personal source [Jesus] of that faith" (p. 248).

257 H. Anderson, *Jesus and Christian Origins: A Commentary on Modern Viewpoints* (New York: Oxford University Press, 1964). Useful survey and suggestions; criticizes the distinction between *Historie* and *Geschichte*; believes that relatively secure knowledge about the historical Jesus can be recovered.

258 J. B. Bedenbaugh, "The First Decade of the New Quest of the Historical Jesus," *LQ* 16 (1964) 239-67. Surveys the contributions of the leading new quest advocates and assesses their major emphases.

259 G. Bornkamm, "Der Auferstandene und der Irdische. Mt 28,16-20," in E. Dinkler, ed., *Zeit und Geschichte* (R. Bultmann Festschrift; Tübingen: Mohr [Siebeck], 1964) 171-91; ET: "The Risen Lord and the Earthly Jesus:

Matthew 28.16-20," in J. M. Robinson, ed., *The Future of Our Religious Past* ([a translation of part of the Bultmann Festschrift] New York: Harper & Row, 1971) 203-29. Argues that the "authority" claim of the risen Christ, coming where it does in a pericope devoid of characteristic apocalyptic and christological details, provides a strong link with the historical Jesus who acted with authority.

260   G. Bornkamm, "The Problem of the Historical Jesus and the Kerygmatic Christ," *SE* 3 [=TU 88] (1964) 33-44. A succinct statement of the points of disagreement between G. Bornkamm and R. Bultmann.

261   C. E. Braaten and R. A. Harrisville, eds., *The Historical Jesus and the Kerygmatic Christ: Essays on the New Quest of the Historical Jesus* (Nashville: Abingdon, 1964). Contains several significant studies, including: R. Bultmann, "The Primitive Christian Kerygma and the Historical Jesus" (pp. 15-42), E. Stauffer, "The Relevance of the Historical Jesus" (pp. 43-53), H. Conzelmann, "The Method of the Life-of-Jesus Research" (pp. 54-68), H. Braun, "The Significance of Qumran for the Problem of the Historical Jesus" (pp. 69-78), C. E. Braaten, "Martin Kähler on the Historic Biblical Christ" (pp. 79-105), H.-W. Bartsch, "The Historical Problem of the Life of Jesus" (pp. 106-141), H. Ott, "The Historical Jesus and the Ontology of History" (pp. 142-71), and V. A. Harvey and S. M. Ogden, "How New is the 'New Quest of the Historical Jesus'?" (pp. 197-242). Many of these studies appeared earlier in German; Braun and Stauffer in H. Ristow and K. Matthiae, eds., *Der historische Jesus und der kerygmatische Christus* (182).

262   R. E. Brown, "After Bultmann, What? An Introduction to the Post-Bultmannians," *CBQ* 26 (1964) 1-30. Reviews and criticizes the new quest; argues that its advocates dismiss material as inauthentic too quickly, unreasonably insisting that burden of proof rests on those who accept material as authentic; also criticizes new quest for ignoring the fourth gospel.

263   G. W. Buchanan, "Jesus and the Upper Class," *NovT* 7 (1964) 195-209. Thinks that Jesus may have come from a background of business, not carpentry.

264   P. J. Cahill, "Rudolf Bultmann and Post-Bultmann Tendencies," *CBQ* 26 (1964) 153-78. Surveys old and new quests, assesses the work of Bultmann's leading pupils, such as E. Käsemann, E. Fuchs, G. Bornkamm, H. Conzelmann, and G. Ebeling; views this work favorably.

265 H. Clavier, "Recherche du Jésus de l'histoire," *RHPR* 44 (1964) 236-44. Reviews historical Jesus research, discusses C. H. Dodd, *Historical Tradition in the Fourth Gospel* (Cambridge: University Press, 1963).

266 E. Dinkler, "Petrusbekenntnis und Satanswort. Das Problem der Messianität Jesu," in E. Dinkler, ed., *Zeit und Geschichte* (R. Bultmann Festschrift; Tübingen: Mohr [Siebeck], 1964) 127-53; ET: "Peter's Confession and the 'Satan' Saying: The Problem of Jesus' Messiahship," in J. M. Robinson, ed., *The Future of Our Religious Past* ([a translation of part of the Bultmann Festschrift] New York: Haper & Row, 1971) 169-202. Argues that when Marcan and Christian elements are removed, we discover that Jesus rebuked Peter for identifying him as the Messiah of popular Jewish expectation (Mark 8:29, 33).

267 A. S. Dunstone, "Ipsissima Verba Christi," *SE* 2 [=TU 87] (1964) 57-64. Criticizes the assumptions and arguments that the gospels do not offer the *ipsissima verba Christi*; believes that the very words of Jesus can be culled from these writings.

268 A. Finkel, *The Pharisees and the Teacher of Nazareth: A Study of their Background, their Halachic and Midrashic Teachings, the Similarities and Differences* (Arbeiten zur Geschichte des Spätjudentums und Urchristentums 4; Leiden: Brill, 1964). Attempts to isolate and compare first-century Pharisaic teaching with what is regarded Jesus' authentic teaching.

269 W. G. Kümmel, "Jesus und Paulus," *NTS* 10 (1962) 163-81. Criticizes the views of W. Schmithals and others; argues that there is more continuity between Jesus and Paul.

270 W. G. Kümmel, "Die Naherwartung in der Verkündigung Jesu," in E. Dinkler, ed., *Zeit und Geschichte* (R. Bultmann Festschrift; Tübingen: Mohr [Siebeck], 1964) 31-46; repr. in Kümmel, *Heilsgeschehen und Geschichte* (E. Grässer, O. Merk, and A. Fritz, eds.; Marburg: Elwert, 1965) 457-70; ET: "Eschatological Expectation in the Proclamation of Jesus," in J. M. Robinson, ed., *The Future of Our Religious Past* ([a translation of part of the Bultmann Festschrift] New York: Harper & Row, 1971) 29-48. Concludes that "an unbiased critical examination of the relevant texts shows unequivocally that Jesus counted on the nearness of the future Reign of God, a future confined to his own generation" (p. 47).

271 E. Lohse, *Die Geschichte des Leidens und Sterbens Jesu Christi* (Gütersloh: Mohn, 1964); ET: *History of the Suffering and Death of Jesus Christ*

(Philadelphia: Fortress, 1967). Sifts through the passion materials to recover the earliest tradition and to show how it has been redacted and interpreted by the evangelists.

272   H. K. McArthur, "Basic Issues: A Survey of Recent Gospel Research," *Interp* 18 (1964) 39-55. Reviews the question of the reliability of the gospels, how the tradition was transmitted, external corroborating materials, authenticity criteria, and where it is possible to reconstruct a portrait of the historical Jesus.

273   W. Neil, "Second Thoughts: The Jesus of History," *ExpTim* 75 (1964) 260-63. Criticizes the skepticism of R. Bultmann and others; believes that the gospels afford ample material for seeing why Jesus' disciples would come to recognize that Jesus the carpenter is Lord.

274   W. Pannenberg, *Grundzüge der Christologie* (Gütersloh: Mohn, 1964; 2nd ed., 1976); ET: *Jesus: God and Man* (Philadelphia: Westminster, 2nd ed., 1977). Challenges the distinction often made between the kerygmatic Christ and the historical Jesus, arguing that New Testament christology is exposition of the historical Jesus.

275   E. Schweizer, "Die Frage nach dem historischen Jesus," *EvT* 24 (1964) 403-19. Argues that although Paul and early Christians were not primarily interested in the Jesus of history, faith without reference to the historical Jesus leads to docetism. The gospels were written to anchor the kerygma in the Jesus of history, and not simply in faith.

276   H. Stock, "Das Verhältnis der Christusbotschaft der synoptischen Evangelien zum historischen Jesus," in E. Dinkler, ed., *Zeit und Geschichte* (R. Bultmann Festschrift; Tübingen: Mohr [Siebeck], 1964) 703-17. Raises the question of how to discuss the critical problem of the relationship between the kerygma and the historical Jesus in the context of religious education.

277   A. Vögtle, "Die historische und theologische Tragweite der heutigen Evangelienforschung," *ZKT* 86 (1964) 385-417. Argues that although the gospels cannot be viewed as biographies of the life of Jesus, much of the historical tradition is reliable and theologically relevant because of the action of the Holy Spirit (John 14—16).

278   J. C. Weber, "Karl Barth and the Historical Jesus," *JBR* 32 (1964) 350-54. Criticizes Barth's position on the historical Jesus; concludes that the question is left unresolved in Barth's theology.

279   H. Wenz, "Der kerygmatisierte historische Jesus im Kerygma," *TZ* 20 (1964) 23-38. Argues that the historical Jesus is part of the kerygma and that R. Bultmann's "Dass" is inadequate for a proper understanding of the kerygma.

280   U. Wilckens, "Hellenistisch-christliche Missionsüberlieferung und Jesustradition," *TLZ* 89 (1964) cols. 517-20. Argues that the Hellenistic-Christian missionary tradition knows of the Jesus tradition only poorly and indirectly.

281   H. C. Wolf, "Kierkegaard and the Quest of the Historical Jesus," *LQ* 16 (1964) 3-40. Relates Kierkegaard's concept of faith to the modern discussion of the problem of the historical Jesus; concludes that historical Jesus is essential to existential faith.

282   M. Zerwick, "Historicida de los Evangelos," *RCB* 1 (1964) 89-104. Argues that the gospel tradition is essentially historical, but not concerned with exact details.

283   R. S. Barbour, "Theologians of Our Time: Ernst Käsemann and Günther Bornkamm," *ExpTim* 76 (1965) 379-83. Discusses the historical method of two leading post-Bultmannian scholars.

284   O. Betz, *Was wissen wir von Jesus?* (Stuttgart and Berlin: Kreuz, 1965); ET: *What Do We Know about Jesus?* (Philadelphia: Westminster, 1968). Challenges the skepticism of R. Bultmann's *Jesus* (77).

285   J. Blank, "Zum Problem der neutestamentlichen Christologie," *UnSanc* 20 (1965) 108-25. Reviews recent discussion of christology and the historical Jesus, especially in relation to Catholic thought.

286   G. Bornkamm, "Jesus," in *Gestalten der Passion* (Sendereihe des Süddeutsche Rundfunks; Stuttgart: Kreuz, 1965) 56-66. Summary of the results of the new quest.

287   W. H. Capps, "Two Contrasting Approaches to Christology," *HeyJ* 6 (1965) 133-44. Compares and evaluates the views of R. Bultmann and O. Cullmann.

288   E. Fuchs, *Glaube und Erfahrung: Zum christologischen Problem im Neuen Testament* (GA 3; Tübingen: Mohr [Siebeck], 1965, 1971). Three of

Fuchs's essays, not previously published, are of relevance to historical Jesus research: "Zur Frage nach dem historischen Jesus. Ein Nachwort" (pp. 1-31), an introductory essay; "Theologische Exegese und philosophisches Seinsverständnis" (pp. 32-48), an assessment of R. Bultmann's *Jesus* (77) and existential self-understanding; and "Der historische Jesus als Gegenstand der Verkündigung" (pp. 433-44), an essay claiming that the Word of God can only come when spoken in the name of Jesus.

289   R. H. Fuller, *The Foundations of New Testament Christology* (New York: Scribner's, 1965). Examines background, Jesus' self-understanding, and the development of New Testament christology in the light of Easter faith.

290   V. P. Furnish, "The Jesus-Paul Debate: From Baur to Bultmann," *BJRL* 47 (1965) 342-81. Examines Pauline epistles for traces of the historical Jesus.

291   M. E. Glasswell, "Jesus Christ," *Th* 68 (1965) 558-63. Examines the distinction between who Jesus *was* and who Jesus *is*.

292   E. Grässer, "Der historische Jesus im Hebräerbrief," *ZNW* 56 (1965) 63-91. Even in Hebrews, whose author is so concerned with the humanity of Jesus, history is swallowed up in the kerygma; three important areas of typology depart from what is known of the historical Jesus.

293   W. G. Kümmel, "Das Problem des geschichtlichen Jesus in der gegenwärtigen Forschungslage," in Kümmel, *Heilsgeschehen und Geschichte* (Marburg Theologische Studien 3; E. Grässer, O. Merk, and A. Fritz, eds.; Marburg: Elwert, 1965) 392-405; originally appeared in H. Ristow and K. Matthiae, eds., *Der historische Jesus und der kerygmatische Christus* (182, pp. 39-53).

294   J. Macquarrie, "A Dilemma in Christology," *ExpTim* 76 (1965) 207-10. Reviews the implications that historical skepticism has for christology; finds in Jesus' death a link between humanity and divinity.

295   B. F. Meyer, "Jesus and the Remnant of Israel," *JBL* 84 (1965) 123-30. Thinks that the idea of "messianic remnant" underlies Jesus' preaching, even though no specific reference is made to it.

296   D. E. Nineham, "Some Reflections on the Present Position with Regard to the Jesus of History," *CQR* 166 (1965) 5-21; repr. in Nineham, et al., *Historicity and Chronology in the New Testament* (SPCK Theological

Collections 6; London: SPCK, 1965) 1-18. In general sympathy with new quest, cautions that true significance of Jesus' life cannot be limited to what is historically verifiable.

297   J. F. Peter, *Finding the Historical Jesus* (New York: Harper & Row, 1965). Concludes that the critic can only arrive at tentative "objective-historical" results, while the believer can have an "existential-historical" encounter with the Christ of the kerygma.

298   J. M. Robinson, "Kerygma and History in the New Testament," in J. P. Hyatt, ed., *The Bible in Modern Scholarship* (Nashville: Abingdon, 1965) 114-50 (with replies by D. M. Smith and F. V. Filson, pp. 151-165); GT: "Kerygma und Geschichte im Neuen Testament," *ZTK* 62 (1965) 294-337. Examines the complexities of "kerygma" and "history" in the New Testament, complexities not adequately taken into account by rigid, even obsolete, scholarly categories.

299   D. T. Rowlingson, "Gospel-Perspective and the Quest of the Historical Jesus," *JBR* 33 (1965) 329-36. Argues that the gospels' preoccupation with Jesus' pre-Easter ministry testifies to the importance of the historical Jesus for the kerygma; concludes that the task must be pursued.

300   D. H. Smith, "Concerning the Duration of the Ministry of Jesus," *ExpTim* 76 (1965) 114-16. Speculates that for several years prior to his baptism, Jesus was actually engaged in a prophetic ministry in Galilee.

301   D. O. Via, "The Necessary Complement to the Kerygma," *JR* 45 (1965) 30-38. Argues that the mere presence of the synoptics in the New Testament canon necessitates the quest of the historical Jesus.

1966-1970

302   O. Betz, "The Christological Problem in New Testament Research of Today," *Encount* 27 (1966) 54-64. Reviews recent major developments; believes that Jesus took upon himself the "messianic woes" of Israel necessary for atonement.

303   J. Blenkinsopp, "Faith or Fact?" *NBlack* 47 (1966) 380-86. Concludes that historical knowledge is necessary, but it cannot replace faith.

304   J. H. Elliott, "The Historical Jesus, the Kerygmatic Christ, and the Escha-
       tological Community," *CTM* 37 (1966) 470-91. Argues that more work
       needs to be done on the problem of the continuity between the Jesus of
       history and the Christ of the kerygma.

305   E. Haenchen, "Die frühe Christologie," *ZTK* 63 (1966) 145-59. Examines
       Paul's understanding of context and significance of dominical tradition.

306   V. A. Harvey, *The Historian and the Believer: The Morality of Historical
       Knowledge and Christian Belief* (New York: Macmillan, 1966). Examines
       the philosophical and hermeneutical complexities involved in many of the
       writings concerned with the historical Jesus, historical knowledge, and
       Christian faith; discusses E. Troeltsch, K. Barth, P. Tillich, R. Bultmann,
       C. H. Dodd, H. R. Niebuhr, and others; very critical of new quest (life of
       Jesus research reviewed on pp. 164-203).

307   H. Hommel, "Herrenworte im Lichte sokratischer Überlieferung," *ZNW* 57
       (1966) 1-23. Compares Jesus' warnings about bodily members that cause
       one to stumble to similar sayings in the socratic tradition.

308   J. D. Kingsbury, "The 'Jesus of History' and the 'Christ of Faith' in Rela-
       tion to Matthew's View of Time—Reactions to a New Approach," *CTM*
       37 (1966) 500-510. Argues that Matthew makes no attempt to present suc-
       cessive stages in Jesus' life, but that Matthew theologically understands
       Jesus' life as the time of fulfillment.

309   J. Macquarrie, "The Pre-Existence of Christ," *ExpTim* 77 (1966) 199-202.
       Proposes how such a doctrine arose from the historical Jesus.

310   R. P. Martin, "The New Quest of the Historical Jesus," in C. F. H. Henry,
       ed., *Jesus of Nazareth: Saviour and Lord* (Grand Rapids: Eerdmans, 1966)
       25-45. Summarizes and evaluates the new quest.

311   R. T. Osborn, "New Hermeneutic?" *Interp* 20 (1966) 400-411. Assesses the
       contributions of E. Fuchs and G. Ebeling; raises questions about relation to
       P. Tillich and Kantian and Heideggerian views.

312   H.-J. Schultz, ed., *Die Zeit Jesu* (Stuttgart: Kreuz, 1966); ET: *Jesus in His
       Time* (Philadelphia: Fortress, 1971). A valuable collection of studies by
       leading scholars on Jesus, his background, and his contemporaries.

313   D. M. Smith, "The Historical Jesus in Paul Tillich's Theology," *JR* 46
       (1966) 131-47. Reviews Tillich's theology; compares it to that of R.
       Bultmann and his pupils.

314   A. Strobel, *Die moderne Jesusforschung* (CH 83; Stuttgart: Calwer, 1966).
       Reviews the work of some of the major contributors to the quest of the
       historical Jesus (e.g., A. Schweitzer, R. Bultmann, E. Käsemann, and H.
       Conzelmann); concludes with a discussion of Schweitzer's famous "either-
       or" questions that had faced the scholars of the nineteenth-century quest.

315   W. Trilling, *Fragen zur Geschichtlichkeit Jesu* (Düsseldorf: Patmos, 1966);
       FT: *Jésus devant l'histoire* (Lire la Bible 15; Paris: Cerf, 1968). Although
       written for the general reader, neatly summarizes the issues; concludes that
       the historical Jesus is enigmatic, even mysterious, and the evangelists have
       interpreted him differently.

316   J. C. Weber, "Jesus' Opponents in the Gospel of Mark," *JBR* 34 (1966)
       214-22. Argues that a core of material goes back to the historical Jesus
       (mostly controversy sayings), but this material does not account for Jesus'
       crucifixion.

317   P. R. Ackroyd, "What Kind of Belief about Jesus?" *ATR* 49 (1967) 281-
       95. Examines the problem of the relationship of history and theology and
       how the church must "translate" the Jesus of history into an expression of
       relevance today.

318   C. K. Barrett, *Jesus and the Gospel Tradition* (London: SPCK, 1967;
       Philadelphia: Fortress, 1968). Fairly optimistic assessment of the general
       reliability of the gospels; concludes that Jesus anticipated suffering and dy-
       ing in behalf of his disciples and the righteous of Israel, but hoped and
       prayed for God's intervention, either immediately before death or soon after.

319   R. Batey, "Ernst Käsemann's Question concerning the Historical Jesus,"
       RestQ 10 (1967) 196-200. Examines the debate between Käsemann and R.
       Bultmann.

320   M. Black, "From Schweitzer to Bultmann: The Modern Quest of the His-
       torical Jesus," *McCQ* 20 (1967) 271-83. Argues that Jesus referred to him-
       self as the Son of Man and predicted his passion and vindication.

321   Th. Boman, *Die Jesus-Überlieferung im Lichte der neuer Volkskunde*
       (Göttingen: Vandenhoeck & Ruprecht, 1967). Applies "ethnology" to the

interpretation of the gospels, arguing that we cannot understand the Jesus tradition unless we appreciate the nature of the Palestinian story-teller.

322   S. G. F. Brandon, *Jesus and the Zealots: A Study of the Political Factor in Primitive Christianity* (New York: Scribner's, 1967). Argues that although Jesus was not himself a zealot, the presence of Simon the Zealot among the twelve indicates that zealot principles were not incompatible with Jesus' views, and this is probably why Jesus was executed by the Romans for sedition. See J. G. Griffiths, *NTS* 19 (1973) 483-85.

323   G. Delling, "Der 'historische Jesus' und der 'kerygmatische Christus,'" in H. Benckert, et al., eds., *Wort und Gemeinde* (E. Schoot Festschrift; Berlin: Evangelische Verlagsanstalt, 1967) 19-42. Argues that the salvific understanding of Jesus' passion and his expressions of authority are to be traced back to the "earthly one" himself, not to the early community.

324   W. R. Farmer, "Historical essay on the Humanity of Jesus Christ," in W. R. Farmer, et al.., eds., *Christian History and Interpretation* (J. Knox Festschrift; Cambridge: University Press, 1967) 101-26. Argues that Jesus rebuked the scribes and Pharisees for criticizing his fellowship with tax collectors and sinners.

325   A. D. Foster, "Gogarten and the Historicity of Christ," *DrewG* 37 (1967) 90-102. Assesses F. Gogarten's thought in relation to R. Bultmann and the new quest; approves of his emphasis of Jesus' obedience as central to christology.

326   A. D. Foster, "Theological Arguments for Christ's Historicity: Parallels with the Theistic Proofs," in W. R. Farmer, et al., eds., *Christian History and Interpretation* (J. Knox Festschrift; Cambridge: University Press, 1967) 57-77. Applies the logic of the ontological, teleological, and moral arguments to establish the historicity of Christ.

327   R. P. C. Hanson, "Assessment of Motive in the Study of the Synoptic Gospels," *ModCh* 10 (1967) 255-69. Criticizes the oft-held critical assumption that theological tendency on the part of an evangelist cancels out historical reliability.

328   W. E. Hull, "The New Quest of the Historical Jesus," *RevExp* 64 (1967) 323-39. Assesses the differences and similarities between the old and new quests; concludes that new quest is essentially different because it is more closely tied to a theological base.

329 J. L. Martyn, "Attitudes Ancient and Modern towards Tradition about Jesus," *Student World* 60 (1967) 359-72; a longer version appears in *USQR* 23 (1968) 129-45. Compares modern attitudes toward historicity of the gospels to those expressed by Ignatius.

330 J. E. Michl, "Probleme einer Geschichte Jesu," in C. Bauer, ed., *Speculum Historiale: Geschichte im Spiegel von Geschichtsschreibung und Geschichtsdeutung* (J. Spörl Festschrift; Freiburg and Munich: Alber, 1967) 513-22. Against the wider context of the problem of historiography, discusses the problems of writing a history of Jesus.

331 D. E. Nineham, "Et hoc genus omne—An Examination of Dr A. T. Hanson's Strictures on Some Recent Gospel Study," in W. R. Farmer, et al., eds., *Christian History and Interpretation* (J. Knox Festschrift; Cambridge: University Press, 1967) 199-222. In response to recent criticism (see A. T. Hanson, *Vindications: Essays on the Historical Basis of Christianity* [London: SCM, 1966] 74-102, in which it is concluded that the skeptical position of Nineham, J. Knox, and others is intolerable), explains how author understands gospel historicity. See Hanson's response in "'Non Liquet': A Rejoinder to Professor Nineham," *ModCh* 11 (1968) 212-22; reasserts that "the divorce between the Jesus of history and the Jesus of faith is neither historically necessary nor theologically justified."

332 G. Quispel, "The Diatessaron and the Historical Jesus," in A. Brelich, et al., eds., *Studi in onore di Alberto Pincherle* (Rome: Ateneo, 1967) 463-72. Points out that since the Gospel of Thomas may contain authentic sayings of Jesus and since Tatian apparently made use of it, the later versions of the *Diatessaron* may yield traditions that can be put to use in the quest of the historical Jesus.

333 E. W. Saunders, *Jesus in the Gospels* (Englewood Cliffs: Prentice-Hall, 1967). Argues that the traditions inherited by the evangelists bear the imprint of Jesus' person and point of view.

334 R. Slenczka, *Geschichtlichkeit und Personsein Jesu Christi: Studien zur christologischen Problematik der historischen Jesusfrage* (FSÖT 18; Göttingen: Vandenhoeck & Ruprecht, 1967). A critical review of the theological motives underlying much of the recent scholarship concerned with the quest; concludes that there is an essential line of continuity from the historical Jesus to the risen Christ.

335   E. Stauffer, *Jesus war ganz anders* (Hamburg: Wittig, 1967). Claims that
       Jesus was the "demythologizer" of his time, a man of protest; what is
       characteristic of Jesus is his uniqueness—he cannot be put into a com-
       monly recognized category.

336   F. W. Beare, "Concerning Jesus of Nazareth," *JBL* 87 (1968) 125-35; repr.
       in R. Batey, ed., *New Testament Issues* (New York: Harper & Row, 1970)
       57-70. Argues that Matthew's gospel cannot be used as a historical source
       without corroboration from other sources.

337   C. E. Carlston, "Biblicism or Historicism? Some Remarks on the Conflict
       between Kähler and Herrmann on the Historical Jesus," *BR* 13 (1968) 26-
       40. Assesses the turn-of-the-century debate between M. Kähler (65) and W.
       Herrmann, which is regarded as still relevant for today; concludes that
       neither approach solves the problem.

338   S. A. Cartledge, *Jesus of Fact and Faith: Studies in the Life of Christ*
       (Grand Rapids: Eerdmans, 1968). Surveys and evaluates major issues in life
       of Jesus research.

339   L. Cerfaux, *Jésus aux origines de la tradition* (Pour une histoire de Jésus 3;
       Paris: Desclée, 1968). Views the gospel tradition as essentially reliable,
       arguing that material is authentic: (1) if it coheres with the context in
       which Jesus ministered and (2) since early Christian tradents were faithful
       in transmitting the Jesus tradition.

340   H. Flender, *Die Botschaft Jesu von der Herrschaft Gottes* (Munich: Kaiser,
       1968). Having searched for the "man" Jesus, concludes that he was essen-
       tially non-apocalyptic, but stood in the tradition of Israel's prophets calling
       on the nation to fulfill its destiny by becoming a cause for universal bless-
       ing.

341   D. Flusser, *Jesus in Selbstzeugnissen und Bilddokumenten* (Rowohlts
       Monographien 140; Hamburg: Rowohlt, 1968); ET: *Jesus* (New York:
       Herder & Herder, 1969); FT: *Jésus* (Paris: Seuil, 1970). Believes that the
       synoptic gospels provide a faithful picture of the historical Jesus; concludes
       that Jesus was a Jewish preacher and miracle worker who fully accepted the
       Jewish law and founded a community to bring about reform and fulfillment
       in Israel, not succession from it.

342   M. Hengel, *Nachfolge und Charisma: Eine exegetisch-religions-
       geschichtliche Studie zu Mt 8:21f. und Jesu Ruf in die Nachfolge* (BZNW

34; Berlin: Töpelmann, 1968); ET: *The Charismatic Leader and His Followers* (New York: Crossroad, 1981). Jesus' summons to discipleship is viewed as unique and is viewed as evidence that Jesus understood himself as Israel's Messiah.

343   W. Marxsen, "Jesus, oder das Neuen Testament," in Marxsen, *Der Exeget als Theologe: Vorträge zum Neuen Testament* (Gütersloh: Mohn, 1968) 246-64. Argues that although critical exegesis is necessary, and the historical Jesus produced by it only faintly resembles the picture we find in the New Testament, neither one can be dispensed with.

344   H. Merkel, "Jesus und die Pharisäer," *NTS* 14 (1968) 194-208. Argues that many of the conflicts between Jesus and the Pharisees are historical and not merely the reflections of later controversy between Judaism and the early church.

345   K. Niederwimmer, *Jesus* (Göttingen: Vandenhoeck & Ruprecht, 1968). Believes that the historical Jesus was in search of a new being (*Dasein*), something that transcends the present; concludes that the apocalyptic Kingdom is an illusion, most of whose aspects Jesus rejected.

346   J. Reumann, *Jesus in the Church's Gospels: Modern Scholarship and the Earliest Sources* (Philadelphia: Fortress, 1968). An informed discussion of the critical issues, useful bibliography; concludes that a conventional biography of Jesus cannot be written.

347   D. T. Rowlingson, *The Gospel-Perspective on Jesus Christ* (Philadelphia: Westminster, 1968). An introductory survey.

348   G. Schille, "Prolegomena zur Jesusfrage," *TLZ* 93 (1968) cols. 481-88. Argues that it is necessary to recognize that there were many early christologies and not a single unified concept.

349   H. Schürmann, *Traditionsgeschichtliche Untersuchungen zu den synoptischen Evangelien* (Kommentare und Beiträge zum Alten und Neuen Testament; Düsseldorf: Patmos, 1968) esp. pp. 83-158. Argues that R. Bultmann's existentialist interpretation of the historical Jesus falsifies the message of the historical Jesus. The main point of Jesus' preaching is not to make available to humankind a new way of being, but to disclose to humankind the nature of God. Thus the emphasis should be theocentric, not anthropocentric.

350   F. T. Trotter, ed., *Jesus and the Historian* (E. C. Colwell Festschrift;
       Philadelphia: Westminster, 1968). The most significant articles would
       include W. H. Brownlee, "Jesus and Qumran" (pp. 52-81), E. L. Titus,
       "The Fourth Gospel and the Historical Jesus" (98-113), H. D. Betz, "Jesus
       as Divine Man" (pp. 114-33), and J. M. Robinson, "Jesus' Parables as God
       Happening" (pp. 134-50).

351   C. C. Anderson, *Critical Quests of Jesus* (Grand Rapids: Eerdmans, 1969).
       Reviews the major contributions to the scholarly quest of the historical
       Jesus; argues that gospel accounts are historically reliable.

352   J. A. Baird, *Audience Criticism and the Historical Jesus* (Philadelphia:
       Westminster, 1969). Concludes that there is a core of carefully preserved
       Jesus tradition in the gospels.

353   M. Bouttier, *Du Christ de l'histoire au Jésus des évangiles* (Avenir de la
       théologie; Paris: Cerf, 1969). An introductory survey that examines the
       views of R. Bultmann, J. Jeremias, and E. Käsemann.

354   H. Braun, *Jesus: Der Mann aus Nazareth und seine Zeit* (Stuttgart: Kreuz,
       1969; 2nd ed., 1984; 3rd. ed., Gütersloh: Mohn, 1988); ET: *Jesus of
       Nazareth: The Man and His Time* (Philadelphia: Fortress, 1979). Argues
       that the essence of Jesus' authority is seen in his emphasis on love and
       grace, which means accepting one's neighbor, and accepting oneself; con-
       cludes that the resurrection was not an "event in space and time."

355   H. Grass, "Historisch-kritische Forschung und Dogmatik," in Grass, *Theo-
       logie und Kritik* (Gesammelte Aufsätze und Vorträge; Göttingen: Vanden-
       hoeck & Ruprecht, 1969) 9-27. A philosophical discussion of the problems
       of relating historical-critical research to Christian dogma, especially in
       reference to historical Jesus and christology; a broad discussion that touches
       on many aspects of historical Jesus research.

356   A. J. B. Higgins, *The Tradition about Jesus* (SJT Occasional Papers 15;
       Edinburgh: Oliver & Boyd, 1969). Assesses the tradition about Jesus in the
       synoptics, the fourth gospel, and the gnostic Gospel of Thomas.

357   L. E. Keck, "Bornkamm's Jesus of Nazareth Revisited," *JR* 49 (1969) 1-
       17. Points out several weaknesses in G. Bornkamm's *Jesus von Nazareth*
       (65).

358   H. K. McArthur, "From the Historical Jesus to Christology," *Interp* 23 (1969) 190-206. Sorts out the logic behind the attempts to find a historical Jesus relevant for Christian faith.

359   H. K. McArthur, *In Search of the Historical Jesus* (New York: Scribner's, 1969). A selection of excerpts from leading scholars.

360   S. McLoughlin, "Gospels and the Jesus of History," *DRev* 87 (1969) 183-200. Review article of X. Léon-Dufour, *The Gospels and the Jesus of History* (248).

361   G. Strecker, "Die historische und theologische Problematik der Jesusfrage," *EvT* 29 (1969) 453-76. Reviews some of the most influential work; concludes that historical findings can never replace the New Testament witness that Jesus is the Christ of faith.

362   W. Trilling, *Fragen zur Geschichtlichkeit Jesu* (Düsseldorf: Patmos, 1969). Discusses several basic questions: Why have attempts to write "lives of Jesus" failed? Can we obtain certain knowledge about Jesus? Was his ministry successful?

363   W. O. Walker, "The Quest for the Historical Jesus: A Discussion of Methodology," *ATR* 51 (1969) 38-56. After reviewing authenticity criteria, argues that a picture of the historical Jesus must place Jesus in first-century Palestinian context, explain his Roman execution, and account for the rise of Christianity.

364   H.-W. Bartsch, *Jesus: Prophet und Messias aus Galiläa* (Antworten 20; Frankfurt: Stimme, 1970). Believes that an adequate link between historical Jesus and Christ of faith can be found.

365   H. Boers, "Jesus and the Christian Faith: New Testament Christology since Bousset's *Kyrios Christos*," *JBL* 89 (1970) 450-56. Reviews the positions of W. Bousset, R. Bultmann, H. Braun, O. Cullmann, F. Hahn, and R. H. Fuller.

366   J. W. Bowman, *Which Jesus?* (Philadelphia: Westminster, 1970). An examination of the various "lives" of the life of Jesus research.

367   O. Cullmann, *Jesus und die Revolutionären seiner Zeit* (Tübingen: Mohr [Siebeck], 1970); ET: *Jesus and the Revolutionaries* (New York: Harper & Row, 1970); FT: *Jésus et les révolutionnaires de son temps* (Neuchâtel:

Delachaux et Niestle, 1970). Argues that in his actions and preaching Jesus brings in a new Kingdom, but he does not call for violence; concludes that Jesus is in some ways more radical than the zealots, less so in other ways.

368 C. H. Dodd, *The Founder of Christianity* (New York: London: Macmillan, 1970); FT: *Le fondateur du christianisme* (Paris: Seuil, 1970). Takes into account the first century Palestinian context well; emphasizes Jesus' personal characteristics and his desire to establish a community worthy of being called "the people of God."

369 E. Fuchs, *Jesus. Wort und Tat* (Vorlesung zum Neuen Testament 1; Tübingen: Mohr [Siebeck], 1970). A series of studies by one of the leading post-Bultmannian scholars in which the view is worked out that the kerygma finds expression in Jesus' conduct toward sinners.

370 E. Käsemann, "Das Thema des Neuen Testaments," in J. C. Hampe, et al., eds., *Hundertfünfundzwanzig Chr Kaiser Verlag München: 1845-1970* (Munich: Kaiser, 1970) 66-83. Argues that historical Jesus is a major presupposition of New Testament theology.

371 H. C. Kee, *Jesus in History: An Approach to the Study of the Gospels* (New York: Harcourt Brace Jovanovich, 1970; 2nd ed., 1977). Reviews the quest of the historical Jesus, the sources, the tendencies of the evangelists, and some of the relevant non-canonical writings.

372 M. Lehmann, *Synoptische Quellenanalyse und die Frage nach dem historischen Jesus* (BZNW 38; Berlin: Töpelmann, 1970). Criticizes the thesis of E. Hirsch; argues that there are no small literary gospels underlying the synoptics; discusses the criteria for determining authenticity.

373 T. Lorenzmeier, "Zum Thema: Historischer Jesus," *EK* 3 (1970) 296-98. A response to W. Schmithals's claim (380) that historical Jesus research is "theologically forbidden."

374 P. Merkley, "New Quests for Old: One Historian's Observations on a Bad Bargain," *CJT* 16 (1970) 203-18. Criticizes the leading advocates of the new quest for misinterpreting and misappropriating the views of the late historian R. G. Collingwood; concludes that these scholars simply do not understand history and historiography.

375 R. Morgan, "Negative Criticism of the Gospels?" *RelS* 6 (1970) 77-88. Argues that "negative" criticism of the gospels, especially as it relates to

the question of the historical Jesus, has the cathartic function of negating the legalistic perversion of Christianity ("this is what Jesus was") and revealing the true character of Christian faith in Jesus ("this is what Jesus means").

376   H. Haag, et al., eds., *Jesus in den Evangelien: Ein Symposion mit Josef Blinzler* (SB 45; Stuttgart: Katholisches Bibelwerk, 1970). Seven essays, the most relevant being those by R. Pesch, "Christliche und jüdische Jesusforschung. Übersicht und kritische Würdigung" (pp. 10-37), and F. Mussner, "Der 'historische' Jesus" (pp. 38-49). The other studies by P. Hoffmann, J. Blinzler, H. Geist, G. Voss, and H. Leroy are concerned with Jesus' preaching in Q, Mark, Matthew, Luke, and John, respectively.

377   K. Rahner, "Bemerkungen zur Bedeutung der Geschichte Jesu für die Katholische Dogmatik," in G. Bornkamm and K. Rahner, eds., *Die Zeit Jesu* (H. Schlier Festschrift; Freiburg: Herder, 1970) 273-83. Discusses the implications that the historical Jesus has for Catholic doctrine.

378   J. Roloff, *Das Kerygma und der irdische Jesus* (Göttingen: Vandenhoeck & Ruprecht, 1970). Argues that certain aspects of the kerygma were manifested in the life of the earthly Jesus (such as violating sabbath laws); claims, contrary to R. Bultmann, that many of the vivid details in the gospels reflect "living memories" and not later unhistorical embellishment.

379   W. Schatz, "Herbert Brauns Jesus-Buch," *Ref* 19 (1970) 189-97. Review article of Braun's *Jesus: Der Mann aus Nazareth und seine Zeit* (354).

380   W. Schmithals, "Kein Streit um des Kaisers Bart. Zur Diskussion über das Bekenntnis zu Jesus Christus," *EK* 3 (1970) 76-82. Claims that historical Jesus research may be possible, even permissible, but it is nevertheless theologically forbidden. See the reply of Lorenzmeier (373).

381   W. Schmithals, "Noch einmal: historischer und biblischer Jesus," *EK* 3 (1970) 416-18. A rejoinder to Lorenzmeier (373).

382   E. Schweizer, *Jesus Christus im vielfältigen Zeugnis des Neuen Testaments* (Munich: Siebenstern, 1970); ET: *Jesus* (London: SCM; Richmond: John Knox, 1971). Emphasizes the uniqueness of Jesus; claims that Jesus repudiated apocalyptic.

383   P. Stuhlmacher, "Kritische Marginalien zum gegenwärtigen Stand der Frage nach Jesus," in D. Rössler, ed., *Fides et Communicatio* (M. Doerne

Festschrift; Göttingen: Vandenhoeck & Ruprecht, 1970) 341-61. Claims
that the present critical stance is unnecessarily skeptical.

384   A. Vögtle, "Jesus von Nazareth," in R. Kottje and B. Moeller, eds., *Oeku-*
      menische Kirchengeschichte I (3 vols.; Mainz: Matthias-Grünewald, 1970)
      1.3-24. Summary article touching on the problem of reconstructing the
      history of Jesus, Jesus and the Baptist, Jesus' ministry, preaching (on
      God's will and the Kingdom), self-understanding, and passion.

                                    1971-1975

385   H.-W. Bartsch, "Théologie et histoire dans la tradition de la vie de Jésus,"
      in E. Castelli, ed., *Révélation et histoire* (Paris: Aubier, 1971) 173-88.
      Reviews the problems in the position of R. Bultmann and in the recent
      developments in the thinking of some of his leading pupils.

386   G. Baumbach, *Jesus von Nazareth im Lichte der jüdischen Gruppenbildung*
      (Aufsätze und Vorträge zur Theologie und Religionsgeschichte 54; Berlin:
      Evangelische Verlagsanstalt, 1971). Compares Jesus to zealots, the Sicarii,
      the Sadducees, and the Pharisees (but not to the Essenes); concludes that
      Jesus offended each of these groups.

387   J. Blank, "Der Christus des Glaubens und der historische Jesus," in E.
      Lessing, ed., *Der Mann aus Galiläa* (Freiburg: Herder, 1971) 199-242; ET:
      "The Christ of Faith and the Historical Jesus," in Lessing, ed., *Jesus:*
      History and Culture of the New Testament (New York: Herder and Herder,
      1971) 195-233. Surveys the problems; outlines Jesus' message and
      ministry of miracles.

388   E. Fascher, "Zur Geschichte der formgeschichtlichen Erforschung des Neuen
      Testaments," in G. Kulicke, et al., eds., *Bericht von der Theologie: Resul-*
      tate, Probleme, Konzepte (Berlin: Evangelische Verlagsanstalt, 1971) 33-
      55. Surveys the history of form-critical research and examines its impact on
      historical Jesus research.

389   J. Gnilka, "Neue Jesusliteratur," *TRev* 67 (1971) cols. 249-56. reviews
      recent books by M. Hengel, O. Cullmann, H. Conzelmann, H. Braun, S.
      Ben-Chorin, and others.

390   P. Grech, "Recent Developments in the Jesus of History Controversy," *BTB* 1 (1971) 190-213. Examines the Bultmannian movement; criticizes assumptions held by R. Bultmann and pupils.

391   M. Hengel, "Kerygma oder Geschichte? Zur Problematik einer falschen Alternative in der neutestamentlichen Forschung aufgezeigt an Hand einiger neuer Monographien," *TQ* 151 (1971) 323-36. Criticizes the widespread assumption that kerygmatic interests necessarily preclude historically reliable tradition.

392   L. E. Keck, *A Future for the Historical Jesus: The Place of Jesus in Preaching and Theology* (Nashville: Abingdon, 1971; Philadelphia: Fortress, 1981). Shows how the results of historical Jesus research can have positive value for Christian faith; critical of the new quest; concludes that the link between the historical Jesus and Christian experience is "trust," i.e., just as Jesus trusted in God, so Christians trust in Jesus and in Jesus' understanding of God.

393   H. Koester, "The Historical Jesus: Some Comments and Thoughts on Norman Perrin's Rediscovering the Teaching of Jesus," in H. D. Betz, ed., *Christology and a Modern Pilgrimage* (Claremont: New Testament Colloquium, 1971) 123-36. Interacting with N. Perrin's *Rediscovering the Teaching of Jesus* (804), discusses the problems of the methodology involved in searching for historical Jesus, with insightful comments on the shortcomings of the dissimilarity criterion.

394   G. E. Ladd, "The Search for Perspective," *Interp* 25 (1971) 41-62. Argues that historical criticism of the gospels fails because it denies an element (i.e., the supernatural) with which the object of its study is inextricably bound up.

395   H. K. McArthur, "The Burden of Proof in Historical Jesus Research," *ExpTim* 82 (1971) 116-19. Argues that the burden of proof rests on the claim to authenticity, except when tradition is found in three or four of the synoptic sources (Mark, Q, L, M).

396   H. Patsch, "Der Einzug Jesu in Jerusalem: Ein historische Versuch," *ZTK* 68 (1971) 1-26. Believes that the synoptic tradition of Jesus' entry into Jerusalem reflects two related, but distinct, traditions: (1) one in which Jesus rode on a donkey and (2) another in which Jesus was acclaimed Messiah by his disciples.

397   É. Trocmé, *Jésus de Nazareth vu par les témoins de sa vie* (Bibliothéque
      Théologique; Neuchâtel: Delachaux & Niestlé, 1971); ET: *Jesus as Seen by
      His Contemporaries* (London: SCM; Philadelphia: Fortress, 1973). A
      critical evaluation of attempts to write a biography of Jesus; proposes steps
      that must be taken to avoid error; concludes that a biography of Jesus is not
      possible, but we can recover the impression that he made on his
      contemporaries.

398   C. C. Anderson, *The Historical Jesus: A Continuing Quest* (Grand Rapids:
      Eerdmans, 1972). A critical assessment of R. Bultmann and the new quest.

399   H.-W. Bartsch, "Theologie und Geschichte in der Überlieferung vom Leben
      Jesu," *EvT* 32 (1972) 128-43. Argues that the life of the historical Jesus
      had a major impact on the practices of the first Christians and on their
      formulation of the tradition, especially as seen in eating together, and their
      attitude toward the Temple.

400   J. Blank, *Jesus von Nazareth: Geschichte und Relevanz* (Freiburg: Herder,
      1972; 4th ed., 1975). A collection of essays, some of which have been
      noted above (see 285,387).

401   W. Eltester, ed., *Jesus in Nazareth* (BZNW 40; Berlin: de Gruyter, 1972).
      Four studies by E. Grässer, A. Strobel, R. Tannehill, and W. Eltester on
      Jesus' Nazareth sermon (Mark 6:1-6; Luke 4:16-30).

402   R. Hiers, "The Historical Jesus and the Historians," *Dial* 11 (1972) 95-100.
      Discusses the contributions, strengths, and weaknesses of the major con-
      tributors to the scholarly quest.

403   H. Jellouschek, "Zur christologischen Bedeutung der Frage nach dem
      historischen Jesus," *TQ* 152 (1972) 112-23. Argues that the quest of the
      historical Jesus must begin with the New Testament's christological state-
      ments and then proceed corrected at every point by historical data.

404   O. Kuss, "'Bruder Jesus.' Zur 'Heimholung' des Jesus von Nazareth in das
      Judentums," *MTZ* 23 (1972) 284-96. Criticizes the studies of Jewish
      scholars (i.e., S. Ben-Chorin, D. Flusser, and E. Lessing) who over-
      emphasize the Jewishness of Jesus, and ignore or treat as unhistorical those
      features that are distinctively Christian.

405   A. M. Ramsey, "Christian Faith and the Historical Jesus," *Th* 75 (1972)
       118-26. Argues that early Christian faith influenced but did not obliterate
       the history of Jesus.

406   W. Schmithals, "Historischer und biblischer Jesus, " in Schmithals, *Jesus
       Christus in der Verkündigung der Kirche* (Neukirchen/Vluyn: Neukirchener,
       1972) 80-90. Offers further defense of his position over against the criti-
       cism of T. Lorenzmeier (see 373,380,381).

407   S. Schulz, "Die neue Frage nach dem historischen Jesus," in H. Baltens-
       weiler and B. Reicke, eds., *Neues Testament und Geschichte: Historisches
       Geschehen und Deutung im Neuen Testament* (O. Cullmann Festschrift;
       Zürich: Theologischer Verlag, 1972) 33-42. Sees research in the area of
       tradition-historical situation of early Christianity as the new question in
       historical Jesus scholarship.

408   H. Schürmann, "Das Weiterleben der Sache Jesu im nachösterlichen Herren-
       mahl. Die Kontinuität der Zeichen in der Diskontinuität der Zeiten," *BZ* 16
       (1972) 1-23. Argues that the essential element of the historical Jesus is to
       be found in his consistent demonstration of the reality of the eschaton and
       what it means for people.

409   G. Strube, ed., *Wer war Jesus von Nazareth? Die Erforschung einer his-
       torischen Gestalt* (Munich: Kindler, 1972). Strube introduces and presents
       ten major contributions to the scholarly quest of the historical Jesus,
       including those by D. F. Strauss, A. Schweitzer, H. J. Cadbury, H. Braun,
       A. Vögtle, E. Käsemann, and M. Hengel.

410   S. Sykes and J. P. Clayton, eds., *Christ, Faith and History* (Cambridge:
       University Press, 1972). Sixteen studies, half of which are relevant to
       historical Jesus research, particularly those by C. F. D. Moule, "The
       Manhood of Jesus in the New Testament" (pp. 95-110), D. Cupitt, "One
       Jesus, Many Christs?" (pp. 131-44), J. P. Clayton, "Is Jesus Necessary for
       Christology? An Antinomy in Tillich's Theological Method" (pp. 147-64),
       P. Carnley, "The Poverty of Historical Scepticism" (pp. 165-90), and G.
       N. Stanton, "The Gospel Traditions and Early Christological Reflection"
       (pp. 191-204).

411   W. Trilling, "Geschichte und Ergebnisse: Der historisch-kritischen Jesus-
       forschung: Der 'historische' Jesus," in F. J. Schierse, ed., *Jesus von
       Nazareth* (Mainz: Matthia-Grünewald, 1972) 187-213. Reviews recent
       results in historical Jesus research.

412   É. Trocmé, "Quelques travaux récents sur le Jésus de l'histoire," *RHPR* 52
       (1972) 489-98. Reviews and evaluates historical Jesus studies published
       from 1961 to 1972.

413   J. Yoder, *The Politics of Jesus* (Grand Rapids: Eerdmans, 1972). Argues
       that one of the significant aspects of Jesus' ministry and teachings centers
       on nonviolent resistance to evil.

414   W. Beilner, "Der Weg zu Jesus: Der Verkündiger und der Verkündigte," in
       A. Paus, ed., *Die Frage nach Jesus* (Graz: Styria, 1973) 69-149. Concludes
       that the person of Jesus cannot be separated from New Testament christo-
       logy, for New Testament christology presupposes the integration of the
       historical Jesus and the Christ of faith.

415   J. Bowker, *Jesus and the Pharisees* (New York: Cambridge University
       Press, 1973). Valuable for its extensive citation of primary source materi-
       als; argues that Jesus offended virtually all groups and was condemned by
       the Sanhedrin as a "rebellious elder."

416   R. Campbell, "History and Bultmann's Structural Inconsistency," *RelS* 9
       (1973) 63-79. Contends that R. Bultmann's understanding of history is
       very wrong; Bultmann's position cannot be consistently maintained apart
       from some historical (i.e., *historisch*) content underlying the kerygma.

417   H. Conzelmann, *Jesus* (Philadelphia: Fortress, 1973); trans. from "Jesus
       Christus," *RGG* 3 (3rd ed., 1959) cols. 619-53. Concise statement of the
       issues; good bibliography.

418   G. Delling, "Die Jesusgeschichte in der Verkündigung nach Acta," *NTS* 19
       (1973) 373-89. Examines the way the history of Jesus is variously
       summarized in the speeches in Acts.

419   B. E. Gärtner, "Den historiske Jesus och trons Krustus: Några reflexioner
       kring Bultmannskolan och Lukas," *SEÅ* 37-38 (1973) 175-84. In response
       to the Bultmannian school of thought, argues that the New Testament
       clearly teaches the personal continuity between the historical Jesus and the
       exalted Christ.

420   E. Grässer, "Christologie und historischer Jesus: Kritische Anmerkungen
       zu Herbert Brauns Christologieverständnis," *ZTK* 70 (1973) 404-19. In

response to H. Braun (354), contends that lying behind New Testament Christology is the exalted Christ, not the "man from Nazareth."

421   E. Grässer, "Motive und Methoden der neueren Jesusliteratur. An Beispielen dargestellt," *VF* 18 (1973) 3-45. Examines recent literature on Jesus, arguing that Jesus cannot be separated from Christ.

422   F. Hahn, "Die Frage nach dem historischen Jesus," *TTZ* 82 (1973) 193-205. Discusses difficulty of getting behind gospels to pre-Easter Jesus; argues that we should examine how Jesus traditions functioned in the life of the early community.

423   J. A. T. Robinson, "The Use of the Fourth Gospel for Christology Today," in B. Lindars and S. S. Smalley, eds., *Christ and Spirit in the New Testament* (C. F. D. Moule Festschrift; Cambridge: University Press, 1973) 61-78. Questions the oft-held assumption that the fourth gospel has no contribution to make to the recovery of the historical Jesus.

424   J. Roloff, "Auf der Suche nach einem neuen Jesusbild. Tendenzen und Aspekte der gegenwärtigen Diskussion, *TLZ* 98 (1973) cols. 561-72. Traces tendencies that have emerged subsequent to the new quest; concludes that Jesus, as well as his preaching, must be studied more closely.

425   F. Schnider, *Jesus, der Prophet* (Göttingen: Vandenhoeck & Ruprecht, 1973). Agrees that one of the earliest titles applied to Jesus was "prophet," but thinks it highly unlikely that this title ever made up the whole of pre-Easter christology.

426   K. Schubert, "Geschichte und Heilsgeschichte," *Kairos* 15 (1973) 89-101. Argues that although history cannot provide the grounds for faith, and certainly not tentative historical research, history is the presupposition of faith.

427   G. Vermes, *Jesus the Jew: A Historian's Reading of the Gospel* (New York: Macmillan, 1973; 2nd ed., 1983). Extensive use of early Palestinian sources; concludes that Jesus is a *hasid*, and so is part of charismatic Judaism.

428   G. Bornkamm, "Jesus Christ," *New Encyclopaedia Britannica* 10 (1974) 145-55. Concise statement from the new quest perspective.

429   J. G. Gager, "The Gospels and Jesus: Some Doubts about Method," *JR* 54
       (1974) 244-72. Concludes that despite success of the criterion of
       dissimilarity, there is too little material and, worst yet, the original setting
       of this meager material cannot be recovered.

430   N. Kehl, "Die Relevanz des historischen Jesus für die Begegnung des
       Christentums mit dem Hinduismus," in G. Oberhammer, ed., *Offenbarung,
       geistige Realität des Menschen* (Leiden: Brill; Vienna: Gerold, 1974) 199-
       219. Argues that many of Christianity's beliefs and practices are rooted in
       the historical Jesus.

431   K. Kertelge, ed., *Rückfrage nach Jesus: zur Methodik und Bedeutung der
       Frage nach dem historischen Jesus* (QD 63; Freiburg and Basel: Herder,
       1974). Six essays by F. Hahn, "Methodologische Überlieferungen zur
       Rückfrage nach Jesus" (pp. 11-77); ET: "Methodological Reflections on the
       Historical Jesus," in Hahn, *Historical Investigation and New Testament
       Faith* (E. Krentz, ed.; Philadelphia: Fortress, 1983) 35-105, F. Lentzen-
       Deis, "Kriterien für die historische Beurteilung der Jesusüberlieferung" (pp.
       78-117), F. Mussner, "Methodologie der Frage nach dem historischen
       Jesus" (pp. 118-47), R. Pesch, "Die Überlieferung der Passion Jesu" (pp.
       148-73), K. Kertelge, "Die Überlieferung der Wunder Jesu und die Frage
       nach dem historischen Jesus" (pp. 174-93), and R. Schnackenburg, "Der
       geschichtliche Jesus in seiner ständigen Bedeutung für Theologie und
       Kirche" (pp. 194-220).

432   H. Küng, *Christ sein* (Munich: Piper, 1974); ET: *On Being a Christian*
       (Garden City: Doubleday, 1984). Viewing the gospels as essentially trust-
       worthy, argues that christology must be founded upon the human Jesus of
       history; concludes that Jesus understood his mission primarily as
       proclaiming his Father's Kingdom, a proclamation which eventually
       provoked the authorities of his time and led to his death. Küng's systematic
       discussion of various questions and topics repeatedly refers to the teaching,
       ministry, and life of Jesus.

433   P. E. Lapide, *Der Rabbi von Nazaret. Wandlungen des jüdischen Jesus-
       bildes* (Trier: Spee, 1974). Examines first-century Palestine, Jewish inter-
       pretation of Jesus from antiquity to present.

434   D. Lührmann, "Jesus: History and Remembrance," in E. Schillebeeckx and
       B. van Iersel, eds., *Jesus Christ and Human Freedom* (Concilium 93; New
       York: Herder and Herder, 1974) 42-55. Discusses the theme of freedom in
       the historical Jesus and the memory of the early church.

435 C. F. D. Moule and H. Willmer, "The Distinctiveness of Christ: A Corre-
spondence," *Th* 77 (1974) 404-12. Argues that Christians selected material
accordingly to their need and experience and were guided by what had happened to Jesus.

436 K. Müller, "Jesus und die Sadduzäer," in H. Merklein and J. Lange, eds.,
Biblische Rand bemerkungen (R. Schnackenburg Festschrift; Würzburg:
Echter, 1974) 3-24. Explores the significance of the Sadducees in the min-
istry of Jesus and in his rejection and death.

437 I. G. Nicol, "Schweitzer's Jesus: A Psychology of the Heroic Will,"
ExpTim 86 (1974) 52-55. Discusses how A. Schweitzer, despite his own
criticism of the approach, produced his own psychology of Jesus.

438 R. Pesch, "Jesus, a Free Man," in E. Schillebeeckx and B. van Iersel, eds.,
Jesus Christ and Human Freedom (Concilium 93; New York: Herder and
Herder, 1974) 56-70. Argues that an essential element in Jesus' faith was
his sense of freedom; in his preaching he called people to the same faith.

439 G. Richards, "Paul Tillich and the Historical Jesus," *SR* 4 (1974/75) 120-
28. Argues that the historical Jesus is theologically unnecessary.

440 E. Schillebeeckx, *Jezus, het verhaal van een levende* (Bloemendaal: Nelis-
sen, 1974); GT: *Jesus: Die Geschichte von einem Lebenden* (Freiburg:
Herder, 1975); ET: *Jesus: An Experiment in Christology* (New York:
Seabury, 1979). Discussion of historical Jesus on pp. 41-397; claims that
behind the church's proclamation is "the concrete person Jesus of
Nazareth," which is "the one and only basis for an authentic christology"
(p. 82); understands Jesus as a leader of a liberation movement, who offered
himself as a servant and who remained silent when condemned in
Jerusalem.

441 H. Schlier, "Zur Frage: Wer ist Jesus?" in J. Gnilka, ed., *Neues Testament
und Kirche* (R. Schnackenburg Festschrift; Freiburg: Herder, 1974) 359-70.
Claims that if the question is framed in a strict historical sense, the question cannot be answered.

442 G. N. Stanton, *Jesus of Nazareth in New Testament Preaching* (SNTSMS
27; Cambridge: University Press, 1974). Argues that there is ample evidence in the New Testament that the early church was interested in the
Jesus of history.

443   H. D. Betz, "Ein judenchristliche Kult-Didache in Matthäus 6,1-18. Über-
       legungen und Fragen im Blick auf das Problem des historischen Jesus," in
       G. Strecker, ed., *Jesus Christus in Historie und Theologie* (H. Conzelmann
       Festschrift; Tübingen: Mohr [Siebeck], 1975) 445-57; ET: "A Jewish-
       Christian Cultic *Didache* in Matt. 6:1-18: Reflections and Questions on the
       Problem of the Historical Jesus," in Betz, *Essays on the Sermon on the
       Mount* (Philadelphia: Fortress, 1985) 55-69. Concludes that the compo-
       nents of Matt 16:1-18 originated in early Jewish Christianity, possibly in
       part derived from Jesus himself (although Betz is highly skeptical of this
       possibility).

444   C. Demke, "Was bringt die Leben-Jesu-Forschung ans Ende?" in J. Rogge,
       ed., *Theologische Versuche 6* (Berlin: Evangelische Verlagsanstalt, 1975)
       37-46. Concludes that the quest of the historical Jesus has come to an end
       if, as its objective, the quest has tried to find a historical Jesus beyond the
       biblical texts.

445   W. Feneberg, "Die Frage nach Bewusstsein und Entwicklung des his-
       torischen Jesus: Eine Erinnerung an Albert Schweitzer," *ZKT* 97 (1975)
       104-16. Argues that preoccupation with social aspects of the historical Je-
       sus has been at the expense of the pyschological. Jesus' growing awareness
       of the nature of the Kingdom, his relation to God, and his sense of personal
       destiny are vital factors in historical Jesus research.

446   D. Lange, *Historischen Jesus oder mythischer Christus. Untersuchungen zu
       den Gegensatz zwischen Friedrich Schleiermacher und David Friedrich
       Strauss* (Gütersloh: Mohn, 1975). Probes the debate between Schleierma-
       cher and Strauss as a way of highlighting major problems in the current
       discussion.

447   G. Strecker, ed., *Jesus Christus in Historie und Theologie* (H. Conzelmann
       Festschrift; Tübingen: Mohr [Siebeck], 1975). The first half of the volume
       (pp. 3-263) is concerned with the historical Jesus. Some of these essays
       include S. Schulz, "Der historische Jesus. Bilanz der Fragen und Lösungen"
       (pp. 3-25), A. Lindemann, "Jesus in der Theologie des Neuen Testaments"
       (pp. 27-58), W. Schmithals, "Jesus und die Apokalyptik" (pp. 59-86), J.
       Becker, "Das Gottesbild Jesu und die älteste Auslegung von Ostern" (pp.
       105-26), H. Thyen, "Der irdische Jesus und die Kirche" (pp.127-42), and J.
       Roloff, "Der mittleidende Hohepriester. Zur Frage nach der Bedeutung des
       irdischen Jesus für die Christologie des Hebräerbriefes" (pp. 143-66).

448 D. G. Wigmore-Beddoes, "The New Quest of the Historical Jesus Seen from a Liberal Christian Viewpoint," in D. G. Wigmore-Beddoes, ed., *Concerning Jesus: A Symposium* (London: Lindsey, 1975) 9-25. Argues that the quest must be continued, for Christian faith is not "safe" unless firmly anchored in the history of Jesus of Nazareth.

1976-1980

449 E. Bammel, "The Jesus of History in the Theology of Adolf von Harnack," *ModCh* 19 (1976) 90-112. Provides a lively discussion of the development of Harnack's thought and how it was received by his contemporaries; concludes that although his picture of the historical Jesus is weak at many points, his balance, or "feeling for proper proportion," is his lasting contribution.

450 H.-W. Bartsch, "Theologie und Geschichte in der Überlieferung vom Leben Jesu," in F. Theunis, ed., *Geschichte, Zeugnis und Theologie* (Wissenschaftliche Beiträge zur kirklich-evangelischer Lehre 58; Hamburg-Bergstedt: Reich, 1976) 72-81. Concludes that the preaching of the early community admittedly concealed the events of the life of Jesus, but the preaching is itself the result of these events.

451 D. Cairns, "Motives and Scope of Historical Inquiry about Jesus," *SJT* 29 (1976) 335-55. Argues that the quest of the historical Jesus is legitimate and aids faith by helping to ascertain its boundaries.

452 B. Casper, ed., *Jesus. Ort der Erfahrung Gottes* (Freiburg: Herder, 1976). Nine essays, of which the following are relevant: M. Theunissen, "ὁ αἰτῶν λαμβάνει. Der Gebetsglaube Jesu und die Zeitlichkeit des Christseins" (pp. 13-68), B. Casper, "Einige sprachphilosophische Überlieferungen im Hinblick auf das Sprechen Jesu" (pp. 69-94), K. Hemmerle, "Die Wahrheit Jesu" (pp. 95-115), and R. Pesch, "Zur Exegese Gottes durch Jesus von Nazaret. Ein Auslegung des Gleichnisses vom Vater und den beiden Söhnen (Lk 15, 11-32)" (pp. 140-89).

453 N. A. Dahl, *Jesus in the Memory of the Early Church* (Minneapolis: Augsburg, 1976). Views gospels as testimonies to Jesus' life and work.

454 D. L. Dungan, "Albert Schweitzer's Disillusionment with the Historical Reconstruction of the Life of Jesus," *PSTJ* 29 (1976) 27-48. Examines

Schweitzer's views of liberal theologians and their understanding of the historical Jesus.

455   B. E. Gärtner, "Der historische Jesus und der Christus des Glaubens: Eine Reflexion über die Bultmannschule und Lukas," in A. Fuchs, ed., *Theologie aus dem Norden* (Freistadt: Plöchl, 1976) 6-18. Noting that biblical scholarship does not stand still, believes that there has been a significant move away from R. Bultmann's skeptical position; draws upon passages from Luke-Acts to show that the risen Lord is clearly identified with the person of Jesus.

456   J. Gnilka, ed., *Wer ist doch Dieser: Die Frage nach Jesus heute* (Theologisches Kontakstudium 4; Munich: Bosco, 1976). Three essays by Gnilka on the problem of the historical Jesus and the resurrection, and two essays by T. Finkenzeller and H. Fries.

457   D. Hill, "Is the Search for the Historical Jesus Religiously Irrelevant?" *ExpTim* 88 (1976) 82-85. Argues that the quest is relevant and necessary.

458   H. W. Hoehner, *Chronological Aspects of the Life of Christ* (Grand Rapids: Zondervan, 1976). Series of studies previously published; argues that Jesus' birth was winter of 5-4 BCE, that Jesus began his ministry in spring or summer of 29 CE, and that he was crucified near Passover in 33 CE.

459   L. E. Keck, "The Historical Jesus and Christology," *PSTJ* 29 (1976) 14-26. Argues that historical Jesus is certainly an integral part of christology; concludes that faith does not depend on historical-critical results.

460   T. Koch, "Albert Schweitzers Kritik des christologischen Denkens und die Sachgemässe Form einer gegenwärtigen Beziehung auf den geschichtlichen Jesus," *ZTK* 73 (1976) 208-40. Assesses Schweitzer's criticism of liberal theology; believes that Schweitzer has not adequately understood Jesus and the potential for adaptation inherent in his teaching.

461   J. P. Mackey, "The Faith of the Historical Jesus," *Horizons* 3 (1976) 155-74. Argues that the historical Jesus believed that God was near all; this was Jesus' message, and its success occasioned the shift from the faith of Jesus (subjective genitive) to faith in Jesus (objective genitive).

462   W. Marxsen, "Die urchristlichen Kerygmata und das Ereignis Jesus von Nazareth," *ZTK* 73 (1976) 42-64. Argues that New Testament christology

reflects two kerygmata; the Jesus-kerygma that looks back to the advent of God's Kingdom through Jesus, and the Christ-kerygma which proclaims that Jesus has been raised and exalted.

463   M. Müller, "Der Jesus der Historiker, der historische Jesus," *KD* 22 (1976) 277-98. Discusses G. E. Lessing's "ugly ditch" and the efforts of N. Grundtvig and S. Kierkegaard to bridge it.

464   H. Staudinger, "Die historische Glaubwürdigkeit der neutestamentlichen Schriften," in H. Pfeil, ed., *Unwandelbares im Wandel der Zeit* (Aschaffenburg: Pattloch, 1976) 129-49. Discusses the theological problems that attend the New Testament's claim that God has made himself known, primarily in Jesus, through unique historical events.

465   W. Thüsing, "Strukturen des christlichen beim Jesus der Geschichte," in E. Klinger, ed., *Christentum innerhalb und ausserhalb der Kirche* (QD 73; Freiburg: Herder, 1976) 100-21. Interacting with K. Rähner, discusses the relationship between the historical Jesus and the christology of the New Testament.

466   É. Trocmé, "Albert Schweitzer et la vie de Jésus," *RHPR* 56 (1976) 28-36. Reviews the work of Schweitzer (71); concludes that he was the most significant biographer of Jesus from E. Renan to R. Bultmann.

467   N. Walter, "Historischer Jesus und Osterglaube: Ein Diskussionsbeitrag zur Christologie," *TLZ* 101 (1976) cols. 321-38. Argues that the post-Easter kerygma should be examined in the light of what is known about the historical Jesus.

468   G. Baumbach, "Fragen der modernen jüdischen Jesusforschung an die christliche Theologie," *TLZ* 102 (1977) cols. 625-36. Examines several questions raised by recent Jewish studies, such as how to determine authentic tradition and the factors that led to Jesus' crucifixion.

469   J. Bloch, "Der historische Jesus und Paulus," in M. Barth, ed., *Paulus: Apostat oder Apostel. Jüdische und christliche Antworten* (Regensburg: Pustet, 1977) 9-30. Examines the development from the teaching of the historical Jesus to Paul's theology, especially in reference to Torah.

470   B. Gerhardsson, *Evangeliernas forhistoria* (Lund: Verbum, 1977); ET: *The Origins of the Gospel Traditions* (Philadelphia: Fortress, 1979). Argues

that Jesus' teaching has been carefully preserved by his disciples whom Jesus had taught according to rabbinic practices.

471   M. Grant, *Jesus: An Historian's Review of the Gospels* (New York: Scribner's, 1977). Believes that critical study of the gospels can reconstruct the essentials of the life of Jesus.

472   K. Grayston, "Jesus: The Historical Question," *DRev* 95 (1977) 254-70. Argues that Paul's portrait of Jesus should serve as point of reference in determining authentic traditions of Jesus.

473   F. H. Klooster, *Quests for the Historical Jesus* (Grand Rapids: Baker, 1977). An adaptation of "Jesus Christ: History and Kerygma," *Presbyterion: Covenant Seminary Review* 1 (1975) 23-50, 80-110. A very conservative assessment of the various quests concluding that the "Now" quest is that of Pannenberg's attempt to argue for the historicity of the resurrection of Jesus.

474   S. Légasse, "Jésus historique et le fils de l'homme: Aperçu sur les opinions contemporaines," in L. Monloubon and H. Cazelles, eds., *Apocalypses et théologie de l'espérance* (Paris: Éditions du Cerf, 1977) 271-98. Assesses recent studies in Jesus and the expression Son of Man.

475   I. H. Marshall, *I Believe in the Historical Jesus* (London: Hodder and Stoughton, 1977). Argues that although the evangelists interpret the tradition, the essential historicity of the tradition is preserved.

476   C. F. D. Moule, *The Origin of Christology* (Cambridge: University Press, 1977). Argues that New Testament christology emerged from the teaching and ministry of historical Jesus, as well as from Easter experience of the disciples.

477   S. Neill, "Jesus and History," in M. Green, ed., *The Truth of God Incarnate* (London: Hodder and Stoughton, 1977) 71-88. Conservative defense of the historicity of the gospel tradition.

478   M. F. Palmer, "Can the Historian Invalidate Gospel Statements? Some Notes on Dialectical Theology," *DRev* 95 (1977) 11-18. Argues that it is not legitimate for dialectical theologians to claim that christology is not in any way subject to historical verification.

479   A. Sand, "Jesus im Urteil jüdischer Autoren der Gegenwart (1930-1976),"
       C 31 (1977) 29-38. Reviews recent major work, Jewish and Christian, in
       which Jesus and his significance for Judaism and Jewish-Christian relations
       are discussed.

480   G. Theissen, *Soziologie der Jesusbewegung. Ein Beitrag zur Entstehungs-
       geschichte des Urchristentums* (ThEx 194; Munich: Kaiser, 1977); ET:
       Sociology of Early Palestinian Christianity (Philadelphia: Fortress, 1978).
       Examines the social aspects of the "Jesus-movement"; Jesus is compared to
       the itinerant charismatic.

481   P. Bilde, "Den nyere evangelieforsknings metoder og sporgsmålet om den
       historiske Jesus," *DTT* 41 (1978) 217-43. Assesses the various emphases
       in historical Jesus research.

482   M. L. Cook, "The Call to Faith of the Historical Jesus: Questions for the
       Christian Understanding of Faith," *TS* 39 (1978) 679-700. Claims that
       history is an essential element in Christian theology and faith.

483   J. A. Duke and D. L. Dungan, "The Lives of Jesus Series," *RSRev* 4
       (1978) 259-73. Duke (pp. 259-62) discusses recent translations of classic
       works concerned with the historical Jesus, while Dungan (pp. 262-73)
       attempts to explain why Protestant Christianity struggles with the problem
       of faith and the Jesus of history.

484   E. F. Harrison, "Current Thinking about the Life of Jesus," in K. S.
       Kantzer, ed., *Evangelical Roots: A Tribute to Wilbur Smith* (Nashville:
       Nelson, 1978) 63-74. Discussion of major contributors and trends in
       historical Jesus research.

485   R. Latourelle, *L'accès à Jésus par les Évangiles* (Tournai: Desclée, 1978);
       ET: *Finding Jesus through the Gospels: History and Hermeneutics* (New
       York: Alba House, 1979). Believes historical Jesus can be found, if one is
       able to discern the presence of Christian influence.

486   H. Leroy, *Jesus. Überlieferung und Deutung* (Erträge der Forshung 95;
       Darmstadt: Wissenschaftliche Buchgesellschaft, 1978). Examines the
       scholarly debate from A. Schweitzer to the seventies; assesses the histori-
       city of the gospels, and probes the relationship between history and
       kerygma.

487   J. Maier, *Jesus von Nazareth in der talmudischen Überlieferung* (Erträge der
       Forschung 82; Darmstadt: Wissenschaftliche Buchgesellschaft, 1978).
       Critical of new quest; makes use of talmudic traditions and concludes that
       there is substantial continuity between the historical Jesus and the christo-
       logical traditions of the early community.

488   J. Blank, "The Image of Jesus in Contemporary Exegesis," in A. Schim-
       mel, ed., *We Believe in One God* (New York: Seabury, 1979) 9-25. Argues
       that Jesus saw himself as an eschatological prophet, studied in the tradition
       of Israel's great prophets, appointed twelve disciples as the inauguration of
       the regathering of the eschatological Israel, and did not claim to be the
       Messiah.

489   D. Hill, "Jesus: 'A Prophet Mighty in Deed and Word'," in Hill, *New Test-
       ament Prophecy* (New Foundations Theological Library; Atlanta: John
       Knox, 1979) 48-69. Argues that Jesus was a unique prophet.

490   T. Holtz, *Jesus aus Nazareth* (Berlin and Leipzig: Union, 1979). Assesses
       social and historical background of first-century Palestine, various ancient
       sources that yield information about Jesus and his time, and various other
       topics.

491   T. Holtz, "Kenntnis von Jesus und Kenntnis Jesu. Eine Skizze zum Ver-
       hältnis zwischen historish-philosophischer Erkenntnis und historisch-
       theologischen Verständnis," *TLZ* 104 (1979) cols. 1-12. Finds adequate
       historical information about Jesus in the gospels, but notes that the real
       problem lies in its interpretation.

492   M. Lattke, "Neue Aspekte der Frage nach dem historischen Jesus," *Kairos*
       21 (1979) 288-99. Reviews three major stages of the scholarly quest for the
       historical Jesus: (1) old quest, (2) R. Bultmann and students, and (3) E.
       Käsemann and new quest.

493   J. P. Mackey, "Christian Faith and Critical History: The Systematician and
       the Exegete," in T. J. Ryan, ed., *Critical History and Biblical Faith: New
       Testament Perspectives* (Villanova: Villanova University, 1979) 59-90.
       Criticizes the tendency among some scholars to locate the origin of christ-
       ology in two or three major "christological moments" (such as the baptism
       and resurrection); Jesus' public ministry must not be underrated.

494 B. F. Meyer, *The Aims of Jesus* (London: SCM, 1979). Offers trenchant criticism of new quest; places emphasis on Jesus' intentions; Jesus was willing, out of his love for others, to die in his attempt to restore Israel.

495 C. Perrot, *Jésus et l'histoire* (Tournai: Desclée, 1979). Argues that Jesus anticipated imminent eschatological judgment, preached repentance and conversion, baptized for forgiveness of sins, was called prophet, but was recognized to be more, and called himself Son of Man, alluding to the power of God present in him.

496 N. Provencher, "L'accès à Jésus de Nazareth selon Alfred Loisy," *EgliseTh* 10 (1979) 239-56. A critical assessment of A. Loisy's views (69).

497 G. N. Stanton, "Rudolf Bultmann: Jesus and the Word," *ExpTim* 90 (1979) 324-28. A critical assessment of R. Bultmann's *Jesus* (77).

498 J. Wirsching, "Martin Kähler: Erbe und Auftrag: Bemerkungen zum Stande der Kähler-Forschung," *TLZ* 104 (1979) cols. 161-71. Reviews M. Kähler in contemporary discussion (65).

499 D. G. Bostock, "Jesus as the New Elisha," *ExpTim* 92 (1980) 39-41. Argues that because Jesus apparently identified John with Elijah (Matt 11:14; Luke 1:17), he may have seen himself as Elisha, Elijah's successor.

500 R. Feneberg and W. Feneberg, *Das Leben Jesu im Evangelium* (QD 88; Freiburg: Herder, 1980). R. Feneberg criticizes the new quest for failing to follow proper form-critical principles, while W. Feneberg complains that undue priority has been given to redaction criticism instead; both claim that the gospel form was inherited by Jesus himself, who attempted to live it out.

501 M. H. Franzmann, "The Quest for the Historical Jesus," *ConcorJ* 6 (1980) 102-6. Believes that the scholarly quest of the historical Jesus is methodologically unsound, theologically illegitimate, and harmful for Christian faith and life.

502 L. E. Keck, "Jesus in New Testament Christology," *AusBR* 28 (1980) 1-20. Calls for a new direction in the study of Jesus and New Testament theology; christological titles should be viewed as metaphors.

503 J. I. H. McDonald, "The New Quest—Dead End: So What about the Historical Jesus?" in E. Livingstone, ed., *Studia Biblica 1978, II. Papers on*

the Gospels (Sheffield: JSOT, 1980) 151-70. After discussing the short-comings of the new quest, proposes moving on with the quest by plotting religious movements, religious roles and religious symbols in Jesus' time; concludes that the quest is an inescapable part of New Testament theology.

504   B. Noack, "Teste Paulo: Paul as the Principal Witness to Jesus and Primi-tive Christianity," in S. Pedersen, ed., *Die Paulinische Literatur und Theo-logie* (Teologiske Studier 7; Göttingen: Vandehoeck & Ruprecht, 1980) 9-28. Concludes that there are strong links between the historical Jesus and the proclamation of the church and that Paul is a major witness to this continuity.

505   M. Ramsey, *Jesus and the Living Past* (Oxford and New York: Oxford University, 1980). Argues that Jesus' life must be viewed "not as an-tecedent to the event of the church but as one event with the origin of the church" (p. 39).

506   J. K. Riches, *Jesus and the Transformation of Judaism* (London: Darton, Longman & Todd, 1980). Argues that Jesus adapted and reinterpreted many of the most important facets of first-century Judaism.

507   M. Trautmann, *Zeichenhafte Handlungen Jesu: Ein Beitrag zur Frage nach dem geschichtlichen Jesus* (Würzburg: Echter, 1980). Concludes that Jesus had a profound sense of the symbolism of his mission, e.g., eating with sinners signifies the salvation of all, the healing of the paralytic signifies God's desire that all people be whole, and the cursing of the fig tree signifies unbelieving Israel's loss of salvation.

                                   1981-1987

508   L. Cantwell, "The Gospels as Biographies," *SJT* 34 (1981) 193-200. Argues that the gospels are not biographies of Jesus, but are biographies of those who had experienced Jesus.

509   R. T. France and D. Wenham, eds., *Studies of History and Tradition in the Gospels* (Gospel Perspectives 2; Sheffield: JSOT, 1981). Ten essays, a few of which are particularly relevant for historical Jesus research including those by R. J. Banks, "Setting 'The Quest for the Historical Jesus' in a Broader Framework" (pp. 61-82), D. A. Carson, "Historical Tradition in the Fourth Gospel: After Dodd, What?" (pp. 83-146), B. D. Chilton,

"Announcement in *Nazara*: An Analysis of Luke 4:16-21" (pp. 147-72), W. L. Craig, "The Empty Tomb of Jesus" (pp. 173-200), R. T. France, "Scripture, Tradition and History in the Infancy Narratives of Matthew" (pp. 239-66), and P. B. Payne, "The Authenticity of the Parables of Jesus" (pp. 329-44).

510   R. A. Guelich, "The Gospels: Portraits of Jesus and His Ministry," *JETS* 24 (1981) 117-25. Observes with approval the recent tendency among conservatives to view gospels as "portraits" of Jesus, rather than as historical records (as in pre-critical times), or as non-historical theological writings (as in skeptical scholarship).

511   D. A. Hagner, "Interpreting the Gospels: The Landscape and the Quest," *JETS* 24 (1981) 23-37. Argues that because the incarnation is historical, historical criticism is necessary.

512   A. E. Harvey, *God Incarnate: Story and Belief* (London: SPCK, 1981). Believes that the narrative of Jesus as found in the gospels is essentially historical.

513   P. W. Hollenbach, "Jesus, Demoniacs, and Public Authorities; a Socio-Historical Study," *JAAR* 49 (1981) 567-88. Concludes that Jesus' ministry of exorcism was a principal cause of conflict with the authorities of his time.

514   E. Käsemann, "The Jesus Tradition as Access to Christian Origins," *Colloquium* 13 (1981) 5-16. Argues that historical facts themselves are not necessarily more important than their later theological interpretation.

515   J. de Kesel, *Le refus decide de l'objectivation: une interprétation du problème du Jésus historique chez Rudolf Bultmann* (Analecta Gregoriana 221; Rome: Gregorian University, 1981). Concludes that in rejecting the historical Jesus, Bultmann has been carried away by the spirit of the modern age; the denial of the historical Jesus strikes at the very heart of Christianity.

516   J. Reumann, "'The Problem of the Lord's Supper' as Matrix for Albert Schweitzer's *Quest of the Historical Jesus*," *NTS* 27 (1981) 475-87. Argues that Schweitzer's focus on the Lord's Supper as the key to the interpretation of Jesus has been much more influential than many have realized (see 71,923).

517   R. Riesner, *Jesus als Lehrer. Ein Untersuchung zum Ursprung der Evan-gelien-Überlieferung* (WUNT 2.7; Tübingen: Mohr [Siebeck], 1981; 2nd ed., 1984). Critical of the assumptions and skepticism of form criticism, argues that the Jesus traditions were preserved by a band of disciples (a "school of Jesus") in like manner to other rabbis and that although similar to his contemporaries in many ways, Jesus' expressions of authority stand out as unique.

518   R. H. Stein, "'Authentic' or 'Authoritative': What is the Difference?" *JETS* 24 (1981) 127-30. Criticizes J. M. Robinson's definition of "authentic" (156).

519   H. Bietenhard, "'Der Menschensohn'—ὁ υἱὸς τοῦ ἀνθρώπου. Sprach-liche, religionsgeschichtliche und exegetische Untersuchungen zu einem Begriff der synoptischen Evangelien," *ANRW* 25/1 (1982) 265-350. Major study on the background of the "Son of Man" sayings in the synoptics.

520   G. Cornfeld, *The Historical Jesus: A Scholarly View of the Man and His World* (New York: Macmillan, 1982; London: Macmillan, 1983). Discusses Jesus' cleansing of the Temple (with insightful archaeological information); concludes that the Sadducees were responsible for having Jesus handed over to the Romans; speculates that Jesus did not die, but swooned while hanging on the cross.

521   J. D. M. Derrett, "Law and Society in Jesus's World," *ANRW* 25/1 (1982) 477-564. Although little is said about Jesus himself (see pp. 484-87), provides a wealth of background discussion on law in first-century Jewish society.

522   W. R. Farmer, *Jesus and the Gospel: Tradition, Scripture, and Canon* (Philadelphia: Fortress, 1982). Believes that we may be optimistic about historical Jesus research: "We have access to a large body of first-rate historical evidence that is decisive in answering important questions about Jesus" (p. 21).

523   G. Ghiberti, "Überlegungen zum neueren Stand der Leben-Jesu-Forschung," *MTZ* 33 (1982) 99-115. Reviews the past and present scholarly quest and then discusses new questions and possibilities for further inquiry.

524   P. Grech, "Le problèm christologique et l'herméneutique," in R. Latourelle and G. O'Collins, eds., *Problèmes et perspectives de théologie fondamen-tale* (Montreal: Bellarmin; Tournai: Desclée, 1982) 155-87; ET: "The

Christological Problem and Hermeneutics," in R. Latourelle and G. O'Collins, eds., *Problems and Perspectives* (New York: Paulist, 1982) 105-32 [appeared originally in Italian in *Problemi e prospettive di teologia fondamentale* (Rome: Editrice Queriniana, 1980)]. After reviewing major contributions to the discussion, concludes that the life of Jesus is the believer's guarantee that his faith is not unreasonable.

525 A. E. Harvey, *Jesus and the Constraints of History* (Philadelphia: Westminster, 1982). Although critical, a more positive assessment of what can be known about Jesus. See the review articles by A. N. Sherwin-White, J. D. G. Dunn, and E. P. Sanders in *JSNT* 17 (1983) 4-24.

526 M. Pesce, "Discepolato gesuana e discepolato rabbinico. Problemi e prospective della comparazione," *ANRW* 25/1 (1982) 351-89. Explores the problems in comparing disciples and discipleship in Jesus with discipleship in the rabbis.

527 R. Riesner, "Der Ursprung der Jesus-Überlieferung," *TZ* 38 (1982) 493-513. Argues that the evidence suggests that the sayings traditions are much more historical than the form critics have allowed.

528 E. P. Sanders, "Jesus, Paul and Judaism," *ANRW* 25/1 (1982) 390-450. Summation of views expressed in *Paul and Palestinian Judaism* (Philadelphia: Fortress, 1977) and *Jesus and Judaism* (574).

529 E. Stauffer, "Jesus, Geschichte und Verkündigung," *ANRW* 25/1 (1982) 3-130. A veritable monograph, discusses the sources, the early stage of Jesus' ministry, his proclamation, opposition, and passion.

530 M. Wilcox, "Jesus in the Light of His Jewish Environment," *ANRW* 25/1 (1982) 131-95. Argues that Jesus performed miracles, called for repentance, and was a pacifistic Messiah.

531 D. E. Aune, *Prophecy in Early Christianity and the Ancient Mediterranean World* (Grand Rapids: Eerdmans, 1983) esp. pp. 153-88. Concludes that many Christian prophetic utterances became part of the dominical tradition.

532 P. M. Beaude, *Jésus de Nazareth* (Paris: Desclée, 1983); trans. in Italian (1983), and in Spanish (1985). Examines historical problems of Jesus; sketches a life.

533   J. Breech, *The Silence of Jesus: The Authentic Voice of the Historical Man* (Philadelphia: Fortress, 1983). Believes that the historical Jesus demonstrated true human freedom, that Jesus was "silent" with regard to many issues that confront and worry people, and that Jesus taught that God is the source of free personhood.

534   J. D. Crossan, *In Fragments: The Aphorisms of Jesus* (San Francisco: Harper & Row, 1983). A form-critical analysis of Jesus' aphorisms in the gospels and in non-canonical sources; believes that in many instances the *ipsissima structura*, though not necessarily the *ipsissima verba*, of the aphorisms have been preserved.

535   R. T. France and D. Wenham, eds., *Studies in Midrash and Historiography* (Gospel Perspectives 3; Sheffield: JSOT, 1983). Three studies are particularly relevant, including those of R. Bauckham, "The Liber Antiquitatum Biblicarum of Pseudo-Philo and the Gospels as 'Midrash'" (pp. 33-76), R. T. France, "Jewish Historiography, Midrash, and the Gospels" (pp. 99-128), and L. Morris, "The Gospels and the Jewish Lectionaries" (pp. 129-56).

536   F. Hahn, *Historical Investigation and New Testament Faith* (Philadelphia: Fortress, 1983). An ET of two previous studies: "Probleme historischer Kritik," *ZNW* 63 (1972) 1-17, and "Methodologische Überlegungen zur Rückfrage nach dem historischen Jesus," in K. Kertelge, *Rückfrage nach Jesus: zur Methodik und Bedeutung der Frage nach dem historischen Jesus* (431, pp.11-77). Criticizes the methodology of the new quest; suggests a new way of viewing the faith perspective of the New Testament writings.

537   M. Hengel, *Between Jesus and Paul: Studies in the Earliest History of Christianity* (London: SCM; Philadelphia: Fortress, 1983). Argues that Jesus saw himself as Israel's Messiah, and believed that his ministry signalled the inauguration of the Kingdom of God.

538   J. M. Robinson, "The Sayings of Jesus: Q," *DrewG* 54 (1983) 26-38. Argues that "Papyrus Q" takes us closer to the historical Jesus than any other source and notes that it is concerned primarily with action, not theology.

539   E. P. Sanders, "Jesus and the Sinners," *JSNT* 19 (1983) 5-36. Argues that Jesus' offense was in his teaching that sinners, having made no atonement, would be received into the Kingdom.

539a E. P. Sanders, "The Search for Bedrock in the Jesus Material," *PIBA* 7 (1983) 74-86. Concludes that an authentic core of sayings is so small it is necessary to turn to Jesus' actions, particularly with respect to the Temple, to begin a reconstruction of the historical Jesus.

540 K. H. Schelkle, "Die Geschichte Jesu," in Schelkle, *Die Kraft des Wortes. Beiträge zu einer biblischen Theologie* (Stuttgart: Katholisches Bibelwerk, 1983) 25-41. A commemorative collection of Schelkle's studies on Jesus. The most relevant include "Die Geschichte Jesu" (pp. 25-42), "Jesus— Lehrer und Prophet" (pp. 43-52), "Auferstehung Jesu. Geschichte und Deutung" (pp. 53-60), and "Das Herrenmahl" (pp. 61-78).

541 G. S. Sloyan, *Jesus in Focus: A Life in Its Setting* (Mystic, CT: Twenty-Third, 1983). Emphasizes the first-century Palestinian setting.

542 A. J. Tambasco, *In the Days of Jesus: The Jewish Background and Unique Teaching of Jesus* (New York: Paulist, 1983). An assessment of the discontinuity of Jesus' teaching with that of John and the rabbis.

543 H.-F. Weiss, *Kerygma und Geschichte: Erwägungen zur Frage nach Jesus im Rahmen der Theologie des Neuen Testaments* (Berlin: Evangelische Verlagsanstalt, 1983). Explores many aspects of the problem of the relation between the Christian kerygma and history, such as the significance of the combination of kerygma and history in Mark, the kerygma in the teaching of the historical Jesus, and christology and its relation to Jesus (bibliography, pp. 106-13).

544 E. Bammel and C. F. D. Moule, eds., *Jesus and the Politics of His Day* (Cambridge: University Press, 1984). Twenty-six studies discussing the question of Jesus' involvement with zealots; contributors include S. G. F. Brandon, B. Reicke, M. Black, W. Grundmann, and others.

545 M. Baumotte, ed., *Die Frage nach dem historischen Jesus. Texte aus drei Jahrhunderten* (Gütersloh: Mohn, 1984). An anthology of major authors, including H. S. Reimarus, D. F. Strauss, E. Renan, A. Schweitzer, M. Dibelius, R. Bultmann, E. Käsemann, M. D. Goulder, and P. Lapide.

546 M. J. Borg, *Conflict, Holiness and Politics in the Teachings of Jesus* (Studies in the Bible and Early Christianity 5; New York and Toronto: Mellen, 1984). Argues that Jesus' ministry was one of conflict with competing groups claiming to know the way to achieve holiness and national renewal. Contrary to these groups which emphasized holiness, Jesus em-

phasized compassion. Consequently he welcomed sinners and outcasts and criticized the exclusive views of others. For a popular version see Borg, *Jesus: A New Vision* (San Francisco: Harper & Row, 1987).

547   G. W. Buchanan, *Jesus, the King and His Kingdom* (Macon: Mercer University, 1984). Believes that Jesus was committed to Jewish theology of conquest and trained his disciples accordingly.

548   G. Eichholz, *Das Rätsel des historischen Jesus und die Gegenwart Jesu Christi* (G. Sauter, ed.; Theologische Bücherei 72; Munich: Kaiser, 1984). In second essay ("Die Frage nach dem historischen Jesus in der gegenwärtigen Forschung," pp. 79-157) assesses the contributions of R. Bultmann, G. Ebeling, and E. Käsemann.

549   R. H. Fuller, "The Historical Jesus: Some Outstanding Issues," *Thomist* 48 (1984) 368-82. Interacting with E. Schillebeeckx (440), examines the question of the relevance of the historical Jesus for christology, the criteria of authenticity, and the content of Jesus' teaching.

550   E. Grässer, "Norman Perrin's Contribution to the Question of the Historical Jesus," *JR* 64 (1984) 484-500. Argues that Perrin's contribution lies in his establishing a middle ground between the positions of R. Bultmann and J. Jeremias.

551   G. Habermas, *Ancient Evidence for the Life of Jesus* (Nashville: Thomas Nelson, 1984). Conservative apologetic for orthodox view of historical Jesus.

552   D. A. Hagner, *The Jewish Reclamation of Jesus: An Analysis and Critique of Modern Jewish Study of Jesus* (Grand Rapids: Zondervan, 1984). Discusses Jewish interpretation of Jesus and the Law, Kingdom of God, righteousness, and Jesus' mission; provides a good bibliography of Jewish works on Jesus and Christianity.

553   B. Jaspert, ed., *Rudolf Bultmanns Werk und Wirkung* (Darmstadt: Wissenschaftliche Buchgessellschaft, 1984) 81-91. Two essays in particular should be noted: E. Grässer, "Albert Schweitzer und Rudolf Bultmann: Ein Beitrag zur historischen Jesusfrage" (pp. 53-69), and C. K. Barrett, "Jesus and the Word" (pp. 81-91).

554   W. Kelber, "The Work of Norman Perrin: An Intellectual Pilgrimage," *JR*
       64 (1984) 452-67. Argues that although Perrin made significant progress
       toward a synthesis of Jesus and tradition, ultimately he was not successful.

555   G. Loughlin, "On Telling the Story of Jesus," *Th* 87 (1984) 323-29.
       Compares the historiographical and mythological versions of the Jesus
       story, concluding that Christians should tell the story as it "accords with
       the Christian's present self-understanding" (p. 328).

556   R. L. Maddox, "The New Quest and Christology," *PerRelSt* 11 (1984) 43-
       55. A critical assessment of the new quest whose advocates, Maddox
       believes, are driven by a functional christology.

557   A. E. McGrath, "Justification and Christology: The Axiomatic Correlation
       between the Historical Jesus and the Proclaimed Christ," *ModTh* 1 (1984)
       45-54. Offers a positive evaluation of M. Kähler's famous dictum: "The
       real Christ is the preached Christ" (65, p. 22).

558   J. Ramisch, "The Debate Concerning the 'Historical Jesus' in the
       Christology of Schillebeeckx," *Semeia* 30 (1984) 29-48. Discusses E.
       Schillebeeckx's use of the "historical Jesus" as a corrective to christology
       (440).

559   W. O. Seal, "Norman Perrin and His 'School': Retracing a Pilgrimage,"
       JSNT 20 (1984) 87-107. Assesses Perrin's work in life of Jesus research
       and christology.

560   T. F. Torrance, "'The Historical Jesus': From the Perspective of a Theolo-
       gian," in W. Weinrich, ed., *The New Testament Age* (vol. 2; B. Reicke
       Festschrift; Macon: Mercer University, 1984) 511-26. Very critical of the
       philosophy underlying much of the quest of the historical Jesus.

561   G. Vermes, *Jesus and the World of Judaism* (Philadelphia: Fortress, 1984).
       A collection of ten previously published essays, intended as a sequel to ear-
       lier study; Jesus is viewed as a *hasid* of first century Palestine, since he is
       presented as a wise teacher, healer, and exorcist.

562   A. F. Zimmermann, *Die urchristlichen Lehrer. Studien zum Tradentenkreis
       der διδάσκαλοι im frühen Urchristentum* (WUNT 2.12; Tübingen: Mohr
       [Siebeck], 1984). Argues that the gospels preserve the sayings of Jesus
       which had been faithfully transmitted by trained disciples, that a Christian

"rabbinate" existed prior to 50 CE, and that the sayings did not originate with the early community, as form critics have often claimed.

563   M. Adinolfi, *L'apostolato dei Dodici nella vita di Gesù* (Turin: Paoline, 1985). Examines historical evidence for Jesus, Jesus' self-understanding, and history and function of the twelve.

564   C. E. Carlston, "Jesus Christ," *HBD* (1985) 475-87. Provides an assessment and summary of the current scholarly position.

565   J. H. Charlesworth, "Research on the Historical Jesus Today: Jesus and the Pseudepigrapha, the Dead Sea Scrolls, the Nag Hammadi Codices, Josephus, and Archaeology," *PrincSB* 6 (1985) 98-115. Raises the question in what ways the pseudepigrapha, Dead Sea scrolls, Nag Hammadi codices, Josephus, and archaeology contribute to historical Jesus research.

566   J. D. G. Dunn, *The Evidence of Jesus* (Philadelphia: Westminster, 1985). Argues that critical scholarship has certainly affected the way that the gospels are viewed, undermining traditional beliefs, but scholarship has not destroyed their reliability.

567   H. Falk, *Jesus the Pharisee: A New Look at the Jewishness of Jesus* (New York: Paulist, 1985). The author gives new expression to a theory of an eighteenth century rabbi in which it is argued that the influence of the Essenes led Jesus and Paul to establish a religion for Gentiles.

568   P. W. Hollenbach, "Liberating Jesus for Social Involvement," *BTB* 15 (1985) 151-57. Argues that Jesus' self-understanding and ministry were greatly influenced by Old Testament Jubilee theology.

569   B. J. Hubbard, "Geza Vermes's Contribution to Historical Jesus Studies: An Assessment," *SBLSemPap* 24 (1985) 29-44. Assesses Vermes's *Jesus the Jew* (427) and *Jesus and the World of Judaism* (561).

570   J.-D. Karaege, "De Reimarus à Ebeling. Esquisse d'une histoire de la question du Jésus historique," *LumVie* 34/175 (1985) 29-40. Criticizes the assumptions and methods of major contributors to the quest, such as H. S. Reimarus and R. Bultmann.

571   K. Lehmann, "Die Frage nach Jesus von Nazareth," in W. Kern, et al., eds., *Handbuch der Fundamentaltheologie* (2 vols.; Freiburg: Herder, 1985) 2.122-44. A summary of the issues involved in historical Jesus research.

572 E. L. Mascall, *Jesus: Who He Is—And How We Know Him* (London: Darton, Longman & Todd, 1985). Concludes that what can be known of Jesus in many ways coheres with the creeds of the church.

573 F. Mussner, "Rückfrage nach Jesus: Bericht über neue Wege und Methoden," in G. Schelbert, et al., eds., *Methoden der Evangelien-Exegese* (Zürich: Benziger, 1985) 165-82. Assesses recent work and new developments in methodologies.

574 E. P. Sanders, *Jesus and Judaism* (Philadelphia: Fortress, 1985). Argues that Jesus was part of Jewish restoration theology; he did not preach repentance (as the Baptist had); died because he threatened to destroy the Temple and build new one in its place.

575 W. Simonis, *Jesus von Nazareth. Seine Botschaft vom Reich Gottes und der Glaube der Urgemeinde. Historisch-kritische Erhellung der Ursprünge des Christentums* (Düsseldorf: Patmos, 1985). A critical survey of life of Jesus research; offers own views of Jesus and his understanding of the Kingdom of God.

576 N. Walter, "Paulus und die urchristliche Jesustradition," *NTS* 31 (1985) 498-522. Argues that Paul's letters reveal that the apostle knew nothing of the narratives of the Jesus tradition and virtually nothing of the sayings.

577 C. M. Watts, "The Intention of Schleiermacher in *The Life of Jesus*," *Encount* 46 (1985) 71-86. Defends F. Schleiermacher against the criticisms of D. F. Strauss (64).

578 F. F. Bruce, *Jesus: Lord & Savior* (The Jesus Library; Downers Grove: Inter-Varsity, 1986). Examines evidence for Jesus, historical setting, basic teaching, ministry, and self-understanding.

579 L. Chouinard, "Trends in Synoptic Christology," *RestQ* 28 (1986) 201-14. Examines the links between synoptic christology and historical Jesus research.

580 F. G. Downing, "Towards a Fully Systematic Scepticism: In the Service of Faith," *Th* 89 (1986) 355-61. Criticizes some of the assumptions and results in historical Jesus research.

581   I. Ellis, "Dean Farrar and the Quest for the Historical Jesus," *Th* 89 (1986)
       108-15. Assesses the merits of F. W. Farrar's *Life of Jesus* (1196).

582   D. Flusser, "Sanders' *Jesus and Judaism*," *JQR* 76 (1986) 246-52. A review
       article of E. P. Sanders, *Jesus and Judaism* (574); in essential agreement.

583   D. Flusser, "Jesus and the World of Judaism," *Judaism* 35 (1986) 361-64.
       A review article of G. Vermes's *Jesus and the World of Judaism* (561).

584   D. Goergen, *The Mission and Ministry of Jesus* (Wilmington: Glazier,
       1986). First of a projected five-volume series concerned with the "theology
       of Jesus"; studies the spirituality and compassion of Jesus.

585   R. J. Hoffmann and G. A. Larve, eds., *Jesus in History and Myth* (Buffalo:
       Prometheus, 1986). Fifteen essays by M. Smith, J. M. Allegro, D. N.
       Freedman, E. Rivkin, and others.

586   R. Kampling, "Jesus von Nazaret—Lehrer und Exorzist," *BZ* 30 (1986)
       237-48. Argues that the combination of teacher and exorcist was uncom-
       mon.

587   V. Kesich, "The Historical Jesus: A Challenge from Jerusalem," *SVTQ* 30
       (1986) 17-42. Review article of G. Cornfeld's *The Historical Jesus* (520).

588   B. C. McGing, "The Governorship of Pontius Pilate: Messiahs and
       Sources," *PIBA* 10 (1986) 55-71. Concludes that gospel portrait of Pilate's
       role in Jesus' death is essentially reliable.

589   J. Neumann, *Der galiläische Messias. Eine Untersuchung über Leben,
       Wirken und Tod des historischen Jesus und den Ursprung des Glaubens an
       die Auferstehung Jesu.* Vol. 1: *Die Entstehung des Christentums* (Ham-
       burg: Johannes Neumann, 1986). Argues that Jesus was stoned and nearly
       killed for opposing Pharisaic law, but later was crucified by Pilate in
       Samaria, and thus should be identified with Samaritan messianic pretender
       described by Josephus (*Ant.* 18.4.1-2 § 85-89).

590   R. A. Rosenberg, *Who Was Jesus?* (New York: University Press of Amer-
       ica, 1986). Reviews Jesus against Jewish perspectives.

591   G. Schille, "Ein neuer Zugang zu Jesus? Das traditionsgeschichtliche Kri-
       terium," *ZZ* 40 (1986) 247-53. Argues that to understand the mind of

Jesus, one must begin with his emphasis of the command to love God and neighbor.

592 W. Stenger, "Sozialgeschichtliche Wende und historischen Jesus," *Kairos* 28 (1986) 11-22. Examines recent models of social analysis and their impact on historical Jesus studies.

593 N. T. Wright, "'Constraints' and the Jesus of History," *SJT* 39 (1986) 189-210. Responding to A. E. Harvey's *Jesus and the Constraints of History* (525), criticizes Harvey's understanding of "constraints," especially his understanding of the constraint of Jewish monotheism and early christology.

594 D. C. Allison, Jr., "Jesus and the Covenant: A Response to E. P. Sanders," *JSNT* 29 (1987) 57-78. Arguing against Sanders, *Jesus and Judaism* (574), concludes that Jesus rejected covenantal nomism.

595 O. Betz, *Jesus der Messias Israel* (WUNT 42; ed. M. Hengel; Tübingen: Mohr [Siebeck], 1987). A collection of several studies, eight of which are specifically concerned with Jesus (see pp. 77-254).

596 B. D. Chilton, "Silver Blaze Rides Again: Two Recent Historical Approaches to Jesus," *Reflections* 84/2 (1987) 8-11. A critical review of G. W. Buchanan's *Jesus: The King and His Kingdom* (547), and E. P. Sanders, *Jesus and Judaism* (574).

597 E. Floris, *Sous le Christ, Jésus. Méthode d'analyse référentielle appliquée aux Évangile* (Paris: Flammarion, 1987). Examines historical Jesus research and argues for a "referential" approach to the gospels (with examples taken primarily from Matthew and Mark).

598 D. J. Harrington, "The Jewishness of Jesus: Facing Some Problems," *CBQ* 49 (1987) 1-13; see also *Bible Review* 3 (1987) 33-41. Examines difficulties of viewing Jesus against the diversity of first-century Judaism.

599 R. A. Horsley, *Jesus and the Spiral of Violence. Popular Jewish Resistance in Roman Palestine* (San Francisco: Harper & Row, 1987). Concludes that Jesus was opposed to violence (thought not a pacifist), calling for social revolution and an end to oppression.

600 B. Lindars, "Jesus Christ Yesterday, Today and Forever," *EpworthRev* 14 (1987) 70-80. Argues that theology must not control historical reconstruction.

601   J. H. Charlesworth, *Jesus Within Judaism* (ABRL; Garden City: Doubleday, 1988). Examines several ancient literatures and aspects of archaeology, concluding that there is a new mood of optimism with regard to Jesus research.

602   C. A. Evans, "The Historical Jesus and Christian Faith: A Critical Assessment of a Scholarly Problem," *CSR* 18 (1988) 48-63. After reviewing major contributions to historical Jesus research, concludes that although similar errors are being repeated, a new phase seems to be emerging.

603   M. D. Hooker, "Traditions About the Temple in the Sayings of Jesus," *BJRL* 70 (1988) 7-19. Contrary to E. P. Sanders (574), claims that Jesus may have intended to cleanse the Temple.

604   D. Ker, "Jesus and Mission to Gentiles," *IBS* 10 (1988) 89-101. Examines Jesus' teaching regarding Gentiles and whether or not he intended to found the Church.

605   P. Stuhlmacher, *Jesus von Nazareth—Christus des Glaubens* (Stuttgart: Calwer, 1988). Explores the problem of how Jesus' preaching gives way to faith in Jesus as Christ.

606   I. M. Zeitlin, *Jesus and the Judaism of His Time* (Oxford: Blackwell; San Francisco: Harper & Row, 1988). Finds that Jesus was a charismatic teacher and revolutionary.

SPECIAL TOPICS

The following topics are closely related to the scholarly quest of the historical Jesus, though they do not always refer to it. The bibliographies in these subsections are much more select.

A. *Demythologization*

1. INTRODUCTION

Although David Strauss's mythological interpretation of the gospels was strongly resisted throughout the nineteenth century, theologians in the twentieth century finally came to recognize the problem of mythology and so sought ways to deal with it. The older liberal approach had been to peel it away, in the search for the kernel of the gospel. But Rudolf Bultmann and his followers argued that myth was to be interpreted, not eliminated. Günther Bornkamm provides one of the most helpful studies on myth and the gospel (see 626). It is interesting to observe, however, that in recent years the problem of myth, or at least its discussion, has virtually dropped out of the historical Jesus debate. In some of the most recent and influential studies, it is hardly referred to at all (e.g., G. Vermes [427,561], E. P. Sanders [574], M. J. Borg [546]).

2. BIBLIOGRAPHY

607   J. G. Herder, *Vom Erlöser der Menschen. Nach unsern drei ersten Evangelien* (Riga: Hartknoch, 1796). Thinks that many of the miracles were symbolic and not literal. See also 55.

608   H. E. G. Paulus, *Philologisch-kritischer und historischer Commentar über das Evanglium des Johannes* (Lübeck: Bohn, 1804). Attempts to rationalize the miracles of the fourth gospel.

609   H. E. G. Paulus, *Das Leben Jesu, als Grundlage einer reinen Geschichte des Urchristentums* (2 vols.; Heidelberg: Winter, 1828). As had Herder (607),

attempts to rationalize the gospel accounts and present the historical Jesus devoid of supernatural (or "mythological") elements. It was against this sort of thinking that D. F. Strauss (58) set himself.

610   B. Bauer, *Kritik der evangelischen Geschichte und der Synoptiker* (2 vols.; Leipzig: Wigand, 1841-42; 2nd ed., 1846). In this work, and in *Kritik der Evangelien und Geschichte ihres Ursprungs* (4 vols.; Berlin: Hempel, 1850-51), argues that Jesus did not exist, while in *Christ und die Cäsaren, der Ursprung des Christentums aus dem römischen Griechentum* (Berlin: Grosser, 1877; 2nd ed., 1879) tries to show that the Jesus story was invented by the Marcan evangelist.

611   A. Drews, *Die Christusmythe* (Jena: Diederichs, 1909; 3rd ed., 1924); ET: *The Christ Myth* (London: Unwin, 1910). Argues that the gospel story of Jesus is completely mythical, that Jesus never lived, and that Paul, the tent-maker of Tarsus, was major developer of the "Christ myth."

612   K. Dunkmann, "The Christ Myth," *BSac* 68 (1911) 34-47 [trans. from *Der Geisteskampf der Gegenwart* (March 1910) 85-94]. Criticizes the advocates of mythological interpretation (such as D. F. Strauss, B. Bauer, and A. Drews).

613   K. Staab, "Wege zur 'Christusmythe' von A. Drews," *Bib* 5 (1924) 26-38. Offers several criticisms of A. Drews's *Die Christusmythe* (611), concluding that the "Christ myth" can perhaps be understood as a philosophical question, but never a historical question.

614   M. Goguel, *Jésus de Nazareth, Mythe ou Histoire?* (Paris: Payot, 1925); ET: *Jesus the Nazarene: Myth or History?* (New York: Appleton, 1926). Although dated, this study is very useful; criticizes the various arguments that Jesus' life is mythical (either that he did not exist or that the gospels cannot give us accurate knowledge of his life and ministry); concludes: "The historical reality of the personality of Jesus alone enables us to understand the birth and development of Christianity, which otherwise would remain an enigma" (p. 316). For a history of the "Christ myth" debate see pp. 1-28.

615   M. Goguel, *Critique et Histoire. À propos de la Vie de Jésus* (Strasbourg: Imperimerie Alsacienne, 1928) [extracted from previous articles in *RHPR*]. Assesses the life of Jesus research, concluding that an adequate history of Jesus can be recovered.

616   H. Windisch, "Das Problem der Geschichtlichkeit Jesu: die Christus-
       mythe," *TRu* 2 (1930) 207-52. Criticizes the "Christ myth" theory of A.
       Drews (611) and others, and the question of Jesus' historicity that these
       writers have raised.

617   R. Bultmann, "Neues Testament und Mythologie," Part II of Bultmann,
       Offenbarung und Heilsgeschehen (BEvT 7; Munich: Kaiser, 1941); repr. in
       H.-W. Bartsch, ed., *Kerygma und Mythos. Ein theologisches Gespräch*
       (620), and as *Neues Testament und Mythologie. Das Problem der
       Entmythologisierung der neutestamentlichen Verkündigung* (BEvT 96; E.
       Jüngel, ed.; Munich: Kaiser, 1985). Classic essay in which it is proposed
       that the New Testament needs to be "demythologized."

618   P. Althaus, "Neues Testament und Mythologie: Zu R. Bultmanns Versuch
       der Entmythologisierung des Neuen Testaments," *TLZ* 67 (1942) cols. 337-
       44. Criticizes R. Bultmann's demythologizing hermeneutic (617).

619   W. G. Kümmel, "Mythische Rede und Heilsgeschehen im Neuen Testa-
       ment," in B. Reicke, ed., *Coniectanea Neotestamentica XI* (A. Fridrichsen
       Festschrift; Lund: Gleerup, 1947) 109-31; repr. in Kümmel, *Heils-
       geschehen und Geschichte* (E. Grässer, et al., eds.; Marburg: Elwert, 1965)
       153-68. Criticizes R. Bultmann's understanding of myth and its role in the
       kerygma.

620   H.-W. Bartsch, ed., *Kerygma und Mythos: Ein Theologisches Gespräche*
       (TF 1; Hamburg-Bergstedt: Reich und Heidrich, 1948; 4th ed., 1960); ET:
       Kerygma and Myth: A Theological Debate (London: SPCK, 1957; 2nd ed.,
       1964). Essays by R. Bultmann, "New Testament and Mythology" (pp. 1-
       44; ET of 617), E. Lohmeyer, "The Right Interpretation of the Mythologi-
       cal" (pp. 124-37), and F. K. Schumann, "Can the Event of Jesus Christ be
       Demythologized?" (pp. 175-90). Probably the most frequently cited volume
       in the years of demythologizing debate that followed. This volume was to
       become the first of nine entitled *Kerygma und Mythos*, published from
       1948-78.

621   P. E. Hughes, "Miracle and Myth," *EvQ* 20 (1948) 184-95. Criticizes the
       views of those whom he calls "mythologists" (R. Niebuhr, K. Barth); dis-
       cusses the miracles of the Old Testament, as well as those of the gospels.

622   J. R. Geiselmann, "Der Glaube an Jesus Christus—Mythos oder
       Geschichte?" *TQ* 129 (1949) 257-77, 418-39. Questions R. Bultmann's
       demythologizing approach (617); believes that it sets up false alternatives.

623   W. G. Kümmel, "Mythos im Neuen Testament," *TZ* 6 (1950) 321-37.
      Disagrees with R. Bultmann (617) and sympathizers; argues that removal
      of myth is not required of the theologian.

624   A. N. Wilder, "Mythology and the New Testament," *JBL* 69 (1950) 113-
      27. In response to R. Bultmann (617), concludes: "If we recognize that the
      central thing in the New Testament is a message concerning the divine
      action, it is a much more difficult thing to discard the so-called mythology"
      (p. 123).

625   W. F. Arndt, "Entmythologisierung," *CTM* 22 (1951) 186-92. A descrip-
      tion and criticism of R. Bultmann's demythologizing hermeneutic (617).

626   G. Bornkamm, "Mythos und Evangelium. Zur Diskussion des Problemes
      der Entmythologisierung der neutestamentlichen Verkündigung," in
      Bornkamm and W. Klaas, *Mythos and Evangelium. Zur Programm R.
      Bultmanns* (ThEx 26; Munich: Kaiser, 1951; 3rd ed., 1953) 3-29=
      Bornkamm, "Evangelium und Mythos. Zur Diskussion des Problemes der
      Entmythologisierung der neutestamentlichen Verkündigung," ZZ 5 (1951)
      1-15; ET: "Myth and Gospel. A Discussion of Demythologizing the New
      Testament Message," in C. E. Braaten and R. A. Harrisville, eds., *Kerygma
      and History: A Symposium on the Theology of Rudolf Bultmann*
      (Nashville: Abingdon, 1962) 172-96. A critical assessment of R. Bult-
      mann's understanding of demythologizing the gospels (617). See also 698.

627   G. Casalis, "Le problèm du mythe," *RHPR* 31 (1951) 330-42. Interacts
      with R. Bultmann (617) and others; reviews last ten years of discussion on
      New Testament and mythology; expresses reservation about a priori
      assumptions.

628   E. Fuchs, "Das entmythologisierte Glaubensärgernis," *EvT* 11 (1951-52)
      398-415; repr. in Fuchs, *Zum hermeneutischen Problem in der Theologie.
      Die existentiale Interpretation* (GA 1; Tübingen: Mohr [Siebeck], 1959)
      211-36. An assessment of R. Bultmann's understanding of demythologiza-
      tion (617).

629   K. Grobel, "Bultmann's Problem of NT 'Mythology'," *JBL* 70 (1951) 99-
      103. An interpretation of R. Bultmann's demythologizing hermeneutic
      (617).

630   W. H. Johnson, "Myth and Miracle at Mid-Century," *TToday* 8 (1951) 313-26. Critical of the attempts to eliminate the miraculous elements of the gospels.

631   A. Nygren, "Kristus och Fördärvsmakterna: Tillika ett ord till Frägan om Kristendomens Avmythologisering," *Svensk Teologisk Kvartalskrift* 27 (1951) 1-11; ET: "Christ and the Forces of Destruction: And a Word concerning the De-mythologizing of Christianity," *SJT* 4 (1951) 363-75, and as "On the Question of De-Mythologizing Christianity," *LQ* 4 (1952) 140-52. Criticizes the assumption that much of New Testament theology is based on myth.

632   R. Schnackenburg, "Von der Formgeschichte zur Entmythologisierung des Neuen Testaments: Zur Theologie Rudolf Bultmanns," *MTZ* 2 (1951) 345-60. Discusses and criticizes R. Bultmann's demythologizing hermeneutic, gnostic construct, and exegesis (617).

633   K. Adam, "Das Problem der Entmythologisierung und die Auferstehung des Christus," *TQ* 132 (1952) 385-410. Argues that the demythologizing hermeneutic has problems with the New Testament teaching that the resurrection of Jesus, as a historical event, lies at the heart of the gospel.

634   H.-W. Bartsch, ed., *Kerygma und Mythos II* (Hamburg: Reich, 1952). Major contributions include those by E. Stauffer, "Entmythologisierung oder Realtheologie?" (pp. 13-28), H. Sauter, "Für und wider Entmythologisierung des Neuen Testamentes" (pp. 41-65), W. G. Kümmel, "Mythische Rede und Heilsgeschehen im Neuen Testament" (pp. 153-69; repr. in Kümmel, *Heilsgeschehen und Geschichte* [E. Grässer, et al., eds., Marburg: Elwert, 1965] 153-68), and R. Bultmann, "Zum Problem der Entmythologisierung" (pp. 177-208; ET: "On the Problem of Demythologization," in 689).

635   S. G. F. Brandon, "Myth and the Gospel," *HibJ* 51 (1952-53) 121-32. Describes and criticizes R. Bultmann's demythologizing hermeneutic, particularly his essay on "New Testament and Mythology" (617).

636   I. Henderson, *Myth in the New Testament* (SBT 7; London: SCM, 1952). Criticizes R. Bultmann's understanding of myth and the need to demythologize the New Testament (617); likens Bultmann's attempt to find a synthesis of Christianity and the modern worldview of his time to that of Thomas Aquinas' attempt to synthesize theology and Aristotelianism.

637   D. Lerch, "Zur Frage nach dem Verstehen der Schrift," *ZTK* 49 (1952) 350-67. Interacts with R. Bultmann's demythologizing hermeneutic and its implications for understanding scripture.

638   W. F. Arndt, "The Faculty at Bethel on the 'Demythologizing' Championed by Professor Dr. Bultmann," *CTM* 24 (1953) 785-808. Critical of R. Bultmann's demythologizing hermeneutic (617), primarily because of dissatisfaction with his understanding of history.

639   S. G. F. Brandon, "De-mythologizing Gospel," *ModCh* 43 (1953) 86-98. Suggests that R. Bultmann's sense of the need for a demythologizing hermeneutic arose because of Christian theologians' misunderstanding that Christianity was essentially historical in the first place; notes that Paul supports his teaching by appeal to experience, not to history.

640   K. Goldammer, "Die Frage der Entmythologisierung im Lichte der Religionsgeschichte und in der Problemstellung der Missionsreligion," *TLZ* 78 (1953) cols. 749-64. Contends that myth and culture are constituent elements of the Christian religion (as they are of all religions), that myth is the language of religion.

641   F. Gogarten, *Entmythologisierung und Kirche* (Stuttgart: Vorwerk, 1953, 4th ed. 1966); ET: *Demythologizing and History* (New York: Scribner's, 1955). Discusses R. Bultmann's demythologizing hermeneutic (617) and tries to explain its relationship to history; defends Bultmann against the charge that he has denied the historicity of Christianity; concludes that the church can no longer return to the creeds of the past.

642   J. Hamer, "Zur Entmythologisierung Bultmanns," *C* 9 (1953) 138-46. Critical assessment of R. Bultmann's demythologizing hermeneutic (617).

643   I. Henderson, "Christology and History: An Issue in the *Entmythologisierung* Controversy," *ExpTim* 65 (1953-54) 367-69. Discusses demythologization in R. Bultmann (617) and F. Gogarten (641).

644   I. Henderson, "Karl Jaspers and Demythologizing," *ExpTim* 65 (1953-54) 291-93. Discusses K. Jaspers's criticisms of R. Bultmann (617,634); Bultmann is being accused of not understanding science, philosophy, or Christian theology.

645   K. Jaspers, "Wahrheit und Unheil der Bultmannischen Entmythologisierung," *Schweizerische Theologische Umschau* 23 (1953) 74-106; repr.

in *Kerygma und Mythos III* (650, pp. 9-46). Criticizes R. Bultmann's understanding of demythologization (617); contends that the Christian gospel itself, even as Bultmann has interpreted it, is no more than myth and that, therefore, Bultmann's theology is "orthodox."

646   A. Kolping, "Sola fide: Aus der Diskussion um Bultmanns Forderung nach Entmythologisierung des Evangeliums," *TRev* 49 (1953) 121-34. Criticizes R. Bultmann's understanding of demythologization (617); considers the implications of his approach for New Testament theology.

647   R. G. Smith, "What is Demythologizing?" *TToday* 10 (1953) 34-44. An early English assessment of R. Bultmann's demythologizing hermeneutic (617).

648   R. F. Aldwinckle, "Myth and Symbol in Contemporary Philosophy and Theology: The Limits of Demythologizing," *JR* 34 (1954) 267-79. Argues that it is not legitimate to view the modern understanding of the world as non-mythological, for science itself is symbol; questions R. Bultmann's understanding of science and history (617).

649   A. Barr, "Bultmann's Estimate of Jesus," *SJT* 7 (1954) 337-54. Interacting with R. Bultmann's contribution to *Kerygma und Mythos* (620), expresses sympathy for what has been attempted, but believes that Bultmann is too extreme in his skepticism.

650   H.-W. Bartsch, ed., *Kerygma und Mythos III* (Hamburg: Reich, 1954; 2nd ed., 1957). Major contributions include those by K. Jaspers, "Wahrheit und Unheil der Bultmannischen Entmythologisierung" (pp. 9-46; see 645), and R. Bultmann, "Zur Frage der Entmythologisierung. Antwort zu Karl Jaspers" (pp. 47-59; see 652).

651   G. Bornkamm, R. Bultmann, and F. K. Schumann, *Die christliche Hoffnung und das Problem der Entmythologisierung* (Stuttgart: Evangelisches Verlagswerk, 1954); ET [of Bultmann's contribution]: "The Christian Hope and the Problem of Demythologizing," *ExpTim* 65 (1953-54) 228-30, 276-78. Tries to show that early Christian apocalyptic hope was thoroughly mythological and that Christians today must demythologize this hope, as indeed the New Testament itself begins to do, and trust their future to God. Responses are offered by Bornkamm and Schumann.

652   R. Bultmann, "Zur Frage der Entmythologisierung," *TZ* 10 (1954) 81-95.
       A reply to K. Jaspers (645); argues that faith is not mythological, the word
       of the gospel gives life. See 650.

653   O. Cullmann, "Le mythe dans les écrits du Nouveau Testament," *Numen* 1
       (1954) 120-35. Criticizes the assumptions and logic operative in R. Bult-
       mann's demythologizing hermeneutic (617); argues that the historical ele-
       ment is essential to Christianity.

654   E. Fuchs, "Entmythologisierung und Säkularisierung," *TLZ* 79 (1954)
       cols. 723-32. In response to F. Gogarten (641) discusses the distinction
       between demythologization and secularization.

655   E. Fuchs, *Das Programm der Entmythologisierung* (Bad Cannstatt:
       Müllerschön, 1954; 3rd ed., 1967). Discusses R. Bultmann's demytholo-
       gizing hermeneutic (617,634) and works out what he thinks is the proper
       application. See also Fuchs, *Hermeneutik* (2nd ed., Bad Cannstatt: Müller-
       schön, 1958).

656   S. E. Johnson, "Bultmann and the Mythology of the New Testament,"
       ATR 36 (1954) 29-47. Raises several questions about R. Bultmann's con-
       cept of demythologization (617,634).

657   W. Pannenberg, "Mythos und Wort: Theologische Überlieferungen zu Karl
       Jaspers' Mythusbegriff," *ZTK* 51 (1954) 167-85. In response to K. Jaspers
       (645), discusses the problem of God's presence and reality in the world.

658   H.-W. Bartsch, ed., *Kerygma und Mythos IV* (Hamburg: Reich, 1955).
       Several essays on demythologization by I. Henderson, H. Ott, S. E. John-
       son, and others.

659   H.-W. Bartsch, ed., *Kerygma und Mythos V* (Hamburg: Reich, 1955).
       Several essays on demythologization and the problem of christology by A.
       Kolping, H. Fries, R. Schnackenburg, K. Adam, R. Marlé, and others.

660   S. G. F. Brandon, "The Historical Element in Primitive Christianity,"
       Numen 2 (1955) 156-67. In response to O. Cullmann (653), criticizes his
       understanding of the historical element in early Christianity, concluding
       that the historical element is itself part of Christian faith.

661 H. Fries, "Das Anliegen Bultmanns im Licht der katholischen Theologie," *C* 10 (1955) 1-13. Offers a critical assessment of R. Bultmann's demythologizing hermeneutic (617,634).

662 H. Fries, *Bultmann—Barth und die katholische Theologie* (Stuttgart: Schwabenverlag, 1955) esp. chap. 3: "Die Theologie der Entmythologisierung" (pp. 75-94); ET: "The Theology of Demythologization" in Fries, *Bultmann—Barth and Catholic Theology* (Duquesne Studies, Theological Series 8; Pittsburgh: Duquesne University, 1967) 90-107. An analysis of R. Bultmann's demythologizing hermeneutic (617,634); is particularly interested in the extent of the influence of existentialism.

663 H. P. V. Nunn, "The Use of Myth and Symbol in Religious Thought," *EvQ* 27 (1955) 81-93. Examines the antecedents, some ancient, of demythologizing.

664 H. Schulte, "'Rettet den Mythos!'" *EvT* 15 (1955) 523-33. In response to K. Goldammer (640), concludes that demythologization is the best way to rescue the mythological content of the New Testament.

665 P. L. Berger, "Demythologization—Crisis in Continental Theology," *RR* 20 (1955-56) 5-24. In response to R. Bultmann's seminal essay (617), reviews the arguments of Bultmann's advocates and critics.

666 J. A. O'Flynn, "New Testament and Mythology," *ITQ* 23 (1956) 49-59, 101-10. A critical assessment of R. Bultmann's position.

667 C. K. Barrett, "Myth and the New Testament: The Greek Word *Mythos*," *ExpTim* 68 (1957) 345-48. Argues that myth is a medium by which theological and philosophical truth is articulated; but the New Testament repudiates the kind of myth that is invented (or newly created) in the sense of falsehoods.

668 C. K. Barrett, "Myth and the New Testament: How far does Myth enter into the New Testament?" *ExpTim* 68 (1957) 359-62. Explains that myth utilizes supernatural beings in telling a narrative; therefore, much of the New Testament is mythical, and much of this myth has been mediated through Jewish apocalyptic.

669 M. Barth, "Introduction to Demythologizing," *JR* 37 (1957) 145-55. In discussion of R. Bultmann's understanding, explores ways that the hermeneutics of demythologization can be put into practice.

670   A. D. Galloway, "Religious Symbols and Demythologising," *SJT* 10 (1957) 361-69. Suggests that the demythologizing hermeneutic sometimes confuses religious symbols with outmoded views of reality, which is what myth really is.

671   J. A. O'Flynn, "New Testament and Mythology," *ITQ* 24 (1957) 1-12, 109-21. An assessment of R. Bultmann's views; discusses *Historie* and *Geschichte* and the meaning of the cross and resurrection.

672   S. M. Ogden, "Bultmann's Project of Demythologizing and the Problem of Theology and Philosophy," *JR* 37 (1957) 156-73. Concludes that R. Bultmann's demythologizing hermeneutic is inconsistent and ought to be modified or altogether rejected.

673   D. M. Stanley, "Rudolf Bultmann: A Contemporary Challenge to the Catholic Theologian," *CBQ* 19 (1957) 347-55. Criticizes R. Bultmann's demythologization of the cross and resurrection; approves of other aspects of Bultmann's thought.

674   M. F. Sulzbach, "The New Testament and Myth," *RL* 26 (1957) 560-71. Argues that New Testament myth attempts to explain how God has encountered humankind.

675   J. H. Thomas, "The Relevance of Kierkegaard to the Demythologising Controversy," *SJT* 10 (1957) 239-52. Believes that R. Bultmann has, as had S. Kierkegaard years before, erred in reducing Christian faith to a philosophy of existence.

676   J. Thompson, "Demythologising," *BibT* 7 (1957) 27-35. Reviews the discussion, concluding that R. Bultmann's approach is dangerous for Christian faith.

677   R. Bultmann, *Jesus Christ and Mythology* (New York: Scribner's, 1958); FT: *Jésus. Mythologie et Démythologisation* (Paris: Seuil, 1968). Brief description of mythology in the New Testament, the beginnings of demythologization of eschatology in the New Testament, and the modern expression of a demythologized Christian message.

678   H. Ott, "Entmythologisierung," *RGG* 2 (3rd ed., 1958) cols. 496-99. A concise summary of demythologization.

679   J. N. Walty, "Bulletin de théologie protestane: L'oeuvre de R. Bultmann,"
       RSPT 42 (1958) 349-70. Examines the work of R. Bultmann and those
       who have discussed his views.

680   K. Grobel, "The Practice of Demythologizing," *JBR* 27 (1959) 17-27. Puts
       into practice R. Bultmann's program of demythologizing, with expositions
       on Matt 11:2-6 and Luke 5:1-11.

681   R. Marlé, *Bultmann und die Interpretation des Neuen Testamentes*
       (Paderborn: Bonifacius-Druckerei, 1959). Assessment of the implications of
       R. Bultmann's demythologizing hermeneutic for New Testament inter-
       pretation.

682   S. M. Ogden, "The Debate on 'Demythologizing,'" *JBR* 27 (1959) 17-27.
       Explains and criticizes R. Bultmann's idea of demythologizing; argues that
       redemption itself is a mythological concept (even if it is regarded in exis-
       tentialist terms); therefore, demythologizing leads to "de-kerygmatizing."

683   J. M. Robinson, "New Testament Faith Today," *JBR* 27 (1959) 233-42.
       Defines the meaning of faith in the context of demythologized gospel and
       existentialism.

684   E. C. Rust, "The Possible Lines of Development of Demythologizing,"
       JBR 27 (1959) 32-40. Interprets R. Bultmann; explains that myth is sym-
       bol, and the gospel can only be explained in mythological language.

685   T. J. J. Altizer, "Demythologizing and Jesus," *RL* 29 (1960) 564-74.
       Argues that "all efforts to abandon, spiritualize, or demythologize the
       eschatology of Jesus and the primitive church must be recognized as
       perilous inasmuch as they invariably lead to a transformation or negation of
       both the person and the message of Jesus himself" (pp. 570-71).

686   A. P. B. Bennie, "Bultmann and the Theological Significance of Myth,"
       ATR 42 (1960) 316-25. Reviews R. Bultmann's understanding of myth;
       concludes that it is not satisfactory.

687   R. Bultmann, "A Chapter in the Problem of Demythologizing," in H. K.
       McArthur, ed., *New Testament Sidelights* (A. C. Purdy Festschrift; Hart-
       ford: Hartford Seminary Foundation, 1960) 1-9. Makes it clear that it is the
       New Testament's worldview that is demythologized, not its thoughts, as
       some have misunderstood him to mean; argues that to speak of God, we
       can only speak of his work in us, in our existence.

688   H.-W. Bartsch, "The Still Unsettled Debate on Demythologizing," *RL* 30 (1961) 167-78. Discusses how the demythologizing debate has provoked controversy in the Lutheran Church; good assessment of the positions of R. Bultmann, his pupils, and his critics.

689   R. Bultmann, "Zum Problem der Entmythologisierung" in E. Castelli, ed., *Il problema della demitizzazione* (Rome: Archivio di Filosofia, 1961) 19-26 (followed by an Italian translation, pp. 27-34); ET: "On the Problem of Demythologizing," *JR* 42 (1962) 96-102; repr. in *New Testament Issues* (ed. R. Batey; New York: Harper & Row, 1970) 35-44. Explains his understanding of the relationship of demythologization to history.

690   P. L. Hammer, "Myth, Faith, and History in the New Testament," *JBR* 29 (1961) 113-18. Criticizes R. Bultmann's definition of myth.

691   J. I. H. McDonald, "The Primitive Community and Truth," *HeyJ* 2 (1961) 30-41. Argues that early Christians carefully preserved the dominical tradition and that therefore the gospels should be viewed as historically reliable, not mythical.

692   S. M. Ogden, *Christ Without Myth: A Study Based on the Theology of Rudolf Bultmann* (New York: Harper & Row, 1961). Critical of R. Bultmann; argues that authentic existence can be realized apart from faith in God or in Christ.

693   H. Anderson, "Existential Hermeneutics: Features of the New Quest," *Interp* 16 (1962) 131-55. A positive assessment of the existentialist hermeneutic; sees it in a mutually supporting role with historical criticism.

694   C. E. Braaten and R. A. Harrisville, eds., *Kerygma and History: A Symposium on the Theology of Rudolf Bultmann* (Nashville: Abingdon, 1962). Contains articles concerned with mythology by C. E. Braaten, E. Ellwein, E. Kinder, W. Künneth, R. Prenter, and G. Bornkamm.

695   H. G. Gadamer, "Zur Problematik des Selbstverständnisses: Ein hermeneutischer Beitrag zur Frage der 'Entmythologisierung'," in K. Oehler, ed., *Einsichten Gerhard Krüger zum 60. Geburtstag* (Frankford: Klostermann, 1962) 71-85. Assesses the contribution that demythologization has made to existentialism and self-understanding.

696 H. Wenz, "Mythos oder historisch ziechenhaftes Heilsgeschehen?" *TZ* 18 (1962) 419-32. Views the facticity of Jesus' miracles, resurrection, and life in general as an important element in christology.

697 H.-W. Bartsch, et al., eds., *Kerygma und Mythos VI* (10 parts; Hamburg: Reich, 1963-78). Some of the most relevant contributions include: Part 1 (1963): R. Bultmann, "Zum Problem der Entmythologisierung" (pp. 20-27; ET in 689); Part 5 (1974): J. M. Robinson, "Hermeneutik des Kerygma als Hermeneutik der Christlichen Freiheit" (pp. 174-80); Part 6 (1975): J. Jeremias, "Die Naherwartung des Endes in den Worten Jesu" (pp. 139-45).

698 G. Bornkamm, "Die Theologie Rudolf Bultmanns in der neueren Diskussion. Zum Problem der Entmythologisierung und Hermeneutik," *TRu* 29 (1963) 33-141="Die Theologie Rudolf Bultmanns in der neueren Diskussion. Literaturbericht zum Problem der Entmythologisierung und Hermeneutik," in Bornkamm, *Geschichte und Glaube* (vol. 1; BEvT 48; Munich: Kaiser, 1968) 173-275. A lengthy discussion of R. Bultmann's understanding of demythologization, his supporters, and his critics; criticizes Bultmann's understanding of the significance of the historical Jesus for the kerygma. Summary of Bultmann's position on pp. 124-41; helpful bibliography on pp. 33-46.

699 H. J. Forstman, "Interpretation of Scripture: IV. Bultmann's Conception and Use of Scripture," *Interp* 17 (1963) 450-65. A positive assessment of R. Bultmann's demythologizing hermeneutic.

700 H. van Oyen, "Judentum und Entmythologisierung," in O. Betz, et al., eds., *Abraham unser Vater: Juden und Christen im Gespräch über den Bibel* (O. Michel Festschrift; Leiden: Brill, 1963) 369-82. Compares R. Bultmann's demythologizing hermeneutic to the hermeneutic of H. Cohen.

701 H. Fries, "Entmythologisierung und theologische Wahrheit," in J. B. Metz, et al., eds., *Gott in Welt* (K. Rahner Festschrift; 2 vols.; Freiburg: Herder, 1964) 1.366-91. Explores the nature of theological truth and how demythologizing recovers it.

702 N. Perrin, "The Challenge of New Testament Theology Today," *Crit* 4 (1965) 25-34. A clear expression of R. Bultmann's position, especially as it relates to M. Kähler's criticism of the liberal quest (65), of the new quest, of Bultmann's critics, and of what tasks yet lie ahead.

703   H. Seebass, "Kirchliche Verkündigung und die sogenannte Entmytholo-
      gisierung," *KD* 11 (1965) 143-63. Finds what he believes are several prob-
      lems with demythologizing.

704   P. Achtemeier, "How Adequate is the New Hermeneutic?" *TToday* 23
      (1966) 101-19. In response to E. Fuchs (655), questions the assumption
      that the question of self is the appropriate question to take to the biblical
      text; also questions the idea that language precedes reality.

705   E. Hübner, "Entmythologisierung als theologische Aufgabe," in E. Busch,
      et al., eds., Παρρησία (K. Barth Festschrift; Zürich: EVZ, 1966) 238-60.
      Reviews the theological task of demythologization, assessing the contribu-
      tions of R. Bultmann and others.

706   U. Luz, "Entmythologisierung als Aufgabe der Christologie," *EvT* 26
      (1966) 349-68. Criticizes R. Bultmann's understanding of myth; concludes
      that myth does not provide verifiable knowledge, only an explanation that
      aids people to understand the world and their experience.

707   G. Delling, "Der 'historische Jesus' und der 'kerygmatische Christus'," in
      H. Benckert, et al., eds., *Wort und Gemeinde* (E. Schoot Festschrift; Berlin:
      Evangelische Verlagsanstalt, 1967) 19-42. An assessment of the new quest
      and the problem of demythologization.

708   N. Perrin, *The Promise of Bultmann* (The Promise of Theology;
      Philadelphia and New York: Lippincott, 1969). Provides a lucid summary
      and assessment of R. Bultmann's understanding of history, faith,
      demythologization, etc.

709   P. Ricoeur, "Die Hermeutik Rudolf Bultmanns," *EvT* 33 (1973) 457-76.
      Exposes what he believes to be the "roots" of the New Testament's
      hermeneutical problems and assesses R. Bultmann's success in dealing with
      them through demythologization.

710   R. Sleeper, "Sense and Nonsense in Theological Myths: An Essay on the
      Limits of Demythologization," in G. McLean, ed., *Traces of God in a Sec-
      ular Culture* (Staten Island: Alba, 1973) 381-403. Relates R. Bultmann's
      understanding of myth (617) to the broader theological-philosophical
      discussion of the existence of God and the question of universal awareness
      of God.

711   R. A. Johnson, *The Origins of Demythologization: Philosophy and Histo-riography in the Theology of Rudolf Bultmann* (Leiden: Brill, 1974). Attempts to understand the antecedents of Bultmann's thought. For a corrective to this work see J. Painter, "'The Origins of Demythologizing' Revisited," *AusBR* 33 (1985) 2-14.

712   P. J. Cahill, "Myth and Meaning: Demythologizing Revisited," in J. W. Flanagan, ed., *No Famine in the Land* (J. L. McKenzie Festschrift; Missoula: Scholars, 1975) 275-91. Suggests that different types of myth need to be identified for there to be validity to demythologizing hermeneutic; some myths carry meaning, some do not.

713   B. A. Gerrish, "Jesus, Myth, and History: Troeltsch's Stand in the Christ-Myth Debate," *JR* 55 (1975) 13-35. Discusses E. Troeltsch's response (72) to A. Drews (611); finds his reasoning faulty in places, sound in others.

714   J. D. G. Dunn, "Demythologizing: The Problem of Myth in the New Testament," in I. H. Marshall, ed., *New Testament Interpretation: Essays on Principles and Methods* (Exeter: Paternoster; Grand Rapids: Eerdmans, 1977) 285-307. Assesses the understanding of myth in D. F. Strauss (58) and R. Bultmann (617); criticizes Bultmann's definition of myth, which he believes makes it impossible to talk of God.

715   K. Zizelkow, "Theologisches Denken heute," *TZ* 33 (1977) 30-40. Assesses the understanding of demythologization in the post-Bultmannian era and the relationship of criticism to confessionalism.

716   J. Runzo, "Relativism and Absolutism in Bultmann's Demythologising Hermeneutic," *SJT* 32 (1979) 401-19. Believes that R. Bultmann's demythologizing hermeneutic involves an "uneasy alliance between historical criticism and philosophical insight" (p. 401); but whatever its problems, demythologizing is necessary.

717   M. J. De Nys, "Myth and Interpretation: Bultmann Revisited," *IJPR* 11 (1980) 27-41. Believes that the main lines of demythologizing must be maintained; the narrative is essential to the meaning of the myth.

718   D. Cairns, "A Reappraisal of Bultmann's Theology," *RelS* 17 (1981) 469-85. Finds that R. Bultmann was inconsistent in the application of his demythologizing hermeneutic, an approach that is harmful to the faith of the church and philosophically impossible.

719   J. Macquarrie, "A Generation of Demythologizing," J. P. van Noppen, ed.,
       Theolinguistics (Brussels: Vrije Universiteit, 1981) 143-58. Bibliographi-
       cal essay.

720   R. Bultmann, *New Testament and Mythology and Other Basic Writings*
       (Philadelphia: Fortress, 1984). An ET of a selection of Bultmann's writ-
       ings.

721   U. Luz, "Rückkehr des mythologischen Weltbildes: Überlegungen bei einer
       neuen Lektüre von Bultmanns Programm der Entmythologisierung," *Ref*
       33 (1984) 448-53. Looking back to R. Bultmann's seminal study in 1941
       (617), ponders the future of demythologization.

722   K. H. Schelkle, "Entmythologisierung in existentialer Interpretation," *TQ*
       165 (1985) 257-66. Reviews recent discussion of demythologization and
       existential interpretation in several areas of critical investigation (creation,
       Jesus' miracles, resurrection, eschatology); concludes that biblical theology
       is indebted to R. Bultmann.

B. *Criteria of Authenticity*

1. INTRODUCTION

   With the rise of form criticism, the critical disposition toward the historical
reliability of the gospel tradition has become much more skeptical. In the minds
of many, the burden of proof rests upon the claim to authenticity. In any case,
several criteria have been proposed and utilized for establishing authentic material
in the gospel tradition. In the General Bibliography below several studies are cited
that discuss the problem of authenticity and the various criteria that have been
proposed. In the Specific Criteria section that follows the criteria themselves are
described and documented.

2. GENERAL BIBLIOGRAPHY

723   F. C. Grant, "The Authenticity of Jesus' Sayings," *Neutestamentliche
       Studien für Rudolf Bultmann* (BZNW 21; W. Eltester, ed.; Berlin: Töpel-
       mann, 1954) 137-43. Makes useful distinctions in the degrees of authenti-
       city.

724   H. K. McArthur, "A Survey of Recent Gospel'Research," *Interp* 18 (1964) 39-55, esp. 47-51.

725   R. H. Fuller, *A Critical Introduction to the New Testament* (London: Duckworth, 1966) 94-98.

726   N. Perrin, *Rediscovering the Teaching of Jesus* (London: SCM; New York, 1967) 15-53. Discusses the criteria of dissimilarity and coherence.

727   W. O. Walker, "The Quest for the Historical Jesus: A Discussion of Methodology," *ATR* 51 (1969) 38-56. Very helpful discussion; assesses several of the criteria of authenticity.

728   M. Lehmann, *Synoptische Quellensanalyse und die Frage nach dem historischen Jesus* (BZNW 38; Berlin: Töpelmann, 1970) 163-205. Examines the synoptic materials as sources for the historical Jesus and how to determine their authenticity.

729   H. K. McArthur, "The Burden of Proof in Historical Jesus Research," *ExpTim* 82 (1970-71) 116-19. Argues that the burden of proof rests on the one who claims authenticity for material that does not enjoy multiple attestation; burden shifts when tradition is multiply attested.

730   M. D. Hooker, "Christology and Methodology," *NTS* 17 (71) 480-87. Criticizes the weaknesses of the criteria of dissimilarity and coherence.

731   R. S. Barbour, *Traditio-Historical Criticism of the Gospels* (London: SPCK, 1972) 1-27. Criticizes the logic and presuppositions of several of the criteria.

732   D. G. A. Calvert, "An Examination of the Criteria for Distinguishing the Authentic Words of Jesus," *NTS* 18 (1972) 209-19. Surveys criteria; suggests that tradition contrary to evangelist's theological tendency may have claim to authenticity.

733   M. D. Hooker, "On Using the Wrong Tool," *Th* 75 (1972) 570-81. Penetrating criticism of some of the criteria.

734   N. J. McEleney, "Authenticating Criteria and Mark 7:1-23," *CBQ* 34 (1972) 431-60, esp. 432-48.

735   R. Latourelle, "Critères d'authenticité historique des Évangiles," *Greg* 55 (1974) 609-38, esp. 6?9-35. Identifies three categories: (1) basic criteria, (2) dependent criteria, and (3) composite criteria.

736   F. Lentzen-Deis, "Kriterien für die historische Beurteilung der Jesusüber-lieferung in den Evangelien," in K. Kertelge, ed., *Rückfrage nach Jesus: zur Methodik und Bedeutung der Frage nach dem historischen Jesus* (QD 63; Freiburg: Herder, 1974) 78-117, esp. 94-102.

737   R. N. Longenecker, "Literary Criteria in Life of Jesus Research: An Evaluation and Proposal," in G. F. Hawthorne, ed., *Current Issues in Biblical and Patristic Interpretation* (M. C. Tenney Festschrift; Grand Rapids: Eerdmans, 1975) 217-29. Surveys criteria; follows up on D. G. A. Calvert's suggestion (732) that material contrary to theological orientation of evangelist may reflect early, widely respected, perhaps authentic, tradition.

738   R. T. France, "The Authenticity of the Sayings of Jesus," in C. Brown, ed., *History, Criticism, and Faith* (Downers Grove: Inter-Varsity, 1976) 101-43. A survey and assessment of criteria.

739   R. H. Stein, "The 'Criteria' for Authenticity," in R. T. France and D. Wenham, eds., *Studies of History and Tradition in the Four Gospels* (Gospel Perspectives 2; Sheffield: JSOT, 1980) 225-63. Best survey of the criteria to date.

740   S. C. Goetz and C. L. Blomberg, "The Burden of Proof," *JSNT* 11 (1981) 39-63. Argue that the burden of proof rests on those who deny the historical reliability of the gospels, since the gospels were written as history.

741   R. H. Stein, "'Authentic' or 'Authoritative'? What is the Difference?" *JETS* 24 (1981) 127-30. Criticizes the oft-held idea that what is truly "authentic" is what is authoritative for Christians, whether or not Jesus himself actually said it.

742   A. E. Harvey, *Jesus and the Constraints of History* (London: Duckworth, 1982) 1-10. Discusses several criteria.

743   M. E. Boring, "Criteria of Authenticity: The Beatitudes as a Test Case," *Forum* 1/4 (1985) 3-38.

744   E. Lohse, "Jesu Worte im Zeugnis seiner Gemeinde," *TLZ* 112 (1987) cols. 705-16. Tries to distinguish the sayings of Jesus from those of the early Church.

745   D. Polkow, "Method and Criteria for Historical Jesus Research," *SBLSem-Pap* (1987) 336-56. Sub-divides the authenticity criteria into 25 categories and examines the Parable of the Mustard Seed in light of them.

3. SPECIFIC CRITERIA AND BIBLIOGRAPHY

(a) Multiple Attestation

The claim to authenticity of a given saying is strengthened, if it is found in two or more traditions (Mark, Q, M, L). F. C. Burkitt identified 31 such sayings. Since the Coptic Gnostic Gospel of Thomas may contain early, even independent tradition, some scholars use it as well. Examples: the lamp saying, in Mark (4:21//Luke 8:16) and Q (Matt 5:15//Luke 11:33); the saying on what is hidden, in Mark (4:22//Luke 8:17), Q (Matt 10:26b//Luke 12:2), and Thomas (§ 5b); the evil generation saying, in Mark (8:12//Matt 16:4) and Q (Matt 12:39b//Luke 11:29b). For further discussion and examples of this criterion see the following:

746   F. C. Burkitt, *The Gospel History and Its Transmission* (Edinburgh: T & T Clark, 1906; 3rd ed., 1911) 147-66.

747   C. H. Dodd, *The Parables of the Kingdom* (London: Nisbet, 1935; 2nd ed., New York: Scribner's, 1961) 20.

748   H. K. McArthur, "The Burden of Proof in Historical Jesus Research," *Exp-Tim* 82 (1970-71) 116-19. Argues (pp. 117-18) that the burden of proof initially rests upon those who claim authenticity, but if material is multiply attested, then the burden shifts to those who deny authenticity.

(b) Multiple Forms

First proposed by C. H. Dodd, the criterion of multiple forms argues that those sayings of Jesus that are found in two or more forms of tradition (e.g., sayings, parables, stories) represent early and widespread tradition and may well reflect authentic material. Examples: the coming of the kingdom of God (Matt 5:17; 9:37-38; 13:16-17; Mark 2:18-20; 4:26-29; Luke 11:14-22; John 4:35); Jesus' mercy to sinners (Matt 11:19; Mark 2:15-17; Luke 15:2); Jesus' teaching regarding the sabbath (Mark 3:1-6; Luke 14:1-6; John 5:9-17; 7:22-24; 9:14-16). For further discussion and examples of this criterion see the following:

749   C. H. Dodd, *History and the Gospel* (New York: Scribner's, 1937) 91-101.

750   J. M. Robinson, "The Formal Structure of Jesus' Message," in W. Klassen and G. F. Snyder, eds., *Current Issues in New Testament Interpretation* (O. Piper Festschrift; New York: Harper & Row, 1962) 91-110, 273-84, see pp. 96-97.

751   H. K. McArthur, "A Survey of Recent Gospel Research," *Interp* 18 (1964) 39-55, see pp. 49-50.

752   W. O. Walker, "The Quest for the Historical Jesus: A Discussion of Methodology," *ATR* 51 (1969) 38-56, see pp. 42-43.

753   D. G. A. Calvert, "An Examination of the Criteria for Distinguishing the Authentic Words of Jesus," *NTS* 18 (1972) 209-19, see p. 217.

754   R. H. Stein, "The 'Criteria' for Authenticity," in R. T. France and D. Wenham, eds., *Studies of History and Tradition in the Four Gospels* (Gospel Perspectives 2; Sheffield: JSOT, 1980) 225-63, see pp. 232-33.

(c) Semitic Features and Palestinian Background

It has been argued, or assumed, that the retention of Semitic and Palestinian features in the Greek gospels points to authenticity, since Jesus' words were originally spoken in Aramaic and in Palestine. However, critics of this criterion point out that the presence of Semitic and Palestinian features may only reflect the early church, which was Palestinian and largely Aramaic-speaking. Examples: Aramaic words and phrases (*bar* ["son"], Matt 16:17; *talitha cum* ["little girl, arise"], Mark 5:41; *ephphatha* ["be opened"], Mark 7:34; *golgotha* ["skull"], Mark 15:22; *eloi eloi lama sabachthani* ["My God, my God, why have you forsaken me?"], Mark 15:34); the "divine passive" and other ways of avoiding the mention of "God" (Matt 5:3-10; 6:9; 13:11; Mark 14:62; 15:16; Luke 7:35); poetic devices (Matt 11:5-6; Mark 9:50; Luke 14:34-35) and word play ("straining out a gnat [*qalma*] and swallowing a camel [*gamla*]," Matt 23:24). For further discussion and examples of this criterion see the following:

755   G. H. Dalman, *Die Worte Jesus mit Berücksichtung des nach kanonischen jüdischen Schrifttums und der aramäischen Sprache erörtert* (Leipzig: Hinrichs, 1898) esp. 13-34; ET: *The Words of Jesus* (Edinburgh: T & T Clark, 1902) 17-42. A classic study; has served as the point of departure for all other studies in this field.

756   C. F. Burney, *The Poetry of Our Lord: An Examination of the Formal Elements of Hebrew Poetry in the Discourse of Jesus Christ* (Oxford: Clarendon, 1925).

757   C. C. Torrey, *The Four Gospels* (New York: Harper, 1933). Both the works of Burney (756) and Torrey have been criticized for exaggerating the extent of the Semitic influence underlying the four gospels (e.g., that the gospels may have originally been written in Aramaic or Hebrew).

758   M. Black, *An Aramaic Approach to the Gospels and Acts* (Oxford: Clarendon, 1946; 3rd ed., 1967) esp. 50-185. A much more balanced discussion of the presence Semitic influence in the gospels.

759   J. Jeremias, *Neutestamentliche Theologie: Erster Teil: Die Verkündigung Jesu* (Gütersloh: Mohn, 1971) esp. 14-45; ET: *New Testament Theology: The Proclamation of Jesus* (London: SCM, 1971) 3-37. A very readable distillation of the work of previous scholars (see 755,756,757,758), with many original and penetrating insights.

760   M. McNamara, *Targum and Testament* (Grand Rapids: Eerdmans, 1972) 94-96. Many examples of the value of the targumic tradition for New Testament interpretation.

761   B. D. Chilton, *A Galilean Rabbi and His Bible: Jesus' Use of the Interpreted Scripture of His Time* (GNS 8; Wilmington: Glazier, 1984). Shows how targumic diction and theme underlie the dominical tradition; many helpful examples.

(d) Proleptic Eschatology

    Johannes Weiss argued years ago that the historical Jesus had a proleptic eschatological understanding, that is, that he believed that the world would end soon and the kingdom of God would dawn. Material that reflects this eschatological outlook, Weiss and others believed, has a strong claim to authenticity. Not all scholars, however, accept this criterion (e.g., see Marcus J. Borg, 546,864). Examples: on the nearness of the kingdom (Matt 4:23; 9:35; Mark 1:15; 8:11; 14:25; Luke 4:43; 8:1); on the coming of the "Son of Man" (Matt 24:27, 44; Luke 11:30; 12:40; 17:24, 30). For further discussion and examples of this criterion see the following:

762   J. Weiss, *Die Predigt Jesu vom Reiche Gottes* (Göttingen: Vandenhoeck & Ruprecht, 1892; 2nd ed., 1900); ET: *Jesus' Proclamation of the Kingdom of God* (Chico: Scholars, 1985). Classic statement of the view; ran contrary to widespread belief that Jesus' preaching was primarily concerned with social reform.

763   A. Schweitzer, *Von Reimarus zu Wrede: Eine Geschichte des Leben-Jesu-Forschung* (Tübingin: Mohr, 1906). Argues for a more consistent application of the criterion of proleptic eschatology; all of Jesus' activity must be seen in the light of this understanding (see comments and bibliography above in 71).

764   T. W. Manson, *The Teaching of Jesus* (Cambridge: University Press, 1931; 2nd ed., 1935) 244-84.

765   W. G. Kümmel, *Verheissung und Erfüllung: Untersuchungen zur eschatologischen Verkündigung Jesu* (Basel: Majer, 1945; 2nd ed., Zürich: Zwingli, 1953) 47-57; ET: *Promise and Fulfillment* (SBT 23; London: SCM, 1957).

766   R. Bultmann, *Theologie des Neuen Testaments* (2 vols.; Tübingen: Mohr [Siebeck], 1948-53; 5th ed., 1965) 1.2-10; ET: *Theology of the New Testament* (2 vols.; New York: Scribner's, 1951-55) 1.3-11.

767   R. Schnackenburg, *Gottes Herrschaft und Reich: Eine biblisch-theologische Studie* (Freiburg: Herder, 1959) 135-48; ET: *God's Rule and Kingdom* (New York: Herder & Herder, 1963).

768   J. Jeremias, *Neutestamentliche Theologie: Erster Teil: Die Verkündigung Jesu* (Gütersloh: Mohn, 1971) 101-5; ET: *New Testament Theology: The Proclamation of Jesus* (New York: Scribner's, 1971).

769   E. P. Sanders, *Jesus and Judaism* (London: SCM; Philadelphia: Fortress, 1985). A provocatively fresh and stimulating presentation of Jesus from this perspective. See comments in 574.

(e) Dissimilarity

The criterion of dissimilarity argues that only material that is dissimilar to, or distinct from, tendencies in Judaism prior to Jesus and tendencies in the church after Jesus may be regarded as having a reasonable claim to authenticity. Obviously this criterion, if applied strictly and apart from other criteria, will exclude much authentic material. For this reason, and for others, the criterion has come under increasing criticism. The parables are considered the most authentic material, for they are distinctive in form and in theme. Examples of specific sayings: casting out demons by the finger of God (Luke 11:20), the kingdom in the midst of people (Luke 17:20-21), violent entry into the kingdom (Matt 11:12). For further discussion and examples of this criterion see the following:

770   R. Bultmann, *Die Geschichte der synoptiker Tradition* (FRLANT 12; Göttingen: Vandenhoeck & Ruprecht, 1921; 2nd ed., 1931; 3rd ed., 1958) 222; ET: *The History of the Synoptic Tradition* (New York: Harper & Row, 1963) 205. Believes that authentic tradition must meet this criterion.

771   E. Käsemann, "Das Problem des historischen Jesus," *ZTK* 51 (1954) 125-53; ET: "The Problem of the Historical Jesus," in Käsemann, *Essays on New Testament Themes* (SBT 41; London: SCM, 1964) 15-47; p. 37: "[Material is authentic] when there are no grounds either for deriving [it] from Judaism or for ascribing it to primitive Christianity."

772   J. M. Robinson, *A New Quest of the Historical Jesus* (SBT 25; London: SCM, 1959; repr. Missoula: Scholars, 1979) 116-19. Positive view of the criterion of dissimilarity.

773   R. H. Fuller, *Foundations of New Testament Christology* (New York: Scribner's, 1965) 18.

774   N. Perrin, *Rediscovering the Teaching of Jesus* (London: SCM; New York:
       Harper & Row, 1967) 39. Believes that authentic tradition must meet this
       criterion. Most of the synoptic examples cited above are discussed on pp.
       63-77.

775   N. Perrin, *What is Redaction Criticism?* (Philadelphia: Fortress, 1969) 71.

776   M. D. Hooker, "On Using the Wrong Tool," *Th* 75 (1972) 570-81. See pp.
       574-75 for penetrating criticism of the criterion of dissimilarity.

777   R. T. France, "The Authenticity of the Sayings of Jesus," in C. Brown,
       ed., *History, Criticism, and Faith* (Downers Grove: InterVarsity, 1976)
       101-43. See pp. 110-14 for criticism of the criterion.

778   D. L. Mealand, "The Dissimilarity Test," *SJT* 31 (1978) 41-50. Argues
       that the criterion of dissimilarity is still the best test, but must be used
       with caution.

779   B. D. Chilton, *A Galilean Rabbi and His Bible: Jesus' Use of the Inter-
       preted Scripture of His Time* (GNS 8; Wilmington: Glazier, 1984). See pp.
       86-87 for criticism of the criterion of dissimilarity.

780   E. P. Sanders, *Jesus and Judaism* (London: SCM; Philadelphia: Fortress,
       1985). See pp. 16-17 for criticism of the criterion of dissimilarity.

(f) Least Distinctive

According to Rudolf Bultmann, "Whenever narratives pass from mouth to
mouth the central point of the narrative and general structure are well preserved;
but in the incidental details changes take place, for imagination paints such details
with increasing distinctiveness" (781, p. 345). Consequently, he and others believe
that the least distinctive tradition has the best claim to authenticity. Not all
scholars, however, agree, for the tendencies of the synoptic tradition have been
found not to develop in consistent patterns, as this criterion must presuppose.
Assuming that Mark was written first and that Matthew and Luke used it as one of
their sources, one should expect greater detail in the later gospels. Sometimes this
is the case (compare Mark 1:4 with Luke 3:2b-3; Mark 1:6 with Matt 3:4);
sometimes it is not (compare Mark 1:39 with Luke 4:44; Mark 1:29-30 with Matt
8:14). Obviously the picture becomes even more inconsistent if Matthew or Luke
should be viewed as prior. For further discussion and examples see the following:

781 R. Bultmann, "The New Approach to the Synoptic Problem," *JR* 6 (1926) 337-62; repr. in Bultmann, *Existence and Faith* (New York: Harper & Row, 1960) 35-54.

782 E. P. Sanders, *The Tendencies of the Synoptic Tradition* (SNTSMS 9; Cambridge: University Press, 1969) 272-75. On p. 272 Sanders observes: "There are no hard and fast laws of the development of the Synoptic tradition. On all counts the tradition developed in opposite directions. It became both longer and shorter, both more and less detailed, and both and more and less Semitic."

783 L. R. Keylock, "Bultmann's Law of Increasing Distinctiveness," in G. F. Hawthorne, ed., *Current Issues in Biblical and Patristic Interpretation* (M. C. Tenney Festschrift; Grand Rapids: Eerdmans, 1975) 193-210. Another critical assessment of Bultmann's position.

(g) Tradition Contrary to Editorial Tendency

Recently it has been suggested that the presence of tradition that is clearly contrary to the editorial tendency of the evangelist has a stronger claim to authenticity. D. G. A. Calvert has stated: "The inclusion of material which does not especially serve his purpose may well be taken as a testimony to the authenticity of that material, or at least to the inclusion of it in the tradition of the Church in such a clear and consistent way that the evangelist was loath to omit it" (785, p. 219). Examples: contrary to Mark's negative portrayal of them, in 1:16-18 and 2:14 the disciples respond promptly to Jesus' summons to discipleship; contrary to his view that the Law is of everlasting value (5:17-20), the Matthean evangelist retains a saying that implies that it has ended with John the Baptist (11:13). For further discussion and examples see the following:

784 C. F. D. Moule, *The Phenomenon of the New Testament* (London: SCM, 1967) 56-76.

785 D. G. A. Calvert, "An Examination of the Criteria for Distinguishing the Authentic Words of Jesus," *NTS* 18 (1972) 209-19.

786 R. N. Longenecker, "Literary Criteria in Life of Jesus Research: An Evaluation and Proposal," in G. F. Hawthorne, ed., *Current Issues in Biblical*

and Patristic Interpretation (M. C. Tenney Festschrift; Grand Rapids: Eerdmans, 1975) 217-29, see pp. 226-27.

(h) Prophetic Criticism

Recently James A. Sanders has suggested that the presence of prophetic criticism may point to authentic tradition. The recovery of such a prophetic hermeneutic is through comparative analysis of the ancient interpretations of Old Testament passages and themes (sometimes called "comparative midrash"). Sanders has stated: "This method of comparative midrash...can be an aid, it seems to me, in piercing back of Luke to Jesus himself" (788, p. 104). The point that Sanders makes is that what Jesus originally intended as prophetic criticism of his own people, later came to be understood statically as criticism of outsiders (i.e., non-Christians), and so was preserved. Examples: Jesus' challenge to assumptions about election in his Nazareth sermon (Luke 4:16-30) and in his Great Banquet parable (14:15-24) probably reflect this prophetic hermeneutic, and so these traditions may represent authentic tradition. For further discussion see the following:

787   J. A. Sanders, "The Ethic of Election in Luke's Great Banquet Parable," in J. L. Crenshaw and J. T. Willis, eds., *Essays in Old Testament Ethics* (New York: Ktav, 1974) 245-271, esp. 253, 266.

788   J. A. Sanders, "From Isaiah 61 to Luke 4," in J. Neusner, ed., *Christianity, Judaism and Other Greco-Roman Cults* (Part One: New Testament; Leiden: Brill, 1975) 75-106, esp. 99-101.

(i) Contradiction

The criterion of contradiction says that those materials that contradict known environmental conditions of first-century Palestine or that contradict materials that have been established as authentic by means of other criteria should be regarded as inauthentic. Examples: the saying about women divorcing their husbands (Mark 10:12), since apparently Jewish women could do no such thing [however, this conclusion is not accepted by all]; the saying about hating one's wife and family (Luke 14:26) may contradict the saying about honoring one's father and mother (Mark 7:9-10); the prophecy of the temple's destruction may represent a *vaticinium ex eventu* (Mark 13:2). For further discussion and examples see the following:

789 D. G. A. Calvert, "An Examination of the Criteria for Distinguishing the Authentic Words of Jesus," *NTS* 18 (1972) 209-19, esp. pp. 212-13.

790 R. H. Stein, "The 'Criteria' for Authenticity," in R. T. France and D. Wenham, eds., *Studies of History and Tradition in the Four Gospels* (Gospel Perspectives 2; Sheffield: JSOT, 1980) 225-63, esp. pp. 248-50.

(j) Consistency (or Coherence)

The consistency criterion is the opposite of the contradiction criterion. Norman Perrin has stated: "Material which is consistent with, or coheres with, material established as authentic by other means may also be accepted" (796, p. 71). This criterion is commonly accepted. Charles Carlston has suggested that such a criterion meet the following two requirements: (1) that the saying "fit reasonably well into the eschatologically based demand for repentance that was characteristic of Jesus' message" (e.g., Mark 1:15; Matt 4:17); and (2) that authentic material should "reflect or fit into the conditions (social, political, ecclesiastical, linguistic, etc.) prevailing during the earthly ministry of Jesus" (794, p. 34). The best known examples that receive support from this criterion are the parables. Sayings that cohere with what on other grounds is regarded as authentic include (see Rudolf Bultmann): coherence with Jesus' eschatological oritentation (Mark 3:24-26, 27), coherence with demand for repentance (Mark 8:35; 10:23b, 25; Luke 9:60a, 62; Matt 7:13-14); coherence with demand for new way of thinking (Mark 7:15; 10:15; Luke 14:11; 16:15; Matt 5:39b-41, 44-48). For further discussion and examples see the following:

791 R. Bultmann, *Die Geschichte der synoptischen Tradition* (FRLANT 12; Göttingen: Vandenhoeck & Ruprecht, 1921; 2nd ed., 1931; 3rd ed., 1958) 110; ET: *The History of the Synoptic Tradition* (New York: Harper & Row, 1963) 105.

792 C. H. Dodd, *The Parables of the Kingdom* (London: Nisbet, 1935; 2nd ed., New York: Scribner's, 1961). With regard to Jesus' parables (p. 1): "Certainly there is no part of the Gospel record which has for the reader a clearer ring of authenticity."

793 J. Jeremias, *Die Gleichnisse Jesu* (Zürich: Zwingli, 1947; 10th ed., Göttingen: Vandenhoeck & Ruprecht, 1984) 5: the parables rest upon "especially firm historical ground." ET: *The Parables of Jesus* (London: SCM, 1963; 3rd ed., New York: Scribner's, 1972).

794 C. E. Carlston, "A *Positive* Criterion of Authenticity?" *BR* 7 (1962) 33-44.

795 N. Perrin, *Rediscovering the Teaching of Jesus* (London: SCM; New York: Harper & Row, 1967), on coherence criterion see p. 43; on reliability of parables tradition see pp. 20-22. See 804 below.

796 N. Perrin, *What is Redaction Criticism?* (Philadelphia: Fortress, 1969).

797 J. Jeremias, *Neutestamentliche Theologie: Erster Teil: Die Verkündigung Jesu* (Gütersloh: Mohn, 1971) 39; ET: *New Testament Theology: The Proclamation of Jesus* (London: SCM, 1971) 30. Argues that in light of the criterion of coherence one may regard the parables as the "bedrock" of the tradition.

C. *The Teaching of Jesus*

1. INTRODUCTION

Although there are many general studies of the teaching of Jesus, because of the complexities of the problems the subject is divided into several subcategories: Parables, the Kingdom of God, the Sermon on the Mount (and Ethics), Prayer, and the Law. Jesus' teaching concerning himself is considered in section D.

2. BIBLIOGRAPHY OF SPECIFIC TOPICS

(a) The Teaching of Jesus: General

798 C. G. Montefiore, *Rabbinic Literature and Gospel Teachings* (London: Macmillan, 1930; New York: Ktav, 1970). Systematically compares the teachings of Jesus and the gospels to that of the rabbis.

799   T. W. Manson, *The Teaching of Jesus: Studies of Its Form and Content* (Cambridge: University Press, 1931; 2nd ed., 1935). Argues that Jesus' teaching is lived out in his life; the Kingdom of God was the sphere in which he lived, moved, and had his being; Jesus summoned the remnant to join him in this sphere.

800   W. G. Kümmel, *Verheissung und Erfüllung: Untersuchungen zur eschatologischen Verkündigung Jesu* (Basel: Majer, 1945; 2nd ed., Zürich: Zwingli, 1953); ET: *Promise and Fulfillment* (SBT 23; London: SCM, 1957). See 860.

801   E. C. Colwell, *An Approach to the Teaching of Jesus* (New York: Abingdon-Cokesbury, 1946). Finds Jesus' teaching radical, original, and emphasizing humility.

802   A. M. Hunter, *The Work and Words of Jesus* (Philadelphia: Westminster, 1950; 2nd ed., 1973). A good introduction for beginning students.

803   J. M. Robinson, "The Formal Structure of Jesus' Message," in W. Klassen and G. F. Snyder, eds., *Current Issues in New Testament Interpretation* (O. Piper Festschrift; New York: Harper & Row, 1962) 91-110, 273-84. Many of Jesus' sayings reflect a two-fold, present and future, perspective.

804   N. Perrin, *Rediscovering the Teaching of Jesus* (New York: Harper & Row, 1967); GT: *Was lehrt Jesus wirklich?* (Göttingen: Vandenhoeck & Ruprecht, 1974). An assessment of Jesus' teaching, primarily the parables, from a post-Bultmannian perspective; one of the first major studies to make comparative use of the Gospel of Thomas.

805   K. Berger, *Die Amen-Worte Jesu* (BZNW 39; Berlin: de Gruyter, 1970). Suggests that the "amen" sayings of Jesus reflect an apocalyptic perspective and convey the sense of an oath; its use implies that the speaker has revelatory insight.

806   J. Jeremias, *Neutestamentliche Theologie: Erster Teil: Die Verkündigung Jesu* (Gütersloh: Mohn, 1971); ET: *New Testament Theology: The Proclamation of Jesus* (New York: Scribner's, 1971). Classic statement of the Semitic background of Jesus' preaching and teaching.

807   F. L. Fischer, *Jesus and His Teaching* (Nashville: Broadman, 1972). Believes that despite the questions raised by criticism, the main themes of Jesus' teaching can be discerned.

808   J. Blank, "Lernprozesse im Jüngerkreis Jesu," *TQ* 158 (1978) 163-77. Argues that although his manner and style of teaching approximate those of his contemporaries, Jesus' sense of authority and criticism of tradition are unique features.

809   R. H. Stein, *The Method and Message of Jesus' Teaching* (Philadelphia: Westminster, 1978). Useful survey of the form and content of Jesus' teaching.

810   R. Hamerton-Kelly, *God the Father: Theology and Patriarchy in the Teaching of Jesus* (Overtures to Biblical Theology; Philadelphia: Fortress, 1979). Believes that Jesus challenged patriarchal assumptions in his time.

811   G. Vermes, *The Gospel of Jesus the Jew* (Newcastle-upon-Tyne: University of Newcastle-upon-Tyne, 1981). Argues that Jesus taught as a holy man and taught that the Kingdom of God was present, and that God was Father.

812   H. Stegemann, "Der lehrende Jesus: Der sogenannte biblische Christus und die geschichtliche Botschaft Jesu von der Gottesherrschaft," *NZST* 23 (1982) 3-20. Believes that Jesus taught the dawn of God's reign whereby a new creation would emerge, and evil, which had gained entry into the world shortly after the original creation, would finally be eradicated.

813   P. Grelot, *Les paroles de Jésus* (Paris: Desclée, 1986). Examines isolated sentences, sentences set in a context, parables, and prayers.

814   L. G. Perdue, "The Wisdom Sayings of Jesus," *Forum* 2/3 (1986) 3-35. A form critical survey and bibliography.

815   J. Schlosser, *Le Dieu de Jésus. Étude exégètique* (Lectio Divina 129; Paris: Cerf, 1987). Examines Jesus' teaching concerning God; Jesus emphasized God's faithfulness.

816   B. D. Chilton, "Jesus and the Repentance of E. P. Sanders," *TynBul* 39 (1988) 1-18. Contrary to Sanders (574), argues that Jesus did preach repentance.

(b) The Parables of Jesus

817   A. Jülicher, *Die Gleichnisreden Jesu* (2 vols.; Freiburg: Mohr, 1888-99; 2nd ed. in 1 vol., Tübingen: Mohr, 1910; repr. 1976). Brought about major turning point in the study of the parables; parables make one basic point and are not to be allegorized; allegorical elements are inauthentic.

818   C. H. Dodd, *The Parables of the Kingdom* (London: Nisbet, 1935; 2nd ed., New York: Scribner's, 1961). Classic study of Jesus' parables; views parable tradition as essentially authentic.

819   W. O. E. Oesterley, *The Gospel Parables in the Light of Their Jewish Background* (New York: Macmillan, 1936). Examines some two dozen parables against their Jewish background.

820   J. Jeremias, *Die Gleichnisse Jesu* (Zürich: Zwingli, 1947; Göttingen: Vandenhoeck & Ruprecht, 10th ed., 1984); ET: *The Parables of Jesus* (London: SCM, 1963; 3rd ed., New York: Scribner's, 1972); for a non-technical summary see Jeremias, *Rediscovering the Parables* (New York: Scribner's, 1966). Masterful study of the parables; much usage of Semitic language and Palestinian background.

821   H. Riesenfeld, "Les paraboles dans la prédication de Jésus selon les traditions synoptique et johannique," *ÉgliseTh* 22 (1959) 21-29; Swedish version: "Liknelserna i den synoptiska och i den johanneiska traditionen," *SEÅ* 25 (1960) 37-61. Argues that Jesus' parables are drawn from Old Testament imagery and religious symbols, and revolve around the themes of the Kingdom of God and the conditions necessary for following Jesus; challenges the conclusion of A. Jülicher in that he finds both symbol and allegory in Jesus' parables.

822   M. Black, "The Parable as Allegory," *BJRL* 42 (1960) 273-87. Argues that Jesus may have employed allegory in some of his parables; should not rule out too hastily the possibility of the presence of authentic allegory.

823   E. Linnemann, *Gleichnisse Jesu: Einführung und Auslegung* (Göttingen: Vandenhoeck & Ruprecht, 1961; 7th ed., 1978); ET: *Parables of Jesus: Introduction and Exposition* (London: SPCK, 1966); *Jesus of the Parables: Introduction and Exposition* (New York: Harper & Row, 1967). Argues that most of Jesus' parables were spoken to opponents; Jesus never allegorized.

824 G. V. Jones, *The Art and Truth of the Parables* (London: SPCK, 1964). Emphasizes the poetic and artistic aspect of the parables; concludes that Jesus did use allegory, hence the interpretation of the parables should not be restricted to one point.

825 N. Perrin, "The Parables of Jesus as Parables, as Metaphors, and as Aesthetic Objects: A Review Article," *JR* 47 (1967) 340-46. Reviews works by E. Linnemann, A. N. Wilder, R. W. Funk, and D. O. Via.

826 D. O. Via, *The Parables: Their Literary and Existential Dimension* (Philadelphia: Fortress, 1967). Identifies parables as "tragic" (those which result in catastrophe) and "comic" (those which end in well-being); concludes that the parables reveal Jesus' understanding of existence.

827 J. M. Robinson, "Jesus' Parables as God Happening," in F. T. Trotter, ed., *Jesus and the Historian* (E. C. Colwell Festschrift; Philadelphia: Westminster, 1968) 134-50. Argues that the parables, in their original form (not the allegorized form often found in the gospels), derive from Jesus.

828 E. C. Blackman, "New Methods of Parable Interpretation," *CJT* 15 (1969) 3-13. Discusses recent studies, especially those which depart from A. Jülicher's hard and fast rule (817) that no authentic parable contains allegory or makes more than one basic point; very favorable with regard to D. O. Via (826).

829 J. D. Kingsbury, "Ernst Fuchs' Existentialist Interpretation of the Parables," *LQ* 22 (1970) 380-95. Further reviews of parable research in "Major Trends in Parable Interpretation," *CTM* 42 (1971) 579-96, and "The Parables of Jesus in Current Research," *Dial* 11 (1972) 101-7.

830 J. D. Crossan, *In Parables: The Challenge of the Historical Jesus* (New York: Harper & Row, 1973). Collection of major studies; sees Jesus as an "oral poet" who challenged the assumptions and worldview of his time; the Kingdom is present and the hearers are invited to participate.

831 C. E. Carlston, "Changing Fashions in Interpreting Parables," *ANQ* 14 (1974) 227-33. After reviewing the contributions of A. Jülicher (817), C. H. Dodd (818), and J. Jeremias (820), discusses some of the newer work on the function and aesthetics of the parables by D. O. Via (826) and E. Linnemann (823) and cautions against interpreting the parables against backgrounds foreign to Jesus and the early church.

832 C. E. Carlston, *The Parables of the Triple Tradition* (Philadelphia: Fortress, 1975). Comparative study of the parables that occur in all three synoptic gospels; although chiefly concerned with the layers of tradition in the gospels, does discuss the meaning of the parables in the ministry of Jesus.

833 N. Perrin, *Jesus and the Language of the Kingdom: Symbol and Metaphor in New Testament Interpretation* (Philadelphia: Fortress, 1976). Believes that the parables are extended metaphors that describe the Kingdom of God, itself a symbol; optimistic that Jesus' original meaning can be recovered.

834 M. Boucher, *The Mysterious Parable: A Literary Study* (CBQMS 6; Washington: Catholic Biblical Association, 1977). Contrary to A. Jülicher's emphasis (817), Boucher believes that all of the parables convey, along with the obvious meaning, an element of mystery. See also M. Boucher, *The Parables* (NTM 7; Wilmington: Glazier, 1981).

835 H. Weder, *Die Gleichnisse Jesu als Metaphern* (Göttingen: Vandenhoeck & Ruprecht, 1978). Traces every parable, in one form or another, back to Jesus; disagrees with A. Jülicher that true parables are always devoid of allegorical ements.

836 W. S. Kissinger, *The Parables of Jesus: A History of Interpretation and Bibliography* (ATLA 4; Metuchen: American Theological Library Association, 1979). Valuable resource tool.

837 C. E. Carlston, "Proverbs, Maxims and the Historical Jesus," *JBL* 99 (1980) 87-105. Argues that many of the 100 proverbial sayings attributed to Jesus reflect Jewish wisdom traditions.

838 D. Flusser, *Die rabbinischen Gleichnisse und der Gleichniserzähler Jesu. 1. Teil: Das Wessen der Gleichnisse* (JC 4; Bern: Lang, 1981). Comparison of Jesus' parables with rabbinic parables; concludes that Jesus' parables teach obedience to Torah, but messianic ideas in the parables are inauthentic, deriving from early church.

839 P. B. Payne, "Jesus' Implicit Claim to Deity in His Parables," *TrinJ* 2 (1981) 3-23. Observes that in many of Jesus' parables Jesus depicts himself in language used in the Old Testament to describe God.

840 R. H. Stein, *An Introduction to the Parables of Jesus* (Philadelphia: Westminster, 1981). Finds four themes in Jesus' parables: (1) the Kingdom of

God as present reality, (2) the call to decision, (3) the nature of God, and (4) final judgment.

841   J. Drury, *The Parables in the Gospels: History and Allegory* (New York: Crossroad, 1985). Has little confidence in tracing the meaning of the parables back to Jesus; their context is the gospels of the church.

842   R. W. Funk, "Poll on the Parables," *Forum* 2/1 (1986) 54-80. A summary of the results of the Jesus Seminar, which met at the University of Redlands in 1986.

843   B. B. Scott, "Assaying the Rock. The Authenticity of the Jesus Parable Tradition," *Forum* 2/1 (1986) 3-53. Concludes that the burden of proof rests on those who deny the authenticity of the parable tradition; examines 27 parables; bibliography.

(c) Jesus' Teaching on the Kingdom of God

844   G. Lundström, *Guds Rike i Jesu Förkunnelse* (Lund: Svenska Kyrkans Diakonistyrelse, 1947); ET: *The Kingdom of God in the Teaching of Jesus* (Edinburgh: Oliver & Boyd, 1963). Reviews history of scholarship, arguing that Jesus taught that the Kingdom of God is both present and coming, and that he himself was King (Messiah).

845   H. Roberts, *Jesus and the Kingdom of God* (London: Epworth, 1955). Argues that the Kingdom of God refers not to a community or realm, but to God's gracious sovereignty ("kingly rule") made present in Jesus

846   R. Schnackenburg, *Gottes Herrschaft und Reich* (Freiburg: Herder, 1959); ET: *God's Rule and Kingdom* (New York: Herder and Herder; Edinburgh and London: Nelson, 1963; London: Search, 1968). Concludes that the Kingdom of God constituted Jesus' central theme in his preaching and teaching; argues that the Kingdom (*pace* C. H. Dodd) is futuristic, but it does require an immediate response.

847   N. Perrin, *The Kingdom of God in the Teaching of Jesus* (Philadelphia: Westminster; London: SCM, 1963). Reviews history of scholarship; favors the views of some of R. Bultmann's leading pupils; interprets the futurity of the Kingdom in existential terms.

848   G. E. Ladd, *Jesus and the Kingdom* (New York: Harper & Row, 1964; London: SPCK, 1966). Argues that according to Jesus' proclamation the Kingdom of God is both realized and yet will come in its fulness in the Eschaton.

849   B. E. Gärtner, "The Person of Jesus and the Kingdom of God," *TToday* 27 (1970) 32-43. Argues that Jesus' ministry is a manifestation of the Kingdom.

850   U. B. Müller, "Vision und Botschaft. Erwägungen zur prophetischen Struktur der Verkündigung Jesu," *ZTK* 74 (1977) 416-48. Argues that Jesus' vision of Satan's fall (Luke 10:18) lies behind his understanding of the Kingdom as a present reality.

851   B. D. Chilton, "Regnum Dei Deus Est," *SJT* 31 (1978) 261-70. On the basis of comparison with Targum Jonathan, concludes that the expression, "Kingdom of God," in Jesus' proclamation implied the presence of God among humankind.

852   B. D. Chilton, *God in Strength: Jesus' Announcement of the Kingdom* (Studien zum Neuen Testament und seiner Umwelt B/1; Freistadt: Plöchl, 1979). Argues that Jesus' announcement of the Kingdom should be understood to mean that God was present "in strength" among people.

853   S. Ruager, *Das Reich Gottes und die Person Jesu* (ANTJ 3; Bern: Lang, 1979). Concludes that Jesus' preaching of the Kingdom was a major factor in his messianic self-understanding; suggests that Jesus viewed himself as Messiah.

854   T. F. Glasson, *Jesus and the End of the World* (Edinburgh: St. Andrews, 1980). Argues that in calling and training disciples, Jesus clearly did not believe that the world was about to end.

855   B. Nordsieck, *Reich Gottes—Hoffnung der Welt. Das Zentrum der Botschaft Jesu* (Neukirchen-Vluyn: Neukirchener Verlag, 1980). Argues that Jesus' proclamation of the Kingdom of God carried with it universal, and not simply nationalistic, implications.

856   J. H. Charlesworth, "The Historical Jesus in Light of Writings Contemporaneous with Him," *ANRW* 25/1 (1982) 451-76. Concludes that Jesus' proclamation of the "Kingdom of God," as recorded in the gospels, coheres with this concept as found in early Jewish sources.

857   H. Merklein, *Jesu Botschaft von der Gottesherrschaft. Eine Skizze* (SB 3;
       Stuttgart: Katholisches Bibelwerk, 1983). Argues that Jesus' concept of the
       Kingdom of God was primarily that of the religious, not political, salva-
       tion of Israel; Jesus understood himself as God's representative to Israel and
       as Israel's representative to God.

858   H. Schürmann, *Gottes Reich—Jesu Geschick. Jesu ureigener Tod im
       Lichte seiner Basileia-Verkündigung* (Freiburg: Herder, 1983); slightly dif-
       ferent collection of studies under same title (Leipzig: St. Benno, 1985). On
       Jesus' understanding of his death in relation to his kingdom proclamation.

859   G. W. Buchanan, *Jesus: The King and His Kingdom* (Macon: Mercer Uni-
       versity, 1984). Argues that Jesus attempted to establish a kingdom through
       military means.

860   B. D. Chilton, ed., *The Kingdom of God in the Teaching of Jesus* (IRT 5;
       Philadelphia: Fortress, 1984). Articles by R. Otto, W. G. Kümmel, N.
       Perrin, B. D. Chilton, and others.

861   G. Lohfink, "Die Korrelation von Reich Gottes und Volk Gottes bei
       Jesus," *TQ* 165 (1985) 173-83. Argues that Jesus believed that the
       Kingdom had begun and that it was to be located in Israel.

862   W. Simonis, *Jesus von Nazareth: Seine Botschaft vom Reich Gottes und
       der Glaube der Urgemeinde* (Düsseldorf: Patmos, 1985). Second half of the
       volume is concerned with the historical Jesus and his preaching of the
       Kingdom (pp. 203-68), which is described as the "secret reign of God" (pp.
       262-68).

863   G. R. Beasley-Murray, *Jesus and the Kingdom of God* (Grand Rapids:
       Eerdmans, 1986). Concludes that in Jesus' appearance and proclamation the
       Kingdom of God has begun to operate on earth; with Jesus' arrival the
       Kingdom is present, not merely foreshadowed, but it is not, however, real-
       ized fully, for the fulness of the Kingdom will arrive some day in the
       future; the Kingdom has begun, but it is yet to be consummated.

864   M. J. Borg, "A Temperate Case for a Non-Eschatological Jesus," *Forum*
       2/3 (1986) 81-102. Argues that when the Son of Man sayings are denied
       authenticity, there are no exegetical grounds for understanding Jesus'
       proclamation of the Kingdom as eschatological; concludes that Jesus' mes-

sage came to be understood as eschatological by the early church because of Jesus' resurrection, an event associated with the Eschaton.

865   J. R. Butts, "Probing the Polling. Jesus Seminar Results on the Kingdom Sayings," *Forum* 3/1 (1987) 98-128. A summary of the results of the Jesus Seminar, which met at the University of Notre Dame.

866   H. M. Evans, "Current Exegesis on the Kingdom of God," *PerRelSt* 14 (1987) 67-77. Review article on recent study by G. R. Beasley-Murray (863).

867   F. Mussner, *Was lehrt Jesus über das Ende der Welt?* (rev. ed., Freiburg: Herder, 1987). Explores Jesus' teaching concerning the end of the age, especially as found in Mark 13.

(d) The Sermon on the Mount and the Ethics of Jesus

868   G. Friedlander, *The Jewish Sources of the Sermon on the Mount* (New York: Bloch, 1911; repr. New York: Ktav, 1969). Citing what are regarded as relevant parallels, suggests how Jesus' original sermon and teachings have been Christianized.

869   H. Windisch, *Der Sinn der Bergpredigt* (Leipzig: Hinrichs, 1929; 2nd ed., 1937); ET: *The Meaning of the Sermon on the Mount* (Philadelphia: Westminster, 1951). Argues that Jesus, much as an orthodox Jew, required a higher ethic of obedience to the Law, perhaps saw himself as an authoritative interpreter of the Law, but not as the Messiah.

870   A. N. Wilder, *Eschatology and Ethics in the Teaching of Jesus* (New York and London: Harper, 1939; 2nd ed., 1950). Argues that Jesus' ethical teachings make up a constituent part of his message; they are not part of an "interim ethic," for Jesus in some ways sensed that the Kingdom of God was present, and not strictly futuristic and apocalyptic. Jesus called for obedience, but also taught that God's grace can make obedience possible.

871   J. Jeremias, *Die Bergpredigt* (CH 27; Stuttgart: Calwer, 1959; 2nd ed., 1960); ET: *The Sermon on the Mount* (London: Athlone, 1961; Philadelphia: Fortress, 1963). Attempts to discover the original setting of the Sermon on the Mount in Jesus' life; concludes that the sermon is made up of smaller units, themselves often summaries of larger sermons. Underlying these units ("apodoses") is the protasis of Jesus' message ("your sins are

forgiven"). Because their sins are forgiven, Jesus can make the ethical demands found in the Sermon on the Mount.

872   T. W. Manson, *Ethics and the Gospel* (London: SCM, 1960). Final chapter is devoted to "the original teaching of Jesus and the ethics of the early church" (pp. 87-103). Central to Jesus' ethic is willingness to serve, even to suffer.

873   G. Strecker, *Der Weg der Gerechtigkeit* (Göttingen: Vandenhoeck & Ruprecht, 1962; 2nd ed., 1966). Argues that Jesus' eschatological preaching has been ethicized by the Matthean evangelist.

874   J. A. Baird, *The Justice of God in the Teachings of Jesus* (Philadelphia: Westminster, 1963). Believes that the idea of the justice of God is central to Jesus' teachings, an idea that stands in continuity with Israel's prophetic tradition.

875   W. D. Davies, *The Setting of the Sermon on the Mount* (Cambridge: University Press, 1964). Argues that although the Sermon on the Mount is itself a literary creation, its contents largely represent the authentic teachings of Jesus; concludes that Jesus not only preached eschatology, but also made ethical demands, making known the True Law, namely, that it is God himself who is the "Law."

876   G. Eichholz, *Auslegung der Bergpredigt* (Neukirchen: Neukirchener Verlag, 1965). A detailed exegesis of the components that make up the Sermon on the Mount; comparison is made with the teachings of Paul.

877   R. H. Hiers, *Jesus and Ethics: Four Interpretations* (Philadelphia: Westminster, 1968). The views of A. Harnack, A. Schweitzer, R. Bultmann, and C. H. Dodd.

878   C. S. Rodd, "Are the Ethics of Jesus Situation Ethics?" *ExpTim* 79 (1968) 167-70. Argues that Jesus' ethics are not situational; Jesus views sin as sin.

879   H.-T. Wrege, *Die Überlieferungsgeschichte der Bergpredigt* (WUNT 9; Tübingen: Mohr [Siebeck], 1968). Attempts to trace various components of the Sermon on the Mount to what their contexts and meanings might have been in Jesus' ministry.

880   D. Greenwood, "Moral Obligation in the Sermon on the Mount," *TS* 31 (1970) 301-9. Argues that Jesus viewed the Mosaic Law as inadequate and sought ways to fulfill (not destroy) it; concludes that what is new in the Sermon on the Mount is the spirit in which the Law is interpreted, as opposed to the way it was interpreted by Jesus' contemporaries.

881   V. P. Furnish, *The Love Command in the New Testament* (Nashville: Abingdon, 1972). Concludes that "Jesus' commandment to *love* the enemy [is what] most of all sets his ethic of love apart from other 'love ethics' of antiquity" (p. 66). This teaching arises in part out of Jesus' proclamation that the Kingdom of God is coming.

882   W. S. Kissinger, *The Sermon on the Mount: A History of Interpretation and Bibliography* (ATLA 3; Metuchen: American Theological Library Association, 1975). Helpful survey and bibliography.

883   U. Berner, *Die Bergpredigt. Rezeption und Auslegung im 20. Jahrhundert* (Göttingener theologischer Arbeiter 12; Göttingen: Vandenhoeck & Ruprecht, 1979). Critical survey of Sermon on the Mount scholarship since 1900.

884   J. Piper, *"Love Your Enemies:" Jesus' Love Command in the Synoptic Gospels and in the Early Christian Paraenesis* (SNTSMS 38; Cambridge: University Press, 1979). Argues that Jesus commanded love of enemies in light of the presence of the Kingdom of God.

885   R. A. Guelich, *The Sermon on the Mount: A Foundation for Understanding* (Waco: Word, 1982). Concludes that although the Sermon on the Mount is a literary creation of the Matthean evangelist, it is made up of traditional materials which go back to Jesus himself.

886   E. Schweizer, *Die Bergpredigt* (Göttingen: Vandenhoeck & Ruprecht, 1982). A paragraph-by-paragraph exposition of the Sermon on the Mount.

887   J. Lambrecht, *Maar Ik zeg u: De programmatische rede van Jezus* (Leuven: Vlaamse, 1983); GT: *Ich aber sage euch. Die Bergpredigt als programmatische rede Jesu* (Stuttgart: Katholisches Bibelwerk, 1984); ET: *The Sermon on the Mount: Proclamation and Exhortation* (GNS 14; Wilmington: Glazier, 1985). Concludes that a "programmatic discourse" of Jesus lies behind the Matthean Sermon on the Mount.

888   P. E. Lapide, *Wie liebt man seine Feinde? mit einer neuübersetzung der Bergpredigt (Mt 5-7) unter Berücksichtigung der rabbinischen Lehrmethoden und der jüdischen Muttersprache Jesu* (Mainz: Grünewald, 1984). An interpretation of the Sermon on the Mount and an attempt to recover the original wording of some of Jesus' sayings.

889   G. Strecker, *Die Bergpredigt. Ein exegetischer Kommentar* (Göttingen: Vandenhoeck & Ruprecht, 1984). A detailed exegesis of the Sermon on the Mount; concludes that although serving the theological interests of the Matthean evangelist, the core of the sermon may be traced back to the preaching of Jesus (see p. 5).

890   C. Bauman, *The Sermon on the Mount: A Modern Quest for Its Meaning* (Macon: Mercer, 1985). Survey of the major studies on the Sermon on the Mount; bibliography.

891   H. D. Betz, *Studien zur Bergpredigt* (Tübingen: Mohr [Siebeck], 1985); ET: *Essays on the Sermon on the Mount* (Philadelphia: Fortress, 1985). Views the Sermon on the Mount as an early pre-Matthean epitome of Jesus' teaching; forthcoming technical commentary in Hermeneia series will present exegetical details.

892   T. L. Donaldson, *Jesus on the Mountain: A Study in Matthean Theology* (JSNTSup 8; Sheffield: JSOT, 1985). Examines the Sermon on the Mount and other mountain episodes in Matthew.

893   G. R. Ginzel, ed., *Die Bergpredigt: jüdisches und christliches Glaubensdokument. Eine Synopse* (Heidelberg: Lambert Schneider, 1985). Synoptic parallels between rabbinic writings and passages of the Sermon on the Mount are provided.

894   H. Weder, *Die "Rede der Reden." Eine Auslegung der Bergpredigt heute* (Zürich: Theologischer Verlag, 1985). An up-to-date exposition of the Sermon on the Mount; believes that most of the sermon's contents ultimately derive from Jesus.

895   G. Lohfink, *Wem gilt die Bergpredigt? Beiträge zu einer christlichen Ethik* (Freiburg: Herder, 1988). Although concerned with other issues, probes the question to whom the Sermon on the Mount was originally addressed.

(e) Jesus and Prayer

896   H. Schürmann, *Das Gebet des Herrn als Schlüssel zum Verstehen Jesu* (Leipzig: St. Benno; Freiburg: Herder, 1957; 4th ed., 1984); ET: *Praying with Christ: The "Our Father" for Today* (New York: Herder & Herder, 1964); FT: *La Prière du Seigneur à la lumière de la prédication de Jésus* (Études Théologiques 3; Paris: l'Orante, 1965). A verse-by-verse exposition of the Lord's Prayer; sees it as an aid in understanding Jesus.

897   J. Jeremias, *The Prayers of Jesus* (SBT 6; London: SCM, 1967). A selection of studies from Jeremias, *Das Vater-Unser im Lichte der neueren Forschung* (CH 50; Stuttgart: Calwer, 1962; 3rd ed., 1965), previously translated as *The Lord's Prayer* (FBBS 8; Philadelphia: Fortress, 1964), and Jeremias, *Abba. Studien zur neutestamentlichen Theologie und Zeitgeschichte* (Göttingen: Vandenhoeck & Ruprecht, 1966) 15-80, 145-52 (pp. 152-71=*Das Vater-Unser*). Especially helpful for Semitic background.

898   R. S. Barbour, "Gethsemane in the Tradition of the Passion," *NTS* 16 (1970) 231-51. Argues that the tradition that Jesus prayed before his passion is strongly attested and should be regarded as authentic tradition.

899   C. A. Blaising, "Gethsemane: A Prayer of Faith," *JETS* 22 (1979) 333-43. Accepting the authenticity of Jesus' Gethsemane prayer, concludes that Jesus prayed not to avoid the crisis, but that it might pass quickly.

900   R. Hamerton-Kelly, "God the Father in the Bible and in the Experience of Jesus," in J. Metz and E. Schillebeeckx, eds., *God as Father?* (Concilium 143; New York: Seabury, 1981) 95-162. Argues that Jesus' understanding of God as Father was one of the most important aspects of Jesus' self-understanding, an aspect that lay at the heart of his teaching and ministry.

901   D. Zeller, "God as Father in the Proclamation and in the Prayer of Jesus," in A. Finkel, ed., *Standing Before God: Studies on Prayer in Scripture and in Tradition* (J. M. Oesterreicher Festschrift; New York: Ktav, 1981) 117-29. Notes that God as Father in Jesus' authentic prayers and teaching tends to appear in wisdom sayings; concludes that Israel is being admonished to restore its filial relationship with God.

902   M. Dorneich, ed., *Vater-Unser Bibliographie—The Lord's Prayer, a Bibliography* (Freiburg: Herder, 1982). A 141 page bibliography of books and articles.

903   R. Schnackenburg, *Alles kann, wer glaubt. Bergpredigt und Vaterunser in der Absicht Jesu* (Freiburg: Herder, 1984). Second half of volume studies the Lord's Prayer.

904   S. Sabugal, *Abba'...La Oración del Señor* (Biblioteca de Autores Christianos 467; Madrid: Editoriàl Catolicà, 1985). Studies the Lord's Prayer in its original setting.

(f) Jesus and the Law (and Old Testament)

905   R. H. Charles, *The Decalogue* (Edinburgh: T & T Clark, 1923). Examines the Jewish background and interpretation of the Ten Commandments, comparing Jesus' understanding of each one.

906   B. H. Branscomb, *Jesus and the Law of Moses* (New York: Smith, 1930). Argues that Jesus elevated the ethical aspects of the Law and relegated the ritual aspects to a secondary position.

907   T. W. Manson, "The Old Testament in the Teaching of Jesus," *BJRL* 34 (1951-52) 312-32. Classic essay; examines the portions of the Old Testament that Jesus quoted, the form of the text cited (Hebrew and targumic traces are present), and his principles of interpretation.

908   R. T. France, *Jesus and the Old Testament* (London: Tyndale, 1971). Argues that Jesus understood himself in the light of various Old Testament personalities (David, Solomon, Elijah, Jonah, Isaiah), institutions (priesthood, covenant), and prophecies (humiliation, service).

909   K. Berger, *Die Gesetzesauslegung Jesu. Ihr historischer Hintergrund im Judentum und im Alten Testament* (WMANT 40; Neukirchen-Vluyn: Neukirchener Verlag, 1972). A massive study, particularly valuable for background material. Most of the discussion on Jesus' understanding of the Law centers on Mark 7:6-13; 10:19; 12:28-34; Matt 19:16-22; Luke 18:18-23.

910   R. J. Banks, *Jesus and the Law in the Synoptic Tradition* (SNTSMS 28; Cambridge: University Press, 1975). Argues that Jesus' attitude toward the Law has been accurately preserved in the synoptic tradition; concludes that Jesus does not oppose the Law, but neither does he try to justify his teachings by appeal to the Law.

911   C. Dietzfelbinger, *Die Antithesen der Bergpredigt* (ThEx 186; Munich: Kaiser, 1975). Argues that Matt 5:21-48 is essentially authentic material that provides important information as to how Jesus understood the Law and his preaching.

912   R. N. Longenecker, *Biblical Exegesis in the Apostolic Period* (Grand Rapids: Eerdmans, 1975). On pp. 51-78 surveys the appearance and function of Old Testament in Jesus' teaching.

913   W. Grimm, *Weil ich dich liebe. Die Verkündigung Jesu und Deuterojesaja* (ANTJ 1; Bern: Lang, 1976). Examines several themes in Jesus' teaching that are based on ideas in Second Isaiah; concludes that Jesus understood himself as the eschatological messenger of good news.

914   M. Hengel, "Jesus und die Torah," *ThB* 9 (1978) 152-72. Emphasizes the several points that distinguish Jesus from his contemporaries.

915   S. Westerholm, *Jesus and Scribal Authority* (Lund: Gleerup, 1978). Compares Jesus against the teachers of the Law of his time; concludes that Jesus taught that God's will sometimes transcends God's Law.

916   J. A. T. Robinson, "Did Jesus Have a Distinctive Use of Scripture?" in R. Berkey and S. Edwards, eds., *Christological Perspectives* (H. K. McArthur Festschrift; New York: Pilgrim, 1982) 49-57; repr. in Robinson, *Twelve More New Testament Studies* (London: SCM, 1984) 35-43. Argues that Jesus' "challenging use" of Scripture is distinctive to Jesus (e.g., Mark 2:25; 9:12; 12:10, 26), and so probably points to authentic tradition.

917   B. D. Chilton, *A Galilean Rabbi and His Bible: Jesus' Use of the Interpreted Scripture of His Time* (GNS 8; Wilmington: Glazier, 1984). A study of the dictional and thematic coherence of Jesus' teaching with early traditions in the Isaiah Targum.

918   D. J. Moo, "Jesus and the Authority of the Mosaic Law," *JSNT* 20 (1984) 3-49. Argues that Jesus obeyed the Law, but also understood it as fulfilled because of his advent.

919   C. A. Evans, "On the Isaianic Background of the Sower Parable," *CBQ* 47 (1985) 464-68. Suggests that the theology of Isa 55:10-11 may lay behind Jesus' Parable of the Sower (Mark 4:3-9).

920   E. P. Sanders, *Jesus and Judaism* (Philadelphia: Fortress, 1985). See esp.
       pp. 245-69. Argues that Jesus accepted the Law and offered no criticism of
       it.

921   R. P. Booth, *Jesus and the Laws of Purity: Tradition History and Legal
       History in Mark 7* (JSNTSup 13; Sheffield: JSOT, 1986). Argues that
       Jesus' emphasis of moral purity over cultic purity gave rise to subsequent
       controversy in the early church.

922   P. Sigal, *The Halakah of Jesus of Nazareth according to the Gospel of
       Matthew* (Lanham: University Press of America, 1986). Argues that Jesus'
       halakah was essentially in agreement with the pre-Jamnian rabbis.

D. *Jesus' Self-Understanding*

1. INTRODUCTION

Research in the life of Jesus often raises the question of how Jesus understood
himself. Did he think of himself as the Messiah, and if he did, in what sense? Did
Jesus call himself the Son of Man, and if he did, what did he mean by this self-
designation? Another question has to do with with his intentions. What did he expect to accomplish in Jerusalem? Did he foresee his death? All of these questions
are fundamental for life of Jesus research. The bibliography represents scholarship
addressed to these questions.

2. BIBLIOGRAPHY

923   A. Schweitzer, *Das Abendmahl im zusammenhang mit dem Leben Jesu und
       der Geschichte des Urchristentums*, 2. Heft: *Das Messianitäts und Leidens-
       geheimnis: Eine Skizze des Lebens Jesu* (Tübingen: Mohr [Siebeck], 1901,
       1956); ET (of 2nd part): *The Mystery of the Kingdom of God. The Secret
       of Jesus' Messiahship and Passion* (New York: Dodd, Mead, 1914; London:
       A & C Black, 1925; New York: Macmillan, 1950; repr. New York:
       Prometheus, 1985). Argues that from his baptism on, Jesus believed that
       God had destined him to be the Messiah. Jesus was willing to suffer, but
       prayed that God would spare him the ordeal.

924   J. Jeremias, *Die Abendmahlsworte Jesu* (Göttingen: Vandenhoeck & Ruprecht, 1935; 3rd ed., 1960); ET: *The Eucharistic Words of Jesus* (Oxford: Oxford University, 1955; rev. ed., London and New York: Scribner's, 1966). Discusses the nature of the Last Supper, when it took place, and what it meant to Jesus and his disciples; concludes that Jesus anticipated his death and understood it to have redemptive significance.

925   S. Hirsch, "Studien zu Matthäus 11:2-26: Zugleich ein Beitrag zur Geschichte Jesus und sur Frage seines Selbsbewusstseins," *TZ* 6 (1950) 241-60. Examines Jesus' self-understanding in light of a series of sayings and controversies, notably the warning concerning Herod.

926   E. Käsemann, "Sätze heiligen Rechtes im Neuen Testament," *NTS* 1 (1955) 248-60; repr. in Käsemann, *Exegetische Versuche und Besinnungen* (2nd ed., 2 vols.; Göttingen: Vandenhoeck & Ruprecht, 1965) 2.69-82; ET: "Sentences of Holy Law in the New Testament," in Käsemann, *New Testament Questions of Today* (Philadelphia: Fortress, 1969) 66-81, esp. 77-78. Views Son of Man sayings as inauthentic.

927   W. Grundmann, "Sohn Gottes," *ZNW* 47 (1956) 113-33. Argues that the belief in Jesus as Son of God derives from Jesus' self-understanding.

928   E. Stauffer, "Messias oder Menschensohn," *NovT* 1 (1956) 81-102. Argues that Jesus called himself "Son of Man" and not "Messiah" to avoid association with popular resistance movements.

929   R. Haubst, "Die Gottesanschauung und das natürliche Erkenntniswachstum Christi," *TQ* 137 (1957) 385-412. Assesses the indications of the growth of Jesus' knowledge and relates these data to theological concerns.

930   P. Vielhauer, "Gottesreich und Menschensohn in der Verkündigung Jesu," in *Festschrift für Günther Dehn* (Neukirchen/Kreis Moers: Erziehungsvereins, 1957) 51-79. Reviews many of the problems that attend Jesus and the Son of Man sayings.

931   I. L. Sanders, "The Origin and Significance of the Title 'The Son of Man' as Used in the Gospels," *Scr* 10 (1958) 49-56. Argues that the title "the Son of Man," perhaps ultimately derived from the Similitudes of Enoch (i.e., 1 Enoch 37—71) and Dan 7:13-14, was Jesus' chosen self-designation because it was neutral and carried no political overtones.

932   H. E. Tödt, *Der Menschensohn in der synoptischen Überlieferung*
       (Gütersloh: Mohn, 1959; 2nd ed., 1963); ET: *The Son of Man in the Syn-*
       optic Tradition (London: SCM; Philadelphia: Westminster, 1965). Judg-
       mental Son of Man sayings are viewed as authentic, but sayings about
       serving and suffering are not.

933   P. W. Meyer, "The Problem of the Messianic Self-Consciousness of
       Jesus," *NovT* 4 (1960) 122-38. Reviews the works of the major
       contributors to the debate, e.g., H. S. Reimarus, A. Schweitzer, W. Wrede,
       E. Schweizer, H. E. Tödt.

934   H. Riesenfeld, "Observations on the Question of the Self-Consciousness of
       Jesus," *SEÅ* 25 (1960) 23-36. Argues that the quest of Jesus' self-under-
       standing is an essential task of historical Jesus research.

935   E. Schweizer, "The Son of Man," *JBL* 79 (1960) 119-29. Concludes that
       Jesus used the ambiguous self-designation "Son of Man" to symbolize
       what Israel's role should be (a righteous servant). Later Christians attached
       christological significance to this self-designation.

936   F. Hahn, *Christologische Hoheitstitel* (FRLANT 83; Göttingen: Vanden-
       hoeck & Ruprecht, 1962; 2nd ed., 1964); ET: *The Titles of Jesus in*
       Christology: Their History in Early Christianity (London: Lutterworth,
       1969). Argues that Jesus called himself the "Son of Man," but only in
       reference to apocalyptic Son of Man. Jesus was born in the line of David
       and so was called the "Son of David."

937   C. P. Ceroke, "The Divinity of Christ in the Gospels," *CBQ* 24 (1962)
       125-39. Concludes that Jesus viewed himself as Messiah and as Son of
       God.

938   O. Betz, "Die Frage nach dem messianischen Bewusstsein Jesu," *NovT* 6
       (1963) 20-48. Argues against R. Bultmann, E. Käsemann, and G.
       Bornkamm, who had argued that Jesus never claimed to be Messiah. Jesus'
       threat to rebuild the Temple provides the best evidence that Jesus did in fact
       understand himself as Israel's Messiah.

939   H. Conzelmann, "Jesu självmedvetande," *SEÅ* 28-29 (1963/64) 39-53; GT:
       "Das Selbstbewusstsein Jesu," in Conzelmann, *Theologie als Schriftausle-*
       gung (BEvT 65; Munich: Kaiser, 1974) 30-41. Concludes that Jesus
       revealed himself through his teaching; claimed no titles for himself.

940   P. Vielhauer, "Jesus und der Menschensohn. Zur Diskussion mit Heinz Eduard Tödt und Eduard Schweizer," *ZTK* 60 (1963) 133-77. Views the Son of Man sayings as inauthentic; they were employed by the evangelists to demonstrate the authority of the earthly Jesus.

941   J. Downing, "Jesus and Martyrdom," *JTS* 14 (1963) 279-93. Argues that because of his rejection, Jesus came to see himself as a martyr whose death would atone for the sins of his people.

942   A. Vögtle, "Exegetische Erwägungen über das Wissen und Selbstbewusstsein Jesu," in J. B. Metz, et al., eds., *Gott in Welt* (K. Rahner Festschrift; 2 vols.; Freiburg: Herder, 1964) 1.608-67; FT: "Réflexions exégètiques sur la psychologie de Jésus," in R. Schnackenburg, ed., *Le Message de Jésus et l'interprétation moderne* (K. Rahner Festschrift; Paris: Les Éditions du Cerf, 1969) 41-114. Interacting with the views of Rahner, examines the baptism of Jesus and concludes that we cannot know whether or not Jesus understood himself as God's Son.

943   A. J. B. Higgins, *Menschensohn—Studien* (Stuttgart: Kohlhammer, 1965) Argues that Jesus saw himself as the Son of Man, to be exalted as heavenly judge.

944   H. M. Teeple, "The Origin of the Son of Man Christology," *JBL* 84 (1965) 213-50. Concludes that the Son of Man sayings did not originate with Jesus or the Jerusalem church, but Hellenistic-Jewish Christianity.

945   P. Vielhauer, "Ein Weg der neutestamentlichen Theologie? Prüfung der Thesen Ferdinand Hahns," *EvT* 25 (1965) 24-72. Critical assessment of the views of F. Hahn (936); disagrees with virtually every aspect of Hahn's conclusions.

946   R. E. C. Formesyn, "Was there a Pronominal Connection for the Bar Nasha Self-Designation?" *NovT* 8 (1966) 1-35. Argues that *bar nasha* ("son of man") derives from the first person pronoun.

947   G. Haufe, "Das Menschensohn-Problem in der gegenwärtigen wissenschaftliche Diskussion," *EvT* 26 (1966) 130-41. Reviewing the major contributions to the modern discussion of the Son of Man problem, concludes that Jesus' authentic Son of Man sayings referred to a being other than himself, who was to come and judge, but that after the resurrection, the early church identified Jesus with this figure.

948   R. Marlow, "The *Son of Man* in recent Journal Literature," *CBQ* 28 (1966)
       20-30. Reviews and summarizes twelve years of publications.

949   I. H. Marshall, "The Synoptic Son of Man Sayings in Recent Discussion,"
       NTS 12 (1966) 327-51. Criticizes those who have denied the authenticity
       of some or all of the Son of Man sayings; concludes that Jesus chose this
       self-designation to hide his messianic identity from his opponents.

950   N. Perrin, "The Son of Man in Ancient Judaism and Primitive Christian-
       ity: A Suggestion," *BR* 11 (1966) 17-28. Argues that there was no apoca-
       lyptic "Son of Man" concept in early Judaism; hence there could not have
       been such a concept in the teaching of Jesus or in his self-understanding.

951   C. L. J. Proudman, "Remarks on the 'Son of Man'," *CJT* 12 (1966) 128-
       31. Argues that Jesus derived the designation "Son of Man" from the
       Similitudes of Enoch (i.e., 1 Enoch 37—71).

952   H. Riedlinger, *Geschichtlichkeit und Vollendung des Wissens Christi* (QD
       32; Freiburg and Vienna: Herder, 1966). Argues that Jesus was aware of his
       messianic mission and of his relationship to God; discusses the problems
       of ascertaining just how much the historical Jesus knew; very concerned
       with the later development of "high christology" and its relation to the New
       Testament writings.

953   F. H. Borsch, *The Son of Man in Myth and History* (The New Testament
       Library; Philadelphia: Westminster, 1967). Compares New Testament Son
       of Man sayings with a variety of related concepts in antiquity.

954   R. E. Brown, "How Much Did Jesus Know?—A Survey of the Biblical
       Evidence," *CBQ* 29 (1967) 315-45. Argues that Jesus anticipated his rejec-
       tion, death, and vindication, and thought of himself as God's agent (not
       necessarily Messiah) for establishing the Kingdom.

955   R. E. Brown, *Jesus, God and Man: Modern Biblical Reflections*
       (Milwaukee: Bruce, 1967). Concerned with the question of deity and self-
       understanding of the historical Jesus.

956   L. Fatum, "Jesu 'selvbevidsthed' og kristologien," *DTT* 30 (1967) 147-82.
       Argues that primitive Christianity read messianic ideas into the passion
       tradition and later the dominical tradition.

957   J. Jeremias, "Die älteste Schicht der Menschensohn-Logien," *ZNW* 58 (1967) 159-72. Compares Son of Man sayings with a variety of related concepts in antiquity.

958   I. H. Marshall, "The Divine Sonship of Jesus," *Interp* 21 (1967) 87-103. Concludes that Jesus understood himself as the unique Son of God.

959   J. Bligh, "Did Jesus Live by Faith?" *HeyJ* 9 (1968) 414-19. Concludes that Jesus wavered in his faith in God, a view not incompatible with the gospel data.

960   R. T. France, "The Servant of the Lord in the Teaching of Jesus," *TynBul* 19 (1968) 26-52. Argues that Jesus understood himself as the Servant of Isaiah 53, as well as the Son of Man of Daniel 7.

961   F. Mussner, "Wege zum Selbstbewusstsein Jesu. Ein Versuch," *BZ* 12 (1968) 161-72. Proposes criteria for finding tradition that authentically reflects Jesus' self-understanding.

962   R. N. Longenecker, "'Son of Man' as a Self-Designation of Jesus," *JETS* 12 (1969) 151-58. Concludes that alluding to Daniel 7, Jesus called himself the Son of Man, an expression connoting suffering and glory.

963   T. A. Mitchell, "Christ as the Ebed Yahweh," *ITQ* 36 (1969) 245-50. Argues that Jesus considered himself to be the Servant of the Lord, with his Son of Man sayings emphasizing suffering and death based on this self-understanding.

964   J. C. O'Neill, "The Silence of Jesus," *NTS* 15 (1969) 153-67. Argues that Jesus did not refer to himself as "Messiah" because to do so was blasphemous; God would recognize one as the true Messiah at enthronement. Jesus' silence is therefore itself part of implicit christology.

965   M. B. Chambers, "Was Jesus Really Obedient unto Death?" *JR* 50 (1970) 121-38. Argues against R. Bultmann's view that Jesus suffered an emotional collapse just prior to his death.

966   R. A. Hammer, "Elijah and Jesus: A Quest for Identity," *Judaism* 19 (1970) 207-18. Concludes that initially Jesus understood himself as Elijah, but only later did he come to think of himself as the Messiah.

967   W. Klassen, "Jesus and the Zealot Option," *CJT* 16 (1970) 12-21. Argues
       that although Jesus was attracted to the zealots' high regard for the Law, he
       eschewed their tendency toward violence.

968   I. H. Marshall, "The Son of Man in Contemporary Debate," *EvQ* 42
       (1970) 67-87. Concludes that the Son of Man tradition in the New
       Testament goes back to Jesus himself.

969   J. Galot, *La conscience de Jésus* (Théologie et Vie; Gembloux: Duculot,
       1971). Believes that Jesus understood himself as the Son of Man, expressed
       authority with "I am" statements, and saw himself as God's Son.

970   F. Neugebauer, *Jesus der Menschensohn: ein Beitrag zur Klärung der Wege
       historischer Wahrheitsfindung im Bereich der Evangelien* (Stuttgart: Cal-
       wer, 1972). Assesses recent work on the question of the Son of Man say-
       ings in the gospels, concluding that Jesus did refer to himself as the Son of
       Man.

971   D. E. Aune, "A Note on Jesus' Messianic Consciousness and
       11QMelchizedek," *EvQ* 45 (1973) 161-65. Argues that the interpretation of
       Isa 52:7 in 11QMelch 15-19 is evidence that preaching good news was un-
       derstood as part of the messianic task. Since Jesus preached good news, he
       may very well have thought of himself as the Messiah.

972   H. Schürmann, "Wie hat Jesus seiner Tod bestanden und verstanden: eine
       methodenkritische Besinnung," in P. Hoffmann, ed., *Orientierung am
       Jesus: zur Theologie der Synoptiker* (J. Schmid Festschrift; Freiburg:
       Herder, 1973) 325-63. Discusses the difficulties encountered in assessing
       whether or not Jesus anticipated his death, and if so, how he interpreted it.

973   F. Wagner, "Systematisch-theologische Erwägungen zur neuen Frage nach
       dem historischen Jesus," *KD* 19 (1973) 287-304. Claims that the new quest
       has made the issue of Jesus' self-consciousness relevant for systematic
       theology.

974   R. Pesch and R. Schnackenburg, eds., *Jesus und der Menschensohn* (A.
       Vögtle Festschrift; Freiburg: Herder, 1975). Twenty-five studies on the
       expression "son of man"; of particular relevance to the question of the
       historical Jesus are those of A. J. B. Higgins, H. Schürmann, R. Pesch, J.
       Gnilka, W. G. Kümmel, K. Kertelge, and F. Hahn.

975 W. Resenhöfft, *Der Tag des Menschensohnes. Die Geschichte Jesu im Wortlaut der Urquellen* (Bern: Lang, 1975). An attempt to sort out the various synoptic traditions, even documents, that express differing understandings of the Son of Man.

976 R. Bauckham, "The Sonship of the Historical Jesus in Christology," *SJT* 31 (1978) 245-60. Argues that Jesus' sense of mission derives from his sense of being God's Son.

977 G. Beckerlegge, "Jesus' Authority and the Problem of his Self-Consciousness," *HeyJ* 19 (1978) 365-82. Reviews the obstacles that make it difficult to determine Jesus' self-understanding; *pace* R. Bultmann, maintains that apart from such knowledge, one cannot assign meaning to Jesus' death.

978 A. J. B. Higgins, *The Son of Man in the Teaching of Jesus* (SNTSMS 39; Cambridge: University Press, 1980). Argues that Jesus expected vindication after his death in the form of his installation as Son of Man who will come in judgment.

979 L. Oberlinner, *Todeserwartung und Todesgewissheit Jesu. Zum Problem eines historischen Begründung* (SBB 10; Stuttgart: Katholisches Bibelwerk, 1980). Concludes that Jesus had not expected to be executed in Jerusalem.

980 D. Stanley, "Go and Tell John What You Hear and See: Jesus' Self-Understanding in the Light of His Earthly Ministry," in F. Eigo, ed., *Who Do People Say I Am?* (Proceedings of the Theology Institute of Villanova University 12; Villanova: Villanova University, 1980) 47-90. Argues that Jesus understood himself as Messiah, had a sense of divine authority, and thought of himself as God's Son.

981 R. G. Gruenler, "Implied Christological Claims in the Core Sayings of Jesus," *SBLSemPap* 20 (1981) 65-77. Applying L. Wittgenstein's phenomenology of persons to Jesus' core sayings (as defined by N. Perrin, 804), concludes that a new approach to investigating Jesus' self-understanding is opened up.

982 B. D. Chilton, "Jesus *ben david*: Reflections on the *Davidssohnfrage*," *JSNT* 14 (1982) 88-112. Discusses in what sense Jesus viewed himself as the "son of David"; concludes that Jesus saw himself as son of David (Mark 12:35), but not in sense of scribal messianic expectation.

983   P. W. Hollenbach, "The Conversion of Jesus: From Jesus the Baptizer to
       Jesus the Healer," *ANRW* 25/1 (1982) 196-219. Argues that Jesus ceased
       baptizing in the tradition of John the Baptist when he experienced a new
       vision, a new sense of mission.

984   R. Leivestad, *Hvem ville Jesus vaere?* (Oslo: Land og Kirke-Gyldendal
       Norsk, 1982); ET: *Jesus in His own Perspective: An Examination of His
       Sayings, Actions, and Eschatological Titles* (Minneapolis: Augsburg,
       1987). Argues that at his baptism Jesus perceived his call to be Messiah, to
       which his subsequent teaching and actions gave witness.

985   R. Leivestad, "Jesus—Messias—Menschensohn. Die jüdischen Heilandser-
       wartungen zur Zeit der ersten römischen Kaiser und die Frage nach dem
       messianischen Selbstwusstsein Jesu," *ANRW* 25/1 (1982) 220-64.
       Assesses the impact that current Jewish messianic beliefs had on Jesus'
       self-understanding.

986   R. C. Newman, "Jesus' Self-Understanding according to the So-Called Q
       Material," in J. Skilton and C. Ladley, eds., *The New Testament Student
       and His Field* (The New Testament Student 5; Phillipsburg: Presbyterian
       and Reformed, 1982) 70-97. Compares and contrasts the understanding of
       the Son of Man tradition in Mark and in Q.

987   H. Stegemann, "Der lehrende Jesus: der sogenannte biblische Christus und
       die geschichtliche Botschaft Jesu von der Gottesherrschaft," *NZST* 24
       (1982) 3-20. Jesus saw himself as bringing about the reign of God through
       his ministry.

988   G. Gerleman, *Der Menschensohn* (Studia Biblica 1; Leiden: Brill, 1983).
       Suggests that "Son of Man" in the Aramaic means "one set apart (from the
       human order)" and thinks that the expression is clarified in the light of
       Davidic traditions.

989   V. Hampel, "Menschensohn und historischer Jesus," *TLZ* 108 (1983) cols.
       233-34. Briefly assesses the statement of the question.

990   S. Kim, *The "Son of Man" as the Son of God* (WUNT 30; Tübingen:
       Mohr [Siebeck], 1983). Argues that the Son of Man sayings represent
       Jesus' attempt to identify himself as Son of God as inoffensively as
       possible.

991   B. Lindars, *Jesus, Son of Man: A Fresh Examination of the Son of Man Sayings in the Gospels in the Light of Recent Research* (London: SPCK, 1983; Grand Rapids: Eerdmans, 1984). Argues that Jesus' use of "Son of Man" had nothing to do with an apocalyptic figure, but only meant "one like me."

992   L. Sabourin, "About Jesus' Self-Understanding," *RSB* 3 (1983) 129-34. Argues that Jesus understood himself as the Servant of God, fulfilling the prophecy of Daniel 7.

993   F. Dreyfus, *Jésus savait-il qu'il était Dieu?* (Paris: Éditions du Cerf; Montreal: Bellarmin, 1984). Believes that Jesus understood himself to be the divine Son of God, an identity he disclosed allusively to his general Jewish audience, shared more extensively with the twelve, and shared even more extensively with Peter, James, and John.

994   W. G. Kümmel, *Jesus der Menschensohn?* (Stuttgart: Steiner, 1984). Provides an excellent bibliography (pp. 41-46) and survey of research on the problem of the Son of Man sayings since H. J. Holtzmann.

995   M. Müller, "The Expression 'the Son of Man' as Used by Jesus," *ST* 38 (1984) 47-64; translated from *DTT* 46 (1983) 201-20. After surveying the scholarly discussion, concludes that the expression "Son of Man" originally meant "I"; the early church came to attach apocalyptic significance to it.

996   R. E. Brown, "Did Jesus Know He Was God?" *BTB* 15 (1985) 74-79. Critical response to F. Dreyfus (993).

997   J. A. Fitzmyer, "*Abba* and Jesus' Relation to God," in F. Refoulé, ed., *À cause de l'évangile* (Paris: Éditions du Cerf, 1985) 15-38. Focusing on Jesus' prayers in which God is addressed as "Abba" (Matt 11:25-27// Luke 10:21-22), concludes that it is probable that it represents something that Jesus actually said.

998   H. F. Bayer, *Jesus' Predictions of Vindication and Resurrection: The Provenance, Meaning and Correlation of the Synoptic Predictions* (WUNT 2, Reihe 20; Tübingen: Mohr [Siebeck], 1986). Concludes that Jesus did predict his suffering and vindication.

999   G. Schwarz, *Jesus "der Menschensohn" : Aramaistische Untersuchungen zu den synoptischen Menschenworte Jesu* (BWANT 119; Stuttgart: Kohlhammer, 1986). A detailed review of the various scholarly positions and

problems involved in determining the original religious background of the
Son of Man expression and what it may have meant in reference to Jesus.

1000   C. Coulot, *Jésus et le disciple. Étude sur l'autorité messianique de Jésus*
(Études Bibliques, n.s. 8; Paris: Gabalda, 1987). Argues that Jesus' messianic self-understanding can be seen in the requirements that he placed
upon his disciples.

E. *The Miracles of Jesus*

1. INTRODUCTION

At one time viewed as later, inauthentic embellishments and so disregarded, the
miracle tradition is now viewed as having a historical basis irrespective of how the
phenomena are to be explained. Current studies focus on the social dimension of
miracles in the life of Jesus and, primarily, in the life of the early church.

2. BIBLIOGRAPHY

1001   R. Bultmann, "Zur Frage des Wunders," in Bultmann, *Glauben und Verstehen* (2 vols.; Tübingen: Mohr [Siebeck], 1954) 1.214-28; ET: "The Problem of Miracle," *RL* 27 (1958) 63-75. Argues that the idea of miracle, as
an event contrary to nature, "can no longer be maintained. Miracle is an act
of God in distinction from a natural event. Faith in God and in miracle
mean exactly the same thing" (p. 69). The only miracle is that of revelation
whereby the hidden God makes himself known. The question of facticity of
Jesus' miracles is irrelevant. The miracle stories testify to the nature of
Christian faith; to respond in faith to God is to believe in God in whatever
manner he may chose to reveal himself.

1002   R. H. Culpepper, "The Problem of Miracles," *RevExp* 53 (1956) 211-24.
Assesses the historical and philosophical problems in the study of the miracles attributed to Jesus.

1003   W. Neil, "The Nature Miracles," *ExpTim* 67 (1956) 369-72. Discusses the
message reflected by the miracle stories.

1004   A. George, "Les miracles de Jésus dans les évangiles synoptiques," *LumVie*
       33 (1957) 7-24. Argues for the authenticity of Jesus' miracles in general;
       reasons that the miracle tradition is too early and widespread to have no
       basis in historical fact.

1005   T. A. Burkill, "The Notion of Miracle with Special Reference to St.
       Mark's Gospel," *ZNW* 50 (1959) 33-73. Argues that many of Jesus' heal-
       ing miracles were psychosomatic, while the nature miracles represent later
       unhistorical legends.

1006   H. van der Loos, *The Miracles of Jesus* (NovTSup 9; Leiden: Brill, 1965).
       A massive study that defines "miracle" and reviews Jesus' miracles in the
       context of his time; concludes that the gospel accounts are historically reli-
       able.

1007   C. F. D. Moule, ed., *Miracles: Cambridge Studies in their Philosophy and
       History* (London: Mowbray, 1965). Twelve studies on miracles in Old and
       New Testaments and ancient world; most relevant for historical Jesus
       research are those by B. Lindars, "Elijah, Elisha and the Gospel Miracles"
       (pp. 61-79), and M. E. Glasswell, "The Use of Miracles in the Markan
       Gospel" (pp. 149-62).

1008   E. Gutwenger, "Die Machterweise Jesu in formgeschichtlicher Sicht," *ZKT*
       89 (1967) 176-90. Argues that miracle traditions that are analogous to say-
       ings established as authentic by form-critical means are probably historical.

1009   F. Mussner, *Die Wunder Jesu. Eine Hinführung* (Schriften zur Katechetik
       10; Munich: Kösel, 1967); ET: *The Miracles of Jesus: An Introduction*
       (Notre Dame: University of Notre Dame, 1968). Argues that the miracles
       of Jesus in the gospels portray the *ipsissima facta Jesu*.

1010   G. Schille, *Die urchristliche Wundertradition. Ein Beitrag zur Frage nach
       dem irdischen Jesus* (Arbeiten zur Theologie 29; Stuttgart: Calwer, 1967).
       Assesses what effect the faith of the early church had on its understanding
       of the miracles of Jesus.

1011   H. Baltensweiler, "Wunder und Glaube im Neuen Testament," *TZ* 23
       (1967) 241-56. Approves of R. Bultmann's understanding of miracle
       (1001); concludes that miracles do not confirm faith; they qualify it.

1012 A. Suhl, *Die Wunder Jesu. Ereignis und Überlieferung* (Gütersloh: Mohn, 1968). Argues that the miracle tradition ultimately is rooted in the historical Jesus, not the life of the early community.

1013 R. Pesch, *Jesu ureigene Taten? Ein Beitrag zur Wunderfrage* (QD 52; Freiburg: Herder, 1970). Explores the possibility of establishing the *ipsissima facta Jesu*, as F. Mussner had argued (1009); concludes that if the *ipsissima verba Jesu* cannot be established, neither can the *ipsissima facta* be established.

1014 C. E. Carlston, "The Question of Miracles," *ANQ* 12 (1971) 99-107. Argues that the miracles of Jesus were manifestations of God, but apart from Christian faith they are subject to diverse and opposing interpretations.

1015 L. Sabourin, "The Miracles of Jesus: Preliminary Survey," *BTB* 1 (1971) 59-80. Raises the question of the significance of the miracle tradition, how it has been interpreted in the gospels.

1016 A. Vögtle, "Jesu Wundertaten vor dem Hintergrund ihrer Zeit," in H. J. Schultz, ed., *Die Zeit Jesu* (Stuttgart: Kreuz, 1966); ET: "The Miracles of Jesus against Their Contemporary Background," in H. J. Schultz, ed., *Jesus in His Time* (Philadelphia: Fortress, 1971) 96-105. Compares Jesus' miracles to miracle traditions outside the New Testament; concludes that they are unique in many respects.

1017 P. J. Achtemeier, "Gospel Miracle Tradition and the Divine Man," *Interp* 26 (1972) 174-97. Examines miracle traditions in Jewish and and non-Jewish Hellenistic sources; explores the question of the divine man concept as an influencing factor in the formation of New Testament miracle traditions.

1018 R. Pesch, "Zur theologischen Bedeutung der 'Machttaten' Jesu. Reflexionen eines Exegeten," *TQ* 152 (1972) 203-13. Examines the theological meaning of Jesus' "acts of power," concluding that the miracle stories cannot be properly evaluated in isolation from the larger question of Jesus' relation to God and the power at work in him.

1019 R. Latourelle, "Authenticité historique des miracles de Jésus: Essai de critériologie," *Greg* 54 (1973) 225-62. Discusses criteria for assessing the historicity of the miracles of Jesus; believes that evidence and logic support their historicity.

1020 R. H. Hiers, "Satan, Demons, and the Kingdom of God," *SJT* 27 (1974) 35-47. Argues that the exorcisms were prepatory for the advent of the Kingdom of God.

1021 L. Sabourin, "The Miracles of Jesus: Jesus and the Evil Powers," *BTB* 4 (1974) 115-75. Concludes that critical criteria support the essential historical reliability of the gospel miracle tradition.

1022 G. Theissen, *Urchristliche Wundergeschichten. Ein Beitrag zur form-geschichtlichen Erforschung der synoptischen Evangelien* (SNT 8; Gütersloh: Mohn, 1974); ET: *The Miracle Stories of Early Christian Tradition* (Philadelphia: Fortress, 1983). A form and social critical analysis of early Christian miracle tradition.

1023 P. J. Achtemeier, "Miracles and the Historical Jesus: A Study of Mark 9:14-29," *CBQ* 37 (1975) 471-91. Argues that it is probable that the miracle tradition underlying Mark 9:14-29 reflects something that Jesus actually did.

1024 L. Sabourin, "The Miracles of Jesus: Healings, Resuscitations, Nature Miracles," *BTB* 5 (1975) 146-200. Concludes that although much of the miracle tradition is based on historical fact, some of it has taken on symbolic value.

1025 G. Petzke, "Die historische Frage nach dem Wundertaten Jesu: Dargestellt am Beilspiel des Exorzismus Mark 9:14-29 Par.," *NTS* 22 (1976) 180-204. Argues that the miracle stories, as illustrated by Mark 9:14-29 and parallels, reflect early Christian propaganda, not history.

1026 O. Betz and W. Grimm, *Wesen und Wirklichkeit der Wunder Jesu. Heilun-gen-Rettungen-Zeichen-Aufleuchtungen. Jes. 60,5 "Da wirst du schauen und strahlen, dein Herz wird beben und weit werden"* (ANTJ 2; Bern: Lang, 1977). Examines Jesus' miracles against the background of miracles in the Bible and later legends.

1027 M. J. Geller, "Jesus' Theurgic Powers: Parallels in the Talmud and Incantation Bowls," *JJS* 28 (1977) 141-55. Argues that parallels with traditions in the Talmud and in the Aramaic, Syriac, and Mandaean incantation bowls suggest that Jesus was viewed as a magician.

1028 X. Léon-Dufour, ed., *Les miracles de Jésus: selon le Nouveau Testament* (Paris: Éditions du Seuil, 1977). Essays by several scholars comparing the miracles of Jesus with ancient miracle traditions.

1029 L. Sabourin, *The Divine Miracles Discussed and Defended* (Rome: Catholic Books, 1977). Repr. of items 1015, 1021, and 1024, plus new chapters on miracles in the early and modern church; concludes that the gospel miracle stories are essentially historical.

1030 R. W. Funk, ed., "Early Christian Miracle Stories," *Semeia* 11 (1978) 1-145. Contributions by P. J. Achtemeier, H. D. Betz, R. W. Funk, and A. C. Wire.

1031 M. Smith, *Jesus the Magician* (San Francisco: Harper & Row, 1978). Argues that historical and comparative research supports the conclusion that Jesus was a magician.

1032 D. Zeller, "Wunder und Bekenntnis: zum Sitz im Leben urchristlicher Wundergeschichten," *BZ* 25 (1981) 204-22. Questions the recent scholarly conclusions about the *Sitz im Leben* of the miracle traditions in the early church (such as the assumption that the miracles served missionary-propagandistic purposes).

1033 J. A. Bühner, "Jesus und die antike Magie: Bemerkungen zu M Smith," *EvT* 43 (1983) 156-75. Discusses M. Smith, *Jesus the Magician* (1031).

1034 H. C. Kee, *Miracle in the Early Christian World: A Study in Socio-historical Method* (New Haven and London: Yale University, 1983) esp. 146-73. Discusses the history of the miracle tradition and how Jesus' miracles may have been interpreted in the first-century context.

1035 C. L. Blomberg, "New Testament Miracles and Higher Criticism: Climbing up the Slippery Slope," *JETS* 27 (1984) 425-38. Observes an emerging consensus among scholars to view the miracles as having metaphorical significance, but not necessarily as being unhistorical.

1036 C. Brown, *Miracles and the Critical Mind* (Exeter: Paternost; Grand Rapids: Eerdmans, 1984). A review of the evolution of critical thinking with regard to miracles; concludes that the miracles of Jesus enjoy historical support and probably should be viewed as factual.

1037 J. Engelbrecht, "Wonders in die Nuwe Testament," *TEv* 17 (1984) 4-11. Compares the miracles of Jesus, Peter, and Paul against the Old Testament miracle stories.

1038 R. Latourelle, "Originalité et fonctions des miracles de Jésus," *Greg* 66 (1985) 641-53. Argues that Jesus' miracles were intended to reveal God and the Kingdom.

1039 D. Smith, "Jesus and the Pharisees in Socio-Anthropological Perspective," *TrinJ* 6 (1985) 151-56. Examines Jesus' healing activities against a Pharisaic background.

1040 D. J. Graham, "Jesus as Miracle Worker," *SBET* 4 (1986) 85-96. Evaluates recent discussion, especially that of G. Vermes, A. E. Harvey, and E. P. Sanders.

1041 R. Latourelle, *Miracles de Jésus et théologie du miracle* (Recherches, n.s. 8; Paris: Cerf; Montreal: Bellarmin, 1986). Examines historicity of Jesus' sayings regarding his miracles.

1042 D. Wenham and C. L. Blomberg, eds., *The Miracles of Jesus* (Gospel Perspectives 6; Sheffield: JSOT, 1986). Twelve studies assess the historical problem of Jesus' miracles and their interpretation in modern scholarship.

1043 H. K. Nielsen, *Heilung und Verkündigung. Das Verständnis der Heilung und ihres Verhältnisses zur Verkündigung bei Jesus und in der ältesten Kirche* (ATD 22; Leiden and New York: Brill, 1987). Explores the relationship between Jesus' healing and preaching.

F. *The Death of Jesus*

1. INTRODUCTION

A major issue in historical Jesus research is understanding the factors, if any, that led to Jesus' trial and crucifixion. The grounds for his execution should help us understand something about his ministry and the influence it had on the people of first-century Palestine.

2. BIBLIOGRAPHY

1044   H. Danby, "The Bearing of the Rabbinical Criminal Code on the Jewish Trial Narratives in the Gospels," *JTS* 21 (1920) 51-76. Concludes that "the Jewish authorities in Jerusalem were empowered to carry out no more than a preliminary investigation of the evidence against their prisoner, and a study of the gospel narratives makes it doubtful whether they can justly be said to have overstepped this permission" (pp. 75-76).

1045   H. Lietzmann, "Der Prozess Jesu," *Sitzungsberichte der Preussischen Akadamie der Wissenschaften in Berlin* 14 (1931) 313-22. Argues that Mark is our only independent source, and that it is unrealiable. Had the Sanhedrin truly condemned Jesus, it would have executed him. Since he was crucified, a non-Jewish form of execution, Jesus' trial and death must have been purely a Roman matter.

1046   S. Zeitlin, *Who Crucified Jesus?* (New York: Harper, 1942). Argues that responsibility for Jesus' death lay primarily with the Romans. See also Zeitlin's studies in *JQR* 31 (1941) 327-69; 32 (1941-42) 175-89, 279-301; 53 (1962) 77-85; 55 (1964) 8-22.

1047   G. D. Kilpatrick, *The Trial of Jesus* (London: Oxford University, 1953). Accepting the Marcan narrative as essentially reliable, concludes that the Sanhedrin interrogated Jesus, condemned him, and handed him over to Pilate for further interrogation.

1048   T. A. Burkill, "The Trial of Jesus," *VC* 12 (1958) 1-18. Concludes that for some unknown reason the Sanhedrin, having interrogated Jesus, handed him over to the Romans, who then prosecuted Jesus on the basis of political charges.

1049   M. Black, "The Arrest and Trial of Jesus and the Date of the Last Supper," in A. J. B. Higgins, ed., *New Testament Essays* (T. W. Manson Festschrift; Manchester: University Press, 1959) 19-33. Argues that "the period occupied by the arrest and trial of Jesus was longer than our Gospels make it out to be" (p. 32).

1050   J. Blinzler, *Der Prozess Jesu. Das jüdische und das römische Gerichtsverfahren gegen Jesus Christus auf Grund der ältesten Zeugnisse dargestellt und beurteilt* (Bibelwissenschaftliche Reihe 4; Stuttgart: Katholisches Bibelwerk, 1951; 4th ed., Regensburg: Pustet, 1969); ET: *The Trial of Jesus*

(Westminster: Newman, 1959). See 4th ed. for bibliography (pp. 453-64). Concludes that there were two trials, one Jewish and one Roman, and both called for death sentence; chief responsibility lay with Jewish authorities.

1051   E. Lohse, "Der Prozess Jesu Christi," in G. Kretschmar and B. Lohse, eds., *Ecclesia und Res Publica* (K. D. Schmidt Festschrift; Göttingen: Vandenhoeck & Ruprecht, 1961) 24-39. A brief version of 1054 below.

1052   P. Winter, *On the Trial of Jesus* (Studia Judaica: Forschungen zur Wissenschaft des Judentums 1; Berlin: de Gruyter, 1961; 2nd ed., rev. and ed. by T. A. Burkill and G. Vermes, 1974). Assesses the Jewishness of Jesus, concludes that he was a Pharisee, was not condemned to death by the Sanhedrin, but by the Romans.

1053   G. Lindeskog, "Der Prozess Jesu im jüdisch-christlichen Religionsgespräch," in O. Betz, et al., eds., *Abraham unser Vater. Juden und Christen im Gesprach über die Bibel* (O. Michel Festschrift; Leiden: Brill, 1963) 325-36. Concludes that "the Jews as a nation have no guilt in the crucifixion of Jesus" (p. 336).

1054   E. Lohse, *Geschichte des Leidens und Sterbens Jesu Christi* (Gütersloh: Mohn, 1964). Concludes that precise details of Jesus' trial and death cannot be recovered, but in all probability Jesus did appear before the Sanhedrin and then was handed over to the Romans.

1055   J. D. M. Derrett, *An Oriental Lawyer Looks at the Trial of Jesus and the Doctrine of Redemption* (London: School of Oriental and African Studies, University of London, 1966). While acknowledging that the Romans assumed the major part of responsibility, believes that some Jewish groups, for differing reasons, may have wished Jesus' death.

1056   W. Koch, *Der Prozess Jesu. Versuch eines Tatsachenberichtes* (Berlin and Köln: Kiepenheuer und Witsch, 1966). Concludes that the responsibility of Jesus' execution lay primarily with Pilate and his office, though certain Jewish leaders cooperated.

1057   A. Bajsic, "Pilatus, Jesus und Barabbas," *Bib* 48 (1967) 7-28. Examines the political factors behind the release of Barabbas and the sentence of Jesus.

1058   S. G. F. Brandon, *Jesus and the Zealots: A Study of the Political Factor in Primitive Christianity* (New York: Scribner's, 1967). Argues that the

Romans executed Jesus for sedition. For more details see 322 above. For further defense of this thesis see 1065 below.

1059 H. Cohn, *Reflections on the Trial and Death of Jesus* (Jerusalem: Israel Law Review Association, 1967). [Extracted from the *Israel Law Review* 2 (1967).] A brief form of a thesis that is worked out in much greater detail in 1060 below; concludes that "both the trial and the execution of Jesus were exclusively Roman" (p. 32).

1060 H. Cohn, *Mishpato u-moto shel Yeshu ha-Notsri* [Hebrew] (Tel Aviv: Dvir, 1968); ET: *The Trial and Death of Jesus* (New York: Harper & Row, 1971). Cohn, a justice of Israel's supreme court, concludes that Jesus was arrested by Romans, but out of courtesy left him under the guard of the Jewish Temple police. The Sanhedrin questions Jesus hoping to find grounds to exonerate him before Pilate. Jesus did not cooperate. In frustration the High Priest tore his robe. Before Pilate Jesus claimed to be Israel's king. Pilate accordingly sentenced him to death.

1061 T. Horvath, "Why was Jesus Brought to Pilate?" *NovT* 11 (1969) 174-84. Concludes that the Jewish leaders brought Jesus to Pilate in order that he might prove himself to be Israel's national deliverer.

1062 H. van der Kwaak, *Het Proces van Jezus. een vergelijkend onderzoek van de beschrijvingen der evangelisten* (Van Gorcum's theologische Bibliotheek 42; Assen: van Gorcum, 1969). Against S. G. F. Brandon (322), argues that Jesus was not associated with the zealots, though his Temple action may have been misconstrued as an attack.

1063 E. Bammel, ed., *The Trial of Jesus* (C. F. D. Moule Festschrift; SBT 13; London: SCM, 1970). Fourteen essays concerned with various aspects of the trial of Jesus, including essays by D. R. Catchpole, "The Problem of the Historicity of the Sanhedrin Trial" (pp. 47-65), J. C. O'Neill, "The Charge of Blasphemy at Jesus' Trial before the Sanhedrin" (pp. 72-77), H. W. Hoehner, "Why did Pilate hand Jesus over to Antipas?" (pp. 84-90), W. Horbury, "The Trial of Jesus in Jewish Tradition" (pp. 103-21), R. Morgan, "'Nothing More Negative': A Concluding Unscientific Postscript to Historical Research on the Trial of Jesus" (pp. 135-46), J. Blinzler, "The Jewish Punishment of Stoning in the New Testament Period" (pp. 147-61), and E. Bammel, "Crucifixion as a Punishment in Palestine" (pp. 162-65).

1064   M. B. Chambers, "Was Jesus Really Obedient unto Death?" *JR* 50 (1970)
       121-38. Challenges R. Bultmann's view that Jesus suffered an emotional
       collapse when he realized that his death was unavoidable.

1065   S. G. F. Brandon, "Jesus and the Zealots: Aftermath," *BJRL* 54 (1971) 47-
       66. In response to his critics, again defends his thesis (322, 1058).

1066   D. R. Catchpole, *The Trial of Jesus: A Study in the Gospels and Jewish
       Historiography from 1777 to the Present Day* (SPB 18; Leiden: Brill,
       1971). Concludes that Jesus had been arrested by Jewish guards and that the
       Sanhedrin met in order to find grounds for accusing him. Jesus was accused
       of claiming to be a son of God, was sentenced to death, and was delivered
       over to Pilate for execution of sentence.

1067   E. Grässer, "'Der politisch gekreuzigte Christus'? Kritische Anmerkungen
       zu einer politischen Hermeneutik des Evangeliums," *ZNW* 62 (1971) 266-
       94. Finds it very doubtful that Jesus had a political agenda.

1068   *Judaism* 20 (1971) 10-74. Several contributions on the trial of Jesus by H.
       Cohn (pp. 10-23), M. S. Enslin (pp. 24-31), D. Flusser (pp. 32-36), R.
       M. Grant (pp. 37-42), S. G. F. Brandon (pp. 43-48), J. Blinzler (pp. 49-
       55), G. S. Sloyan (pp. 56-68), and S. Sandmel (pp. 69-74).

1069   W. Horbury, "The Passion Narratives and Historical Criticism," *Th* 75
       (1972) 58-71. Probes the reasons why the early church was interested in the
       details of the passion.

1070   H. D. Lange, "The Relationship Between Psalm 22 and the Passion Narra-
       tive," *CTM* 43 (1972) 610-21. Argues that Jesus quoted parts of Psalm 22
       while hanging on the cross and that by doing so he was following Jewish
       custom.

1071   J. Wilkinson, "The Physical Cause of the Death of Christ," *ExpTim* 83
       (1972) 104-7. Concludes that Jesus' death came early because he voluntar-
       ily surrendered his life. See criticism of this view offered by R. O. Ball and
       K. Leese, *ExpTim* 83 (1972) 248.

1072   G. Baumbach, "Die Stellung Jesu im Judentum seiner Zeit," *FZPT* 20
       (1973) 285-305. Argues that Jesus was not part of the zealots, but his ex-
       treme actions calling for renewal, such as cleansing the Temple, led to
       misunderstanding his intentions, with the result that he was executed for
       sedition.

1073   J. H. Charlesworth, "Jesus and Jehohana: An Archaeological Note on Crucifixion," *ExpTim* 84 (1973) 147-50. A description of the skeletal remains
of one Jehohana, who apparently was crucified between 6 and 66 CE, and its
relevance for understanding the crucifixion of Jesus; helpful bibliography.

1074   G. S. Sloyan, *Jesus on Trial: The Development of the Passion Narratives
and their Historical and Ecumenical Implications* (J. Reumann, ed.;
Philadelphia: Fortress, 1973). Concludes that Jesus in all probability
appeared before Jewish and Roman authorities, was mocked by Roman soldiers, and was denied by Peter. These are likely authentic traditions, for it is
highly unlikely that the early church would have invented them.

1075   J. G. Sobosan, "The Trial of Jesus," *Journal of Ecumencial Studies* 10
(1973) 70-93. Argues that the gospel portrait of Pilate as weak and vacil-
lating is not convincing; the crowd shouting for Jesus' crucifixion may
have been supporters of Barabbas.

1076   P. E. Davies, "Did Jesus Die as a Martyr-Prophet?" *BR* 19 (1974) 37-47.
Concludes that Jesus was willing to accept death as a martyr-prophet.

1077   T. F. Glasson, "Davidic Links with the Betrayal of Jesus," *ExpTim* 85
(1974) 118-19. Suggests that Davidic tradition may have colored the
passion story, especially relating to Judas' act of betrayal.

1078   H. Schützeichel, "Der Todesschrei Jesu. Bemerkungen zu einer Theologie
des Kreuzes," *TTZ* 83 (1974) 1-16. Concludes that Jesus probably did cry
out on the cross and his cry may have included the first part of Psalm 22,
which became an interpretive key for the early church.

1079   F. Chenderlin, "Distributed Observance of the Passover—A Hypothesis,"
Bib 56 (1975) 369-93. The week of Jesus' death may have involved more
than one set date for the observance of Passover. See also Chenderlin, *Bib*
57 (1976) 1-24.

1080   E. Rivkin, "Beth Din, Boulé, Sanhedrin: A Tragedy of Errors," *HUCA* 46
(1975) 181-99. Argues that the Sanhedrin which interrogated Jesus was not
the *Beth Din* of his time, but the *Boulé*. For further details see 1092 below.

1081   J. M. Ford, "'Crucify him, crucify him' and the Temple Scroll," *ExpTim*
87 (1976) 275-78. Suggests that 11QTemple provides one external support
for the gospel narrative of Jesus' crucifixion.

1082 C.-I. Foulon-Piganiol, "Le rôle du peuple dans le procès de Jésus. Une hypothése juridique et théologique," *NRT* 108 (1976) 627-37. Suggests comparing Jesus' interrogation before the Sanhedrin and handing over to Pilate to Jeremiah's similar experience of being charged by the prophets and priests and then judged by the magistrates and people (Jer 26:8, 11, 16).

1083 M. Hengel, *"Mors turpissima crucis.* Die Kreuzigung in der antiken Welt und die 'Torheit' des 'Wortes vom Kreuz'," in W. Pöhlmann and P. Stuhlmacher, eds., *Rechfertigung* (E. Käsemann Festschrift; Tübingen: Mohr [Siebeck], 1976) 125-84; ET: *Crucifixion: In the Ancient World and the Folly of the Message of the Cross* (London: SCM; Philadelphia: Fortress, 1977). Significant discussion of Jesus' crucifixion and its background.

1084 J. J. Heaney, "A Different Kind of Memorial," *RL* 46 (1977) 450-59. Suggests that Jesus, out of a sense of fear and isolation, may have asked his disciples to remember him.

1085 J. A. Fitzmyer, "Crucifixion in Ancient Palestine, Qumran Literature, and the New Testament," *CBQ* 40 (1978) 493-513. Observes that recent archaeological finds suggest that the Romans may not have been the only people to have practiced crucifixion in the first century.

1086 R. L. Overstreet, "Roman Law and the Trial of Christ," *BSac* 135 (1978) 323-32. Concludes that it was out of cowardice that Pilate gave in to the demands for Jesus' death.

1087 J. D. M. Derrett, "The Iscariot, *Mesira,* and the Redemption," *JSNT* 8 (1980) 2-23. Argues that Judas' betrayal was an act of *mesira*, the handing over of a Jew to the Gentiles for punishment (as Joseph had been handed over to Gentiles by his brothers).

1088 D. Cohn-Sherbok, "A Jewish Note on *to proterion tes eulogias,*" *NTS* 27 (1981) 704-9. Argues that Jesus pronounced his blessing over the fourth cup, not the third.

1089 O. Betz, "Probleme des Prozesses Jesu," *ANRW* 25/1 (1982) 565-647. A detailed investigation of Jesus' trial; notes several problems in the gospel accounts.

1090   J. Carmichael, *The Death of Jesus* (New York: Horizon, 1982). Examination of the legal and political factors in Jesus' execution. Argues that Jesus was executed for fomenting rebellion against Rome.

1091   H.-W. Kuhn, "Die Kreuzesstrafe während der frühen kaiserzeit. Ihre wirklichkeit und Wertung in der Umwelt des Urchristentums," *ANRW* 25/1 (1982) 648-793. Monograph-length study, complete with indices; investigates crucifixion in antiquity.

1092   E. Rivkin, *What Crucified Jesus? The Political Execution of a Charismatic* (Nashville: Abingdon, 1984). Argues that the Sanhedrin that condemned Jesus was not the prestigious *Beth Din* (house of judgment), but an *ad hoc* group of persons loyal to Caiaphas, himself an apppointee of Pilate; believes that Pilate executed Jesus with little concern over his guilt or innocence.

1093   C. Grappe, "Essai sur l'arrière-plan pascal des récits de la dernière nuit de Jésus," *RHPR* 65 (1985) 105-25. Argues that Jesus died on the 14th of Nissan when the lambs were being sacrificed in the Temple.

1094   D. Hill, "Jesus before the Sanhedrin—On what Charge?" *IBS* 7 (1985) 174-86. Concludes that in all probability Jesus was crucified as a deceiver of the people.

1095   F. Watson, "Why was Jesus Crucified?" *Th* 88 (1985) 105-12. Argues that Jesus was likely crucified as a political criminal for speaking against the Temple and having aroused great alarm among Jewish and Roman leaders.

1096   P. Lapide, *Wer war Schuld an Jesu Tod?* (Gütersloh: Mohn, 1987). Argues that it was Pilate who was primarily responsible for the execution of Jesus; traces the factors involved in changing Pilate's guilt into a picture of reluctant complicity with Jewish demands.

1097   H. Ritt, "'Wer war Schuld am Tod Jesu?' Zeitgeschichte, Recht und theologische Deutung," *BZ* 31 (1987) 165-75. Argues that responsibility for Jesus' death lies with Pilate and a few Sadducees who do not represent the Jewish nation as a whole.

1098   O. Betz, "The Temple Scroll and the Trial of Jesus," *SWJT* 30 (1988) 5-8. 11QTemple 6-13 shows that crucifixion was sometimes the penalty for threats against the Temple.

1099 K. Kertelge, ed., *Der Prozess gegen Jesus. Historische Rückfrage und theo-logische Deutung* (QD 112; Freiburg: Herder, 1988). A collection of eight essays on various aspects of Jesus' trial, including essays by J. Gnilka, K. Müller, and G. Schneider.

1100 G. Schwarz, *Jesus und Judas. Aramaistische Untersuchungen zur Jesus-Judas-Überlieferung der Evangelien und der Apostelgeschichte* (BWANT 123; Stuttgart: Kohlhammer, 1988). Based on an Aramaic analysis of the traditions, concludes that Judas did not betray Jesus, but handed him over to the authorities just as Jesus had instructed him.

G. *The Resurrection of Jesus*

1. INTRODUCTION

The interpretations of the resurrection of Jesus have run the gamut; virtually every theory conceivable has been proposed. Rudolf Bultmann and pupils have understood the resurrection as beyond the reach of historical criticism (*pace* Ethelbert Stauffer). The resurrected Jesus lives, it has been argued, in the preaching of the kerygma. One of the major proponents for the bodily resurrection of Jesus is Wolfhart Pannenberg; note also the work of William Craig, one of Pannenberg's students. Recently Pinchas Lapide, a Jewish scholar, has argued for the bodily resurrection of Jesus.

2. BIBLIOGRAPHY

1101 E. Stauffer, "Der Auferstehungsglaube und das leere Grab," *ZRGG* 6 (1954) 146-48. Significant review of H. von Campenhausen's *Der Ablauf der Ostereignisse und das leere Grab* (Heidelberg: Winter, 1952).

1102 W. Nauck, "Die Bedeutung des Leeren Grabes für den Glauben an den Auferstandenen," *ZNW* 47 (1956) 243-67. Argues that the empty tomb tradition is historical, but it does not provide a basis for faith; rather it clarifies the meaning of the resurrection faith.

1103 C. F. D. Moule, "The Post-Resurrection Appearances in the Light of Festival Pilgrims," *NTS* 4 (1957) 58-61. Suggests that pilgrimages to festivals may account for wide geographical range of post-resurrection appearances.

1104   W. C. Robinson, "The Bodily Resurrection of Christ," *TZ* 13 (1957) 81-101. Offers several lines of argument in defense of the bodily resurrection of Jesus.

1105   H. E. W. Turner, "The Resurrection," *ExpTim* 68 (1957) 369-71. Rules out explanations that deny the reality of Jesus' resurrection; concludes that New Testament accounts are essentially reliable.

1106   S. M. Pavlinec, "Zur Grundlegung des Osterglaubens," *ComVia* 1 (1958) 267-74. Concludes that the empty tomb tradition is legendary, but the appearances are factual.

1107   R. Russell, "Modern Exegesis and the Fact of the Resurrection," *DRev* 76 (1958) 251-64, 329-43. Defends the reliability of the gospels' witness to the resurrection of Jesus.

1108   A. Descamps, "La structure des récits évangeliques de la résurrection," *Bib* 40 (1959) 726-41. Concludes that the resurrection narratives derive from different forms, not fragments, of the tradition.

1109   J. Dupont, "Ressuscité le troisième jour," *Bib* 40 (1959) 742-76. Explores the origin of the "third day" tradition.

1110   R. H. Fuller, "The Resurrection of Jesus Christ," *BR* 4 (1960) 8-24. Concludes that the empty tomb tradition is not historical, but arose in the early church as *didache* for new converts.

1111   E. C. Rust, "Interpreting the Resurrection," *JBR* 29 (1961) 25-34. Argues that the evidence compels us to interpret the resurrection of Jesus as bodily.

1112   J. W. D. Smith, "The Resurrection of Christ: Myth or History?" *ExpTim* 72 (1961) 370-75. Argues that the resurrection narratives contain elements of both myth and history.

1113   R. A. Harrisville, "Resurrection and Historical Method," *Dial* 1 (1962) 30-37. Seeks a mediating position between mythologizing approach of R. Bultmann, on the one hand, and the historicizing approach of E. Stauffer, on the other.

1114   G. E. Ladd, "Resurrection and History," *Dial* 1 (1962) 55-56. A reply to Harrisville (1113); see also 1117.

1115   E. Schick, "Die Bemühungen der neueren protestantischen Theologie um den Zugang zu dem Jesus der Geschichte, in besondere zum Faktum seiner Auferstehung," *BZ* 6 (1962) 256-68. Concludes that Jesus' resurrection is historical, but was a transcendant act that cannot be fully comprehended.

1116   J. Sint, "Die Auferstehung Jesu in der Verkündigung der Urgemeinde," *ZKT* 84 (1962) 129-51. Argues that the historicity of the resurrection of Jesus should be affirmed and that through faith its true meaning is found. See *Theology Digest* 12 (1964) 33-39.

1117   G. E. Ladd, "The Resurrection and History," *RL* 32 (1963) 247-56. Argues that Jesus' resurrection is a historical event, an instance of immortality breaking into the human sphere of mortality.

1118   W. Marxsen, *Die Auferstehung Jesu als historische und als theologisches Problem* (Gütersloh: Mohn, 1964); repr. in Marxsen, et al., *Die Bedeutung der Auferstehungsbotschaft für den Glauben an Jesus Christ* (Gütersloh: Mohn, 1966) 9-39. Responses are offered by U. Wilckens, "Die Überlieferungsgeschichte der Auferstehung Jesu" (pp. 41-63) and G. Delling, "Die Bedeutung der Auferstehung Jesu für den Glauben an Jesus Christus. Ein exegetischer Beitrag " (pp. 65-90), with a summary by H.-G. Geyer, "Die Auferstehung Jesu Christi. Ein Überblick über die Diskussion in der gegenwärtigen Theologie" (pp. 91-117); ET: *The Significance of the Message of the Resurrection for Faith in Jesus Christ* (C. F. D. Moule, ed.; London: SCM; Naperville: Allenson, 1968). In what proved to be a controversial essay, Marxsen argues that in "seeing" Jesus (1 Cor 15:8) the disciples did not actually see the risen Christ in a literal sense. The early community came to interpret the Easter experience in terms of resurrection ideas.

1119   H. Anderson, "The Easter Witness of the Evangelists," in H. Anderson and W. Barclay, eds., *New Testament in Historical and Contemporary Perspectives* (G. C. H. Macgregor Festschrift; Oxford: Blackwell, 1965) 35-55. Argues that it is not profitable to attempt to reconstruct the sequence of Easter events. The importance of the resurrection narratives lies in their affirmation that the Jesus of history and the risen Christ are one and the same.

1120 H.-W. Bartsch, *Das Auferstehungszeugnis. Sein historisches und seine theologisches Problem* (TF 41; Hamburg: Herbert Reich, 1965). Critical response to W. Marxsen (1118).

1121 D. P. Fuller, *Easter Faith and History* (Grand Rapids: Eerdmans, 1965). Appreciative of the work of W. Pannenberg (1123,1133), argues for the historicity of the resurrection; sees this question as a major issue in the question of the historical Jesus.

1122 N. Q. Hamilton, "Resurrection Tradition and the Composition of Mark," *JBL* 84 (1965) 415-21. Suggests that Mark may have composed the empty tomb narrative, not as apologetic for the resurrection but to explain Jesus' translation as risen Christ about to embark on a second phase of ministry in Galilee.

1123 W. Pannenberg, "Did Jesus Really Rise from the Dead?" *Dial* 4 (1965) 128-35. Argues that the resurrection of Jesus was a historical event, even though the word used to describe it—"resurrection"—is a metaphorical expression borrowed from apocalyptic.

1124 P. Benoit, *Passion et Résurrection du Seigneur* (Lire la Bible 6; Paris: Cerf, 1966); ET: *The Passion and Resurrection of Jesus Christ* (New York: Herder & Herder, 1969). A detailed commentary on the passion and resurrection narratives of the gospels; accepts the fourth gospel as reliable, even as based on eye-witness testimony.

1125 D. P. Fuller, "The Resurrection of Jesus and the Historical Method," *JBR* 34 (1966) 18-24. Concludes that Jesus was resurrected; historical method would suggest this conclusion because there is no Jewish understanding or expectation of an individual resurrection prior to the general resurrection.

1126 E. Gutwenger, "Zur Geschichtlichkeit der Auferstehung Jesu," *ZKT* 88 (1966) 257-82. Argues for the authenticity of the empty tomb tradition.

1127 K. Runia, "Resurrection and History," *RTR* 25 (1966) 41-52. Concludes that the resurrection of Jesus is historical, provides proof of the kerygma, but not proof in the sense that an objective historian can demonstrate the event, only proof in the sense that it provides a basis for Christian faith.

1128 S. H. Hooke, *The Resurrection of Christ as History and Experience* (London: Darton, Longman & Todd, 1967). Accepting the essential historicity of the resurrection narratives, Hooke argues that the transfiguration experience prepared the disciples for Easter.

1129 G. G. O'Collins, "Is the Resurrection an 'Historical' Event?" *HeyJ* 8 (1967) 381-87. Argues that the resurrection places Jesus outside the realm of observable history; concludes that the experience of the disciples was historical, but the resurrection itself, strictly speaking, was not.

1130 W. Andersen, *Die biblische Auferstehungsbotschaft als Frage an unseren Gottesglauben* (Arbeiten zur Theologie 33; Stuttgart: Calwer, 1968). Reviews recent discussion; concludes that the New Testament presents Jesus' resurrection as God's invitation to people to enter a new life.

1131 J. H. Hayes, "Resurrection as Enthronement and the Earliest Church Christology," *Interp* 22 (1968) 333-45. Argues that the earliest understanding of Jesus' resurrection was in terms of Davidic enthronement.

1132 W. Marxsen, *Die Auferstehung Jesu von Nazareth* (Gütersloh: Mohn, 1968); ET: *The Resurrection of Jesus of Nazareth* (London: SCM; Philadelphia: Fortress, 1970). Concludes that the confession, "Jesus is risen," originally was not in reference to an event in the past; the resurrection tradition that emerges in the New Testament reflects an interpretation of Easter in terms of the human experience of living and dying.

1133 W. Pannenberg, "Dogmatische Erwägungen zur Auferstehung Jesu," *KD* 14 (1968) 105-11. Argues that the resurrection was a historical event, but one that cannot be the object of historical inquiry because of its transcendant and eschatological nature.

1134 R. R. Bater, "Towards a More Biblical View of the Resurrection," *Interp* 23 (1969) 47-65. Assesses the assumptions and results of critical inquiry into the resurrection of Jesus.

1135 E. Gutwenger, "Auferstehung und Auferstehungsleib Jesu," *ZKT* 91 (1969) 32-58. Reviews the contributions of W. Marxsen (1118,1132) and several others; notes the problems of Jesus' resurrected body.

1136 F. Mussner, *Die Auferstehung Jesu* (Munich: Kösel, 1969). Responding to Marxsen (1118,1132) and others, argues that the wrong questions are being asked; concludes that the New Testament affirms that Jesus of Nazareth was dead, buried, and raised to a new form of existence, affirmations with which historical criticism should deal directly.

1137 E. Posset, "La résurrection," *NRT* 91 (1969) 1009-44. Considers the philosophical, semantic, historical, and exegetical dimensions of the resurrection of Jesus.

1138 R. Schnackenburg, "Zur Aussageweise 'Jesus ist (von den Toten) auferstanden'," *BZ* 13 (1969) 1-17. Examines in what ways the resurrection of Jesus is similar to or different from early Jewish views; concludes that unlike the Jewish view, Jesus was not raised back into this life, but into the new life to come.

1139 J. J. Smith, "Resurrection Faith Today," *TS* 30 (1969) Discusses the empty tomb tradition and 1 Cor 15:1-11.

1140 J. C. DeYoung, "Event and Interpretation of the Resurrection," in S. Kistemaker, ed., *Interpreting God's Word Today* (Grand Rapids: Baker, 1970) 127-75. From a conservative reformed perspective criticizes various interpretations of the resurrection and its historicity in R. Bultmann, G. Bornkamm, W. Pannenberg, and others.

1141 C. F. Evans, *Resurrection and the New Testament* (SBT 2 [2nd series]; London: SCM, 1970). Concludes that the corporeality of Jesus' resurrection, though not important, cannot be ruled out.

1142 D. Whitaker, "What Happened to the Body of Jesus? A Speculation," *ExpTim* 81 (1970) 307-10. Speculates that the resurrection was not physical, but tomb was empty because of grave robbers.

1143 J. Blank, "Der historische Jesus und die Kirche," *Wort und Wahrheit* 26 (1971) 291-307. Argues that the resurrection provides the vital link between the historical Jesus and the church.

1144 R. H. Fuller, *The Formation of the Resurrection Narratives* (New York: Macmillan, 1971; 2nd ed., Philadelphia: Fortress, 1980). Traces the development of earliest resurrection faith and the development of the resurrection narratives, concluding that something outside of the disciples must have happened, something one might describe as "meta-historical."

1145 G. Friedrich, "Die Auferweckung Jesu, eine Tat Gottes oder ein Interpretament der Jünger?" *KD* 17 (1971) 153-87. In response to W. Marxsen

(1118,1132), concludes that ὤφθη in 1 Cor 15:8 implies that the disciples saw something real, and it is evidence, though admittedly not proof, of the resurrection of Jesus as historical event.

1146 A. Richardson, "The Resurrection of Jesus Christ," *Th* 74 (1971) 146-54. Interacting with W. Pannenberg and followers, believes that the historical resurrection of Jesus is the only plausible explanation of the evidence.

1147 H. Burhenn, "Pannenberg's Argument for the Historicity of the Resurrection," *JAAR* 40 (1972) 368-79. Criticizes the view of W. Pannenberg for asking the modern reader to assume that God can be part of recoverable historical information.

1148 R. G. Crawford, "The Resurrection of Christ," *Th* 75 (1972) 170-76. Discusses K. Barth's criticism of R. Bultmann; sides with Barth; concludes that resurrection is a unique event in history.

1149 W. O. Walker, "Christian Origins and Resurrection Faith," *JR* 52 (1972) 41-55. Explores the factors that contributed to early Christianity's understanding of Jesus' death and resurrection.

1150 J. Finkenzeller, "Die Auferstehung Christi und unsere Hoffnung," in A. Paus, ed., *Die Frage nach Jesus* (Graz: Styria, 1973) 181-270. Places the discussion of resurrection faith in a broad, theological-philosophical context; reviews virtually every item of debate.

1151 M. Hengel, "Ist der Osterglaube noch zu retten?" *TQ* 153 (1973) 252-69. Easter faith, *pace* R. Pesch (1153), could only derive from a new experience, and the resurrection of Jesus was that new experience.

1152 W. Kasper, "Der Glaube an die Auferstehung Jesu vor dem Forum historischer Kritik," *TQ* 153 (1973) 229-41. Argues that R. Pesch's view (1153) is incorrect and is too indebted to parallels of questionable relevance.

1153 R. Pesch, "Zur Entstehung des Glaubens an die Auferstehung Jesu. Ein Vorschlag zur Diskussion," *TQ* 153 (1973) 201-28. Argues that Easter faith is to be traced back to the messianic contents of Jesus' ministry, not to the empty tomb and appearance traditions. In the same issue of *TQ* (pp. 270-83) Pesch responds to the criticisms of W. Kasper (1152), K. H. Schelkle (1154), P. Stuhlmacher (1155), and M. Hengel (1151).

1154 K. H. Schelkle, "Schöpfung des Glauben?" *TQ* 153 (1973) 242-43. Argues
      that R. Pesch (1153) has misunderstood 1 Cor 15:3-8.

1155 P. Stuhlmacher, "'Kritischer müssten mir die historisch-kritischen sein!'"
      TQ 153 (1973) 244-51. Alluding to the words of K. Barth ("For me histor-
      ical criticism must be more critical!"), argues that R. Pesch (1153) has
      misunderstood the empty tomb tradtion and the meaning of ὤφθη in 1 Cor
      15:5.

1156 H.-W. Bartsch, "Der Ursprung des Osterglaubens," *TZ* 31 (1975) 16-31.
      Against R. Pesch (1153), argues that the Easter faith of the disciples rests
      in the resurrection appearances of Jesus, not in messianic understanding of
      Jesus before Easter.

1157 L. Sabourin, "The Resurrection of Jesus," *BTB* 5 (1975) 262-93. Reviews
      several recent studies; concludes that scholars are increasingly open to
      accepting the historicity of the resurrection.

1158 J. D. Crossan, "Empty Tomb and Absent Lord," in W. Kelber, ed., *The
      Passion in Mark* (Philadelphia: Fortress, 1976) 135-52. Argues that the
      evangelist Mark "created the tradition of the Empty Tomb as the precise and
      complete redactional conclusion for his Gospel (16:1-8)" (p. 135).

1159 M. D. Goulder, "The Empty Tomb," *Th* 99 (1976) 206-14. Suggests that
      Mark 16:1-8 is a midrash reflecting traditions from Josh 10:16-27 (death
      and burial), Daniel 12 (resurrection), and other Old Testament passages.

1160 J. Kremer, "Entstehung und Inhalt des Osterglaubens. Zur neuesten
      Diskussion," *TRev* 72 (1976) 1-14. Reviews the position of R. Pesch
      (1153) and the critical responses to it (1151,1152,1154,1155,1156).

1161 J. P. Galvin, "Resurrection as Theologia Crucis Jesu: The Foundational
      Christology of Rudolf Pesch," *TS* 38 (1977) 513-25. Reviews the dialogue
      between R. Pesch (1153) and others (see 1151,1152,1154,1155,1156) and
      notes that his attempt to link christology to the pre-Easter Jesus (and not
      simply to Easter) is important and needs to be pursued.

1162 P. Lapide, *Auferstehung. Ein jüdisches Glaubenserlebnis* (Stuttgart: Cal-
      wer, 1977); ET: *The Resurrection of Jesu: A Jewish Perspective* (Minnea-
      polis: Augsburg, 1983). Argues that although Jesus and his resurrection
      were a Jewish affair, the resurrection does not make him Israel's Messiah.

1163 R. H. Stein, "Was the Tomb Really Empty?" *JETS* 20 (1977) 23-29. Concludes that several compelling arguments can be made in favor of the gospel tradition that the tomb was found empty.

1164 S. Ben-Chorin, "Auferstehung. Bemerkungen zu einem apologetischen Pamphlet," *ZRGG* 30 (1978) 259-62. Criticizes Lapide's argument for the historicity of Jesus' resurrection (1162).

1165 C. A. Evans, "Mark's Use of the Empty Tomb Tradition," *Studia Biblica et Theologica* 8/2 (1978) 50-55. *Pace* J. D. Crossan (1158), concludes that the empty tomb story in Mark was not created by the evangelist, but derives from older tradition.

1166 K. H. Schelkle, "Auferstehung Jesu: Geschichte und Deutung," in A. Winter, et al., eds., *Kirche und Bibel* (E. Schick Festschrift; Paderborn: Schöningh, 1979) 389-96. Argues that there may remain uncertainty as to the historicity of the resurrection, but there can be no mistaking the historical result of the resurrection.

1167 W. R. Clark, "Jesus, Lazarus, and Others: Resuscitation or Resurrection?" *RL* 49 (1980) 230-41. Believes that the New Testament understands the resurrection of Jesus and others (Lazarus, widow's son) as essentially the same; concludes that the assumption that all but Jesus are merely resuscitated and will die again is incorrect.

1168 J. P. Galvin, "A Recent Jewish View of the Resurrection," *ExpTim* 91 (1980) 277-99. A critical review of P. Lapide's work (1162).

1169 E. Schweizer, "Resurrection: Fact or Illusion?" *HBT* 1 (1980) 137-59; German version: "Auferstehung—Wirklichkeit oder Illusion?" *EvT* 41 (1981) 2-19. Claims that the history of Israel and the early Christian witness to the resurrection of Jesus offer strong support to the reality of resurrection.

1170 W. L. Craig, "The Empty Tomb of Jesus," in R. T. France, ed., *Studies of History and Tradition in the Gospels* (Gospel Perspectives 2; Sheffield: JSOT, 1981) 173-200. Argues that the evidence for the reliability of the empty tomb tradition is compelling (see 1184).

1171 W. L. Craig, *The Son Rises: The Historical Evidence for the Resurrection of Jesus* (Chicago: Moody, 1981). Elaborates on thesis in 1170; surveys and rebuts alternative explanations (see 1184).

1172 K. Grayston, "The Empty Tomb," *ExpTim* 92 (1981) 263-67. Claims that the empty tomb tradition is not essential to the resurrection tradition.

1173 H.-W. Bartsch, "Inhalt und Funktion des urchristlichen Osterglauabens," *ANRW* 25/1 (1982) 794-843, with supplemental bibliographies by H. Rumpeltes (pp. 844-73) and T. Pola (pp. 873-90). Significant discussion of the antecedents to the resurrection of Jesus.

1174 G. Ghiberti, *La risurrezione di Gesù* (Biblioteca minima di cultura religiosa 30; Brescia: Paideia, 1982). Believes that Mark 16:1-8 is historically reliable.

1175 H. Hempelmann, *Die Auferstehung Jesu Christi—eine historishe Tatsache? Eine engagierte Analyse* (Wuppertal: Brockhaus, 1982). Argues for the historicity of the resurrection.

1176 L. Oberlinner, "Die Verkündigung der Auferweckung Jesu im geöffneten und leere Grab," *ZNW* 73 (1982) 159-82. Argues that the empty tomb tradition arose as a consequence of the Easter proclamation; it played no part in its basis.

1177 J. M. Robinson, "Jesus: From Easter to Valentinus (or to the Apostles' Creed)," *JBL* 101 (1982) 5-37. Concludes that the earliest resurrection experience was probably that of a luminous Christ, such as is found in Mark 9:2-8, Acts 9:3, and, in much greater detail, Rev 1:13-16. Because of exploitation of this tradition by an incipient gnosticizing tendency, the Marcan evanglist relocated the luminous tradition to a mid-point in his gospel (the transfiguration) and omitted a description of the resurrection at the conclusion of his gospel narrative. See the response of G. G. O'Collins (1180).

1178 R. Pesch, "Zur Entstehung des Glaubens an die Auferstehung Jesu: ein neuer Versuch," *FZPT* 30 (1983) 73-98. Argues that Jesus' Son of Man sayings merged with Easter "Son of Man visions" and gave rise to resurrection faith (see 1153).

1179 H. Staudinger, "The Resurrection of Jesus Christ as Saving Event and as 'Object' of Historical Research," *SJT* 36 (1983) 309-26. Concludes that although historical certainty is impossible, the unity of the early traditions and other considerations argue for the essential veracity of the early church's claim that Jesus had been raised from the dead.

1180 G. G. O'Collins, "Luminous Appearances of the Risen Christ," *CBQ* 46 (1984) 247-54. Contrary to J. M. Robinson (1177), believes that the luminous appearance traditions of the resurrection do not represent the earliest form of resurrection faith.

1181 G. R. Osborne, *The Resurrection Narratives: A Redaction Study* (Grand Rapids: Baker, 1984). Accepts the essential historicity of the resurrection narratives; thinks that Mark's gospel originally had an account of a resurrection appearance (which Osborne attempts to reconstruct on pp. 64-65).

1182 P. Perkins, *Resurrection: New Testament Witness and Contemporary Reflection* (Garden City: Doubleday, 1984). A major study; compares the various Jewish beliefs about resurrection; concludes that the empty tomb tradition (Mark 16:1-8) represents the evangelist's attempt to bring Jesus' earthly ministry to a close.

1183 J. Perret, *Ressuscité? Approche historique* (Paris: FAC-éditions, 1984). Concludes that one cannot reject the resurrection for historical reasons.

1184 W. L. Craig, "The Historicity of the Empty Tomb of Jesus," *NTS* 31 (1985) 39-67. Finds several lines of evidence that argue strongly for the historicity of the empty tomb tradition (see 1170).

1185 S. T. Davis, "Was Jesus Raised Bodily?" *CSR* 14 (1985) 140-52. Argues that there is no compelling evidence or reason to understand Jesus' resurrection in any other sense than bodily.

1186 D. A. S. Fergusson, "Interpreting the Resurrection," *SJT* 38 (1985) 287-305. Assesses "radical," "liberal," and "traditional" views of the resurrection of Jesus; concludes that for "high" christology to be maintained, defense of the resurrection more or less along traditional lines is needed.

1187 H. Kessler, *Sucht den Lebenden nicht beiden Toten. Die Auferstehung Jesu Christi in biblischer, fundamentaltheologischer und systematischer Sicht* (Düsseldorf: Patmos, 1985). Examines biblical background to resurrection faith, the original resurrection faith of Jesus' followers, and the significance of modern faith in the resurrection.

1188 J. Hallman, "The Resurrection of Jesus and the Origin of Christology," *Encount* 47 (1986) 219-31. Assesses the communal aspect of understanding the resurrection.

1189 B. W. Henault, "Empty Tomb or Empty Argument: A Failure of Nerve in Recent Studies of Mark 16?" *SR* 15 (1986) 177-90. Argues that because of a failure to apply the canons of historical investigation to Mark 16:1-8, several scholars have accepted the historicity of the empty tomb tradition.

1190 W. G. Kümmel, "Eine jüdisch Stimme zur Auferstehung Jesu," *TRu* 51 (1986) 92-97. Reviews contributions by P. Lapide (1162), S. Ben-Chorin (1164), and J. P. Galvin (1161,1168).

1191 B. Lindars, "Jesus Risen: Bodily Resurrection But No Empty Tomb," *Th* 89 (1986) 90-96. Concludes that the empty tomb tradition is inauthentic, part of later Christian interpretation of the resurrection of Jesus.

1192 L. Oberlinner, ed., *Auferstehung Jesu—Auferstehung der Christen. Deutung des Osterglaubens* (QD 105; Freiburg: Herder, 1986). Several studies on various aspects of the resurrection of Jesus with contributions by I. Broer, L. Oberlinner, I. Maisch, P. Friedler, D. Zeller, and J. M. Nützel.

1193 W. L. Craig, "Pannenbergs Beweis für Auferstehung Jesu," *KD* 34 (1988) 78-104. Although accepting much of Pannenberg's position, it is argued that the historicity (or "extramental") aspect of Jesus' resurrection should not be denied.

1194 J. P. Galvin, "The Origin of Faith in the Resurrection of Jesus: Two Recent Perspectives," *TS* 49 (1988) 25-44. Interacting with R. Pesch and H. Verweyan, weaknesses and strengths are assessed.

H. *Lives of Jesus*

1. INTRODUCTION

There is no intention to offer even a sampling of the thousands of lives of Jesus that have been written since the publication of Reimarus' fragments. Those in the bibliography below are included because they have made significant contributions to the scholarly quest of the historical Jesus or because they are representative of various schools of thought. Some of the lives that were cited in the bibliography of Section 2 will not be repeated here (see H. S. Reimarus [51], D. F. Strauss [58], H. J. Holtzmann [61], E. Renan [62], etc.; for surveys see W. S. Kissinger [19], D. L. Pals [15], and A. Schweitzer [7] in Section 1).

2. BIBLIOGRAPHY

1195 F. E. D. Schleiermacher, *Das Leben Jesu* (K. A. Rütenik, ed.; Berlin: Georg Reimer, 1864); ET: *The Life of Jesus* (J. C. Verheyden, ed.; Philadelphia: Fortress, 1975). Most of the material comes from Schleiermacher's 1832 lecture notes; first major theologian to lecture publicly (beginning in 1819) on the scholarly problem of the life of Jesus; views Jesus as fully human.

1196 F. W. Farrar, *Life of Christ* (New York: Dutton, 1874); trans. into French, German, and many other languages. Perhaps the best of the Victorian lives of Jesus; believes that much of the gospel tradition derives from eye-witnesses.

1197 B. Weiss, *Das Leben Jesu* (2 vols.; Berlin: Hertz, 1882; Stuttgart and Berlin: Cotta, 1902); ET: *The Life of Christ* (3 vols.; Edinburgh: T & T Clark, 1883-84). Believes that Jesus' messianic consciousness gradually matured; only toward the end of his ministry did Jesus come to realize that he would have to die, for the death of the Baptist had opened up that possibility to his thinking.

1198 A. Edersheim, *The Life and Times of Jesus the Messiah* (2 vols.; New York: Randolph; London: Longmans, 1883; repr. Grand Rapids: Eerdmans, 1943). Rich with Jewish background; harmonizing approach.

1199 W. Beyschlag, *Das Leben Jesu* (2 vols.; Halle: Strein, 1885-86, 1912). Believes that Jesus was conscious of his unique authority and was aware that his teaching was sourced in divine revelation; emphasizes a distinction between the "teaching of Jesus" and the apostolic "teaching about Christ."

1200 F. Delitzsch, *Ein Tag in Capernaum* (Leipzig: Naumann, 1873); ET: *A Day in Capernaum* (New York: Funk and Wagnalls, 1887). Based on comparative background study; offers a portrait of what a typical day in Jesus' Galilean ministry would have been like.

1201 W. Rauschenbusch, *Das Leben Jesu* (Cleveland: Ritter, 1895). Classic life of Jesus from old liberal perspective.

1202   P. W. Schmidt, *Die Geschichte Jesu* (2 vols.; Tübingen: Mohr, 1899).
       Vol. 1 offers a life of Jesus; vol. 2 discusses various critical issues and
       offers hundreds of technical notes to go along with the paragraphs of vol. 1.

1203   O. Holtzmann, *Das Leben Jesu* (Tübingen and Leipzig: Mohr, 1901); ET:
       The Life of Jesus (London: A. & C. Black, 1904). Sees Jesus as a prophet
       and great teacher, but not as supernatural Son of God; utilizes Mark, por-
       tions of Matthew, Luke, and the Gospel of the Hebrews.

1204   W. Bousset, *Jesus* (Halle: Gebauer-Schwetschke, 1904; 3rd ed., Tübingen:
       Mohr, 1907); ET: *Jesus* (Crown Theological Library 14; New York: Put-
       nam; London: Williams and Norgate, 1906). Argues that Jesus had a vision
       at his baptism, heard the voice of God speak, sensed his calling to preach,
       and went to Jerusalem with a "dim impulse and consciousness that there his
       destiny would be accomplished" (p. 15).

1205   E. D. Burton, *The Life of Christ* (Chicago: University of Chicago, 1907).
       Surveys background issues; describes a life of Jesus.

1206   G. Papini, *Storia di Cristo* (Firenze: Vallechi, 1921, 1970); ET: *Life of
       Christ* (New York: Harcourt, Brace, 1923, 1927); FT: *Histoire du Christ*
       (Paris: Payot, 1923); GT: *Lebensgeschichte Jesu* (Munich: Allgemeine,
       1924). Lively account; reminiscent of Victorian lives of Jesus.

1207   A. Schlatter, *Die Geschichte des Christus* (Stuttgart: Calwer, 1921; 2nd
       ed., 1923; 3rd ed., 1977). First three chapters deal with background and
       topical issues; the fourth chapter summarizes Jesus' ministry (Jesus' self-
       understanding, the disciples, the events in Jerusalem); fifth chapter briefly
       discusses Easter faith; concludes that historical Jesus is the basis for New
       Testament theology.

1208   M. Goguel, *La Vie de Jésus* (Paris: Payot, 1925); ET: *The Life of Jesus*
       (New York: Macmillan, 1933). See 76.

1209   R. Bultmann, *Jesus* (Berlin: Deutsche Bibliothek, 1926); ET: *Jesus and the
       Word* (New York: Scribner's, 1934, 1958); FT: *Jésus. Mythologie et
       Démythologisation* (Paris: Seuil, 1968). See 77.

1210   S. J. Case, *Jesus: A New Biography* (Chicago: University Press, 1927).
       Describes Jesus as essentially a prophet of religious and social reform; see
       78.

1211   M. J. Lagrange, *L'évangile de Jésus-Christ* (Paris: Gabalda, 1928; ET: *The Gospel of Jesus Christ* (2 vols.; London: Burns, Oates, and Washbourne, 1938). Assessing the historical reliability of all four gospels, produces a biography that attempts to assemble and harmonize all of the gospel materials.

1212   J. Mackinnon, *The Historic Jesus* (London and New York: Longmans, Green, 1931). A liberal life of Jesus; see 80.

1213   F. C. Burkitt, *Jesus Christ: An Historical Outline* (London and Glasgow: Blackie and Son, 1932). A life of Jesus based on the Gospel of Mark; see 82.

1214   C. A. H. Guignebert, *Jésus* (Paris: Renaissance, 1933); ET: *Jesus* (London: Paul, Trench, Trübner, 1935; New York: University Books, 1956). An engaging biographical account that is replete with critical questions and comments; amazingly insightful redaction-critical comments.

1215   H. J. Cadbury, *The Peril of Modernizing Jesus* (New York: Macmillan, 1937). The second half of volume presents life of Jesus (pp. 86-193); discusses Jesus in the light of the "limitations" of his society and religion; see 83.

1216   P. Gardner-Smith, *The Christ of the Gospels* (Cambridge: Heffer and Sons, 1938). Believes that Jesus sensed his mission at his baptism and understood that his death would establish a new covenant.

1217   M. Dibelius, *Jesus* (Berlin: de Gruyter, 1939); ET: *Jesus* (Philadelphia: Westminster, 1949; repr. 1963). See 84.

1218   H. J. Cadbury, *Jesus: What Manner of Man?* (New York: Macmillan, 1947; London: SPCK, 1962). See 91.

1219   G. S. Duncan, *Jesus, Son of Man* (London: Nisbet, 1947). See 92.

1220   E. J. Goodspeed, *A Life of Jesus* (New York: Harper, 1950; Westport: Greenwood, 1979). Believes that Jesus journeyed to Jerusalem with hope of victory, yet anticipated rejection and death.

1221   A. M. Hunter, *The Work and Words of Jesus* (Philadelphia: Westminster, 1950; London: SCM, 1951; 2nd ed., 1973). Reviews the scholarly discussion, then sketches a life of Jesus, concluding that Jesus was aware of his mission as uniquely authorized of God and that his death would establish a new covenant.

1222 T. W. Manson, *The Beginning of the Gospel* (London and New York: Oxford University, 1950). A life of Jesus based on the Gospel of Mark, with interspersed paragraphs of comment.

1223 H. A. Guy, *The Life of Christ* (London: Macmillan, 1951). A life of Jesus that summarizes and discusses the synoptics, with the Johannine narrative portions appearing in an appendix.

1224 T. W. Manson, *The Servant-Messiah: A Study of the Public Ministry of Jesus* (Cambridge: University Press, 1953). See 104.

1225 V. Taylor, *The Life and Ministry of Jesus* (London: Macmillan, 1954; Nashville: Abingdon, 1955, 1968). Bases his life of Jesus on Mark, a source believed to be essentially reliable; concludes that Jesus knew that he was the Messiah, but not as the Jewish people understood it. Jesus journeyed to Jerusalem in anticipation of rejection and death. See 119.

1226 W. Grundmann, *Die Geschichte Jesu Christi* (Berlin: Evangelische Verlagsanstalt, 1956; 2nd ed., 1959). Believes that Jesus sensed an authority that placed him above Moses, but he presented himself as Israel's Messiah of humility. See 122.

1227 E. Stauffer, *Jesus. Gestalt und Geschichte* (Bern: Francke, 1957). Although very conservative, it is a sophisticated weaving together of materials from all four gospels. See 133.

1228 W. Barclay, *The Mind of Jesus* (London: SCM, 1960). One of the better popular books; to a great extent reflects the thinking of the old quest; concludes that Jesus understood himself as the suffering Son of Man.

1229 E. W. Bauman, *The Life and Teaching of Jesus* (Philadelphia: Westminster, 1960). Believes that the gospels are essentially reliable; notes the presence of "legend," behind which a kernel of history is usually to be found; concludes that Jesus knew that he faced death in Jerusalem.

1230 E. W. Saunders, *Jesus in the Gospels* (Englewood Cliffs: Prentice-Hall, 1967). A critical life of Jesus; argues that the "dominant consciousness of Jesus" was his belief that his destiny was to suffer as the Lord's Servant. See 333.

1231 D. Flusser, *Jesus in Selbstzeugnissen und Bilddokumenten* (Rowohlts Monographien 140; Hamburg: Rowohlt-Taschenbuch, 1968); ET: *Jesus* (New York: Herder and Herder, 1969); FT: *Jésus* (Paris: Seuil, 1970). Arguing that Jesus had been an Essene, attempts to write a biography of Jesus. See 341.

1232 E. F. Harrison, *A Short Life of Christ* (Grand Rapids: Eerdmans, 1968). A life of Jesus based on all four gospels, which are viewed as reliable sources.

1233 J. G. Kallas, *Jesus and the Power of Satan* (Philadelphia: Westminster, 1968). Argues that the historical Jesus was oriented "Satanward" in his thought and ministry, i.e., as Satan's opponent.

1234 C. H. Dodd, *The Founder of Christianity* (New York: Macmillan; London: Collier-Macmillan, 1970). See 368.

1235 D. Guthrie, *Jesus the Messiah* (Grand Rapids: Zondervan, 1972). A life of Jesus written from a very conservative perspective; see also Guthrie's *A Shorter Life of Christ* (Grand Rapids: Zondervan, 1978).

1236 M. Burrows, *Jesus in the First Three Gospels* (Nashville: Abingdon, 1977). Assumes that the synoptic gospels are essentially historical and that their chronology is historical.

1237 J. Marsh, *Jesus in His Lifetime* (London: Sidgwick & Jackson, 1981). Reviews the problem of the historical Jesus, Jesus' background in Jewish Palestine; reconstructs what may be known of Jesus' life; concludes that Jesus became aware of his sonship at his baptism and sensed his mission to Israel and to the Gentiles as well.

1238 G. Theissen, *Der Schatten des Galiläers. Historische Jesusforschung in erzählender Form* (Munich: Kaiser, 1986); ET: *The Shadow of the Galilean: The Quest of the Historical Jesus in Narrative Form* (Philadelphia: Fortress, 1987). A narrative portrait of Jesus and his time; emphasizes social and religious background.

I. *Non-Canonical Historical Sources*

1. INTRODUCTION

The primary sources for the life of Jesus are, of course, the gospels of the New Testament; however, there is some Jesus tradition elsewhere in the New Testament. Most of this tradition is found in Acts (1:4b-5, 7-8; 9:4b, 5b, 6b, 11-12, 15-16; 11:16b; 18:9b-10; 20:35b; 22:7b, 8b, 10b, 18, 21; 23:11b; 26:14b, 15b-18), in Paul's letters to the church at Corinth (1 Cor 7:10; 11:24b, 25b; 2 Cor 12:9a), and in the Apocalypse (1:8a, 11, 17b-3:22; 22:7a, 12-13, 16, 20). In post-New Testament Christian writings the Jesus tradition expands greatly, mostly in the form of apocryphal gospels. In non-Christian circles, however, Jesus tradition is limited, though what is extant is not without significance. Some scholars, most notably Joachim Jeremias, believe that some of the non-canonical tradition may very well derive from Jesus. Those sayings thought to be authentic are referred to as the *agrapha*, or "unwritten" sayings of Jesus (i.e., not written in the four canonical gospels). Jeremias (1240, pp. 49-87) has identified 21 potentially authentic *agrapha*, of which a few examples are cited below:

> On the same day he saw a man performing a work on the Sabbath. Then he said to him: "Man! If you know what you are doing, you are blessed. But if you do not know, you are cursed and a transgressor of the Law." (from Codex D, following Luke 6:5)

> "He who is near me is near the fire; he who is far from me is far from the Kingdom." (from Origen, *Homilies on Jeremiah* 20.3; also found in the Gospel of Thomas § 82)

> "No one can obtain the kingdom of heaven who has not passed through temptation." (from Tertullian, *On Baptism* 20)

> "You have rejected the Living One who is before your eyes, and talk idly of the dead." (from Augustine, *Against the Enemy of the Law and the Prophets* 2.4.14)

> "There will be dissensions and squabbles." (Justin, *Dialogue with Trypho* 35.3)

> "Ask for the great things, and God will add to you the little things." (first quoted by Clement of Alexandria, *Stromateis* 1.24.158)

Much of the remainder of the non-canonical tradition is, in contrast with the four Gospels, considerably more elaborate; some of it is fantastic, even grotesque.

Selections from (a) Christian Apocryphal sources, (b) Gnostic Sources, (c) Josephus, (d) the Slavonic Josephus, (e) other Jewish Sources, (f) Roman Historians and Writers, (g) Thallus and Mara bar Serapion, and (h) the Qur'an will be given in the subsections below, following the General Bibliography.

2. GENERAL BIBLIOGRAPHY

1239 W. Bauer, *Das Leben Jesu im Zeitalter der neutestamentlichen Apokryphen* (Tübingen: Mohr [Siebeck], 1909). Analyzes contents of apocryphal writings; topics concern Jesus' parents, John the Baptist, Jesus' ministry, Last Supper, crucifixion, resurrection, and teachings.

1240 J. Jeremias, *Unbekannte Jesusworte* (Gütersloh: Mohn, 1948; 4th ed., 1965); ET: *Unknown Sayings of Jesus* (London: SPCK, 1958).

1241 R. Dunkerley, *Beyond the Gospels* (Baltimore: Penguin, 1957). Convenient collection of most of the relevant items.

1242 F. F. Bruce, *Jesus and Christian Origins outside of the New Testament* (London: Hodder and Stoughton; Grand Rapids: Eerdmans, 1974). Surveys traditions pertaining to Jesus and Christian origins in pagan writers, Josephus, the rabbis, apocryphal gospels, the Qur'an and Islamic tradition, and archaeology.

1243 J. A. Pagola Elorza, *¿Que podemos saber del Jésus histórico?* (Curso de Christología 2; Madrid: Fundación Santa Maria, 1982). Surveys the extrabiblical sources of Jesus and then deals with the historical Jesus problem.

1244 J. H. Charlesworth, "Research on the Historical Jesus Today: Jesus and the Pseudepigrapha, the Dead Sea Scrolls, the Nag Hammadi Codices, Josephus, and Archaeology," *PrincSB* 6 (1985) 98-115. Provides a much fuller discussion in 601.

1245 R. W. Funk, *New Gospel Parallels* (2 vols.; Philadelphia: Fortress, 1985). Extremely valuable tool providing a synopsis not only of the four New Testament gospels, but of several other ancient "gospels" as well.

1246 D. Wenham, ed., *The Jesus Tradition Outside the Gospels* (Gospel Perspectives 5; Sheffield: JSOT, 1985). Several essays examine Jesus tradition in Paul, James, 1 Peter, Gospel of Thomas, Apostolic Fathers, apocryphal gospels, early Jewish and classical authors; bibliography.

3. SPECIFIC SOURCES AND BIBLIOGRAPHY

(a) Christian Apocryphal Sources

The New Testament Apocrypha is made up of more than one hundred documents (see J. H. Charlesworth [1253]); many of these documents are "gospels," "acts," or "apocalypses." There are several fragmentary gospels (mostly deriving from the Oxyrhynchus Papyri 1, 654, 655, 840, 1224, and Papyrus Egerton 2), various Jewish Christian gospels, including the Gospel of the Nazarenes, the Gospel of the Ebionites, and the Gospel of the Hebrews, the infancy gospels, and dozens of other gospels named after various apostolic worthies (see M. R. James [1247], E. Hennecke [1248], and R. W. Funk [1245]). Excerpts from two of the more significant gospels are cited below.

(1) The Gospel of Peter (see 1248, pp. 185-86) provides us with several large fragments narrating the death, burial, and resurrection of Jesus:

> Now in the night in which the Lord's day dawned, when the soldiers, two by two in every watch, were keeping guard, there rang out a loud voice in heaven, and they saw the heavens opened and two men come down from there in a great brightness and draw near to the sepulchre. That stone which had been laid against the entrance to the sepulchre started of itself to roll and gave way to the side, and the sepulchre was opened, and both the young men entered in. When now those soldiers saw this, they awakened the centurion and the elders—for they also were there to assist the watch. And whilst they were relating what they had seen, they saw again three men come out from the sepulchre, and two of them sustaining the other, and a cross following them, and the heads of the two reaching to heaven, but that of him who was led by them by the hand overpassing the heavens. And they heard a voice out of the heavens crying, "Thou hast preached to them that sleep," and from the cross there was heard the answer, "Yea." (9:35-10:42)

(2) The Secret Gospel of Mark (from a letter of Clement of Alexandria to Theodore, see 1249, pp. 16-17) allegedly provides additional information about the young man clothed with the linen cloth (cf. Mark 14:51-52), the very one who

may have met the women at the tomb (cf. Mark 16:5). The relevant part of the fragment reads as follows:

> And they came into Bethany, and a certain woman, whose brother had died, was there. And, coming, she prostrated herself before Jesus and says to him, "Son of David, have mercy on me." But the disciples rebuked her. And Jesus, being angered, went off with her into the garden where the tomb was, and straightway a great cry was heard from the tomb. And going near Jesus rolled away the stone from the door of the tomb. And straightway, going in where the youth was, he stretched forth his hand and raised him, seizing his hand. But the youth, looking upon him, loved him and began to beseech him that he might be with him. And going out of the tomb they came into the house of the youth, for he was rich. And after six days Jesus told him what to do and in the evening the youth comes to him, wearing a linen cloth over [his] naked [body]. And he remained with him that night, for Jesus taught him the mystery of the kingdom of God. And thence, arising, he returned to the other side of the Jordan.

1247 M. R. James, *The Apocryphal New Testament* (Oxford: Clarendon, 1924). Provides translations of much of the New Testament Apocrypha.

1248 E. Hennecke and W. Schneemelcher, *Neutestamentliche Apokryphen in deutscher Übersetzung* (3 vols.; Tübingen: Mohr [Siebeck], 1959-64); ET: *New Testament Apocrypha* (2 vols.; Philadelphia: Westminster, 1974), esp. vol. 1: "Gospels and Related Writings." Indispensable tool for the study of the New Testament Apocrypha; texts and bibliography. On the Gospel of Peter see pp. 183-87. On pp. 88-89 Jeremias cites eleven *agrapha* that he thinks have the strongest claim to authenticity.

1249 M. Smith, *The Secret Gospel: The Discovery and Interpretation of the Secret Gospel according to Mark* (New York: Harper & Row, 1973). For a critical edition of the Secret Gospel see M. Smith, *Clement of Alexandria and a Secret Gospel of Mark* (Cambridge: Harvard University, 1973).

1250 W. L. Lane, "A Critique of Purportedly Authentic Agrapha," *JETS* 18 (1975) 29-35. Discusses criteria for determining the authenticity of the *agrapha*; concludes that when examined in light of these criteria, the best of the *agrapha* look doubtful.

1251 R. Cameron, *The Other Gospels: Non-Canonical Gospel Texts* (Philadelphia: Westminster, 1982). Texts of seventeen apocryphal gospels; annotated bibliography for each.

1252 J. D. Crossan, *Four Other Gospels: Shadows on the Contours of Canon* (New York: Seabury, 1985). A series of exegetical studies utilizing the Gospel of Thomas, Papyrus Egerton 2, the Secret Gospel of Mark, and the Gospel of Peter.

1253 J. H. Charlesworth, *The New Testament Apocrypha and Pseudepigrapha: A Guide to Publications, with Excurses on Apocalypses* (with J. R. Mueller; ATLA 17; Metuchen and London: American Theological Library Association, 1987). A massive bibliography on the New Testament Apocrypha; lists over 100 apocryphal texts.

(b) Gnostic Sources

The best known of the Coptic Gnostic sources is the Gospel of Thomas (NHL II,*2*). The Coptic version appears to be a translation of a Greek collection of sayings, some fragments of which are extant (Oxyrhynchus Papyri 1, 654, and 655) dating back to the second century. In the Nag Hammadi library Thomas appears as the second tractate in codex 2 (pages 32-51). Most scholars divide it into 114 sayings. The tractate begins with the prologue: "These are the secret sayings which the living Jesus spoke and which Didymos Judas Thomas wrote down." Much of the material in Thomas parallels the New Testament gospels (and other New Testament writings). Some of it is clearly later Gnostic tradition, while some of it may represent genuine dominical tradition (such as logion 82, cited above, and logia 64 and 65). In most of the tractates in which Jesus appears he is presented as the mysterious revealer of heavenly knowledge and secrets. We see this in the Book of Thomas the Contender (NHL II,*7*), the Sophia of Jesus Christ (NHL III,*4*), the Apocalypse of Paul (NHL V,*2*), the First Apocalypse of James (NHL V,*3*), the Acts of Peter and the Twelve Apostles (NHL VI,*1*), the Apocalypse of Peter (NHL VII,*3*), the Letter of Peter to Philip (NHL VIII,*2*), the Gospel of Mary (BG 8502,*1*), and in the two tractates which are cited below. A typical example is seen in the Apocryphon of James (NHL I,*2*; see 1256, pp. 30-31):

> [...] the twelve disciples [were] all sitting together and recalling what the Savior had said to each one of them, whether in secret or openly, and [putting it in] in books—[But I] was writing that which was in [my book]—lo, the Savior appeared, [after] departing from [us while we] gazed after him. And after five hundred and fifty days since he had risen from the dead, we said to him, "Have you departed and removed yourself from us?"

> But Jesus said, "No, but I shall go to the place from whence I came. If you wish to come with me, come!"

They all answered and said, "If you bid us, we come."

He said, "Verily I say unto you, no one will enter the kingdom of heaven at my bidding, but (only) because you yourselves are full. Leave James and Peter to me that I may fill them." And having called these two, he drew them aside and bade the rest occupy themselves with that which they were about. (page 2, lines 7-39)

This account is quite similar to one found in the Apocryphon of John, a tractate that must have been quite popular in early Gnostic circles, judging by its appearance three times in the Nag Hammadi library (NHL II,*1*; III,*1*; IV,*1*). John, son of Zebedee and brother of James, was in the Temple one day where he was asked by a Pharisee where his master had gone. "John" goes on to narrate (NHL II,*1*, supplemented from the other copies; see 1256, p. 105):

[When] I, [John], heard these things [I turned] away from the temple [to a desert place]. And I grieved [greatly in my heart saying], "How [then was] the savior [appointed], and why was he sent [in to the world] by [his Father..].?"

Straightway, [while I was contemplating these things,] behold, the [heavens opened and] the whole creation [which is] below heaven shone, and [the world] was shaken. [I was afraid, and behold I] saw in the light [a youth who stood] by me. While I looked [at him he became] like an old man. And he [changed his] likeness (again), becoming like a servant....

He said to me, "John, John, why do you doubt, or why [are you] afraid? You are not unfamiliar with this image, are you?—that is, do not be timid!—I am the one who [is with you (pl.)] always. I [am the Father], I am the Mother, I am the Son...." (page 1, line 17—page 2, line 14)

1254   A. Guillaumont, et al., *The Gospel according to Thomas* (Leiden: Brill; New York: Harper, 1959). Provides Coptic text and ET of Thomas, and index of biblical parallels.

1255   J. E. Ménard, *L'Évangile selon Thomas* (NHS 5; Leiden: Brill, 1975). Excellent critical study of the Gospel of Thomas.

1256   J. M. Robinson, ed., *The Nag Hammadi Library* (Leiden: Brill; San Francisco: Harper & Row, 1977; 3rd ed., 1988). An ET of the entire (Coptic Gnostic) Nag Hammadi find, plus two related tractates (BG 8502, *1* and *4*).

1257   E. M. Yamauchi, *Pre-Christian Gnosticism: A Survey of the Proposed Evidences* (Grand Rapids: Eerdmans, 1973; 2nd ed., Grand Rapids: Baker, 1983). A scholarly assessement of the relationship of early Gnosticism and

Christianity; criticizes the contention that New Testament christology is substantially dependent upon Gnostic mythology or that Gnosticism antedates Christianity.

1258   K. Rudolf, *Die Gnosis: Wesen und Geschichte einer spätantiker Religion* (Göttingen: Vandenhoeck & Ruprecht, 1977; 2nd ed., 1980); ET: *Gnosis: The Nature and History of Gnosticism* (San Francisco: Harper & Row, 1983). A scholarly survey of the Gnostic literature (Coptic and Mandaean); believes (*pace* Yamauchi) that the New Testament understanding of Jesus has been significantly influenced by early Gnosticism.

(c) Josephus

In two places (according to the Greek MSS. of his works) the first-century Jewish historian (Flavius) Josephus mentions Jesus (on John the Baptist, see *Jewish Antiquities* 18.5.2 § 116-119). The passages are as follows (based on L. H. Feldman, *Josephus* [LCL 9; London: Heinemann, 1969] 49-51, 495-99):

And so he [Ananus the High Priest] convened the judges of the Sanhedrin and brought before them a man called James, the brother of Jesus who was called the Christ, and certain others. He accused them of having transgressed the law and delivered them up to be stoned. (*Jewish Antiquities* 20.9.1 § 200-203)

About this time there lived Jesus, a wise man, if indeed one ought to call him a man. For he was one who wrought surprising feats and was a teacher of such people as accept the truth gladly. He won over many Jews and many of the Greeks. He was the Messiah. When Pilate, upon hearing him accused by men of the highest standing among us, had condemned him to be crucified, those who had in the first place come to love him did not give up their affection for him. On the third day he appeared to them restored to life, for the prophets of God had prophesied these and countless other marvellous things about him. And the tribe of Christians, so called after him, has still to this day not disappeared. (*Jewish Antiquities* 18.3.3 § 63-64)

Although few dispute the authenticity of the first passage, most scholars suspect that the second passage, if not entirely an interpolation, has been edited by a later Christian. For if Josephus had truly believed the things found in this passage, then it is indeed strange that he mentions Jesus nowhere else. J. Klausner (*Jesus of Nazareth* [New York: Macmillan, 1925] 55-56) has offered this hypothetical reconstruction (minus parenthetical comments and Greek text):

Now, there was about this time Jesus, a wise man; for he was a doer of wonderful works, a teacher of such men as receive the truth with pleasure. He drew over to him both many of the Jews and many of the Gentiles. And when Pilate, at the suggestion of the principal men among us, had condemned him to the cross, those that loved him at the first ceased not so [to do]; and the race of Christians, so named from him, are not extinct even now.

For a different emendation see:

1259 R. Eisler, *The Messiah Jesus and John the Baptist* (London: Methuen; New York: Dial, 1931) 62.

The question of the authenticity of this passage (known as the *Testimonium Flavium* [or *Flavianum*]), either in whole or in part, has been debated for centuries. Defenders of the authenticity of the passage include the following:

1260 F. C. Burkitt, "Josephus and Christ," *TTij* 47 (1913) 135-44.

1261 A. Harnack, "Der jüdische Geschichtschreiber Josephus und Jesus Christus," *Internationale Monatsschrift für Wissenschaft und Technik* 7 (1913) cols. 1037-68. See also Harnack, *Geschichte der altchristlichen Literatur bis Eusebius* (part 1; Leipzig: Hinrichs, 1893) 858-60, (part 2; Leipzig: Hinrichs, 1897) 581; repr. 1958.

1262 F. Dornseiff, "Lukas der Schriftsteller, mit einem Anhang: Josephus und Tacitus," *ZNW* 35 (1936) 145-48.

1263 F. Dornseiff, "Zum Testimonium Flavium," *ZNW* 46 (1955) 245-50.

1264 J. Salvador, "É Autêntico o 'Testimonium Flavianum'?," *RCB* 2 (1978) 137-51.

Those who view the passage as a whole as an inauthentic interpolation include the following:

1265 S. Zeitlin, "The Christ Passage in Josephus," *JQR* 18 (1927-28) 231-55; repr. in Zeitlin, *Solomon Zeitlin's Studies in the Early History of Judaism* (vol. 1; New York: Ktav, 1973) 407-31. For a general study see Zeitlin, *Josephus on Jesus* (Philadelphia: Dropsie College, 1931), and see his summary in *JQR* 21 (1930-31) 377-417.

Those who view the passage as original, but redacted, include:

1266 H. St. J. Thackeray, *Josephus, the Man and the Historian* (New York: Jewish Institute of Religion, 1929) 136-49;

1267 F. Scheidweiler, "Das Testimonium Flavianum," *ZNW* 45 (1954) 230-43.

1268 A. Pelletier, "L'originalité du témoignac de Flavius Joséphe sur Jésus," *RSR* 52 (1964) 177-203.

1269 S. G. F. Brandon, "The Testimonium Flavium," *History Today* 19 (1969) 438.

1270 Z. Baras, "Testimonium Flavium: The State of Recent Scholarship," in M. Baras and Z. Baras, eds., *Society and Religion in the Second Temple Period* (Jerusalem: Masada, 1977) 303-13, 378-85.

1271 A.-M. Dubarle, "Le témoignage de Joséphe sur Jésus d'après des publications récentes," *RB* 84 (1977) 38-58; abbreviated version in *BTS* 154 (1973) 22-23.

1272 P. Bilde, "Josefus' beretning om Jesus," *DTT* 44 (1981) 99-135.

1273 L. H. Feldman, "The *Testimonium Flavium*: The State of the Question," in R. F. Berkey and S. A. Edwards, eds., *Christological Perspectives* (H. K. McArthur Festschrift; New York: Pilgrim, 1982) 179-99, 288-93.

Other studies:

1274 H. Montefiore, *Josephus and the New Testament* (Contemporary Studies in Theology 6; London: Mowbray, 1962).

1275 P. Winter, "Bibliography to Josephus, Antiquitates Judaicae, XVIII, 63, 64," *JHS* 2 (1969-70) 292-96.

1276 D. Hill, "Jesus and Josephus' 'Messianic Prophets'," in E. Best, ed., *Text and Interpretation* (M. Black Festschrift; Cambridge: University Press, 1979) 143-54;

1277 J. N. Birdsall, "The Continuing Enigma of Josephus' Testimony about Jesus," *BJRL* 67 (1985) 609-22.

L. H. Feldman's observation (1273) that the *Testimonium Flavium* was apparently unknown to most of the early fathers argues strongly for the inauthenticity of the present form of the passage, for had this form existed at the end of the first century, it is quite likely that Christian apologists would have cited it often. Although Eusebius knows of this passage (*Ecclesiastical History* 1.11.7-8; *Demonstration of the Gospel* 3.5), according to Origen (*Commentary on Matthew* 10.50.17; *Against Celsus* 1.47) Josephus did not regard Jesus as the Messiah. The absence in the Arabic version, moreover, of the very lines suspected of being interpolations adds more support to the contention that the passage has been tampered with. The Arabic version of the *Testimonium Flavium* (cf. Agapius, *Book of the Title*) reads as follows (see 1278, p. 16):

> Similarly Josephus the Hebrew. For he says in the treatises that he has written on the governance [?] of the Jews: "At this time there was a wise man who was called Jesus. And his conduct was good, and [he] was known to be virtuous. And many people from among the Jews and the other nations became his disciples. Pilate condemned him to be crucified and to die. And those who had become his disciples did not abandon his discipleship. They reported that he had appeared to them three days after his crucifixion and that he was alive; accordingly he was perhaps the Messiah concerning whom the prophets have recounted wonders."

1278 S. Pines, *An Arabic Version of the Testimonium Flavianum and its Implications* (Jerusalem: Israel Academy of Sciences and Humanities, 1971).

(d) The Slavonic Josephus

In the Slavonic, or Old Russian, version of Josephus' *Jewish War* several passages are found that make reference to the Baptist, Jesus, and early Christians (passages which are without parallel in the Greek MSS. of Josephus). Scholarly opinion is divided over the question of their authenticity. A few of the most relevant passages include the following (see 1281, pp. 106-10):

(1) On the ministry, trial, and crucifixion of Jesus (follows *Jewish War* 2.9.3, between § 174 and 175):

> At that time also a man came forward,—if even it is fitting to call him a man [simply]. His nature as well as his form were a man's; but his showing forth was more than [that] of a man. His works, that is to say, were godly, and he wrought wonder-deeds amazing and full of power. Therefore it is not possible for me to call him a man [simply]. But again, looking at the existence he shared with all, I would also not call him an angel.

And all that he wrought through some kind of invisible power, he wrought by word and command.

Some said of him, that our first Lawgiver has risen from the dead and shows forth many cures and arts. But others supposed [less definitely] that he is sent by God.

Now he opposed himself in much to the Law and did not observe the Sabbath according to ancestral custom. Yet, on the other hand, he did nothing reprehensible nor any crime; but by word solely he effected everything.

And many from the folk followed him and received his teachings. And many souls became wavering, supposing that thereby the Jewish tribes would set themselves free from the Roman hands.

Now it was his custom often to stop on the Mount of Olives facing the city. And there also he avouched his cures to the people. And there gathered themselves to him of servants a hundred and fifty, but of the folk a multitude.

But when they saw his power, that he accomplished everything that he would by word, they urged him that he should enter the city and cut down the Roman soldiers and Pilate and rule over us. But that one scorned it.

And thereafter, when knowledge of it came to the Jewish leaders, they gathered together with the High-priest and spake: "We are powerless and weak to withstand the Romans. But as withal the bow is bent, we will go and tell Pilate what we have heard, and we will be without distress, lest if he hear it from others, we be robbed of our substance and ourselves be put to the sword and our children ruined." And they went and told it to Pilate.

And he sent and had many of the people cut down. And he had that wonder-doer brought up. And when he had instituted a trial concerning him, he perceived that he is a doer of good, but not an evil-doer, nor a revolutionary, nor one who aimed at power, and set him free. He had, you should know, healed his dying wife.

And he went to his accustomed place and wrought his accustomed works. And as again more folk gathered themselves together round him, then did he win glory though his works more than all.

The teachers of the Law were [therefore] envenomed with envy and gave thirty talents to Pilate, in order that he should put him to death. And he, after he had taken [the money], gave them consent that they should themselves carry out their purpose.

And they took him and crucified him according to the ancestral law.

(2) On the crucifixion and resurrection of Jesus (follows *Jewish War* 5.5.4 §
214):

> [The Temple curtain] had, you should know, been suddenly rent from the top to
> the ground, when they delivered over to death through bribery the doer of
> good, the man—yea, him who through his doing was no man. And many other
> signs they tell which came to pass at that time. And it was said that after he
> was put to death, yea after burial in the grave, he was not found. Some then as-
> sert that he is risen; but others, that he has been stolen by friends. I, however,
> do not know which speak more correctly.... But others said that it was not
> possible to steal him, because they had put guards all round his grave—thirty
> Romans, but a thousand Jews.

(3) An inscription concerning Jesus inserted in *Jewish War* 5.5.2 § 195):

> And over these tablets [at one of the gates leading into the Temple] with
> inscriptions hung a fourth tablet with inscription in these [Greek, Roman, and
> Jewish] characters, to the effect: Jesus has not reigned as king; he has been
> crucified by the Jews because he proclaimed the destruction of the city and the
> laying waste of the Temple.

(4) In reference to a prophecy of a coming world ruler (inserted at *Jewish War*
6.5.4, replacing § 313):

> Some indeed by this understood Herod, but others the crucified wonder-doer
> Jesus, others say again Vespasian.

1279 A. J. Berendts, *Die Zeugnisse vom Christentum im slavischen "De bello
judaico" des Josephus* (TU 29 [=n.s. 14]; Leipzig: Hinrichs, 1906). A critical discussion of the relevant passages in Slavonic Josephus; argues that
they are authentic.

1280 J. Frey, *Der slavische Josephusbericht über die urchristliche Geschichte
nebst seinen Parallelen* (Dorpat: Mattiesen, 1908). Argues that the peculiar
passages in Slavonic Josephus are early interpolations.

1281 G. R. S. Mead, *The Gnostic John the Baptizer* (London: Watkins, 1924).
See pp. 97-119 for discussion and ET of the relevant passages peculiar to
the Slavonic MSS.

1282 H. St. J. Thackeray, *Josephus* (LCL 3; London: Heinemann, 1928) 635-58.
Provides an ET of relevant passages from Slavonic Josephus.

1283   J. M. Creed, "The Slavonic Version of Josephus' History of the Jewish
       War," *HTR* 25 (1932) 277-319. Studies the Slavonic "additions" and
       suspects that they are spurious.

1284   J. W. Jack, *The Historic Christ* (London: CLarke, 1933). Views the
       Slavonic additions as very late and completely worthless.

1285   R. Dunkerley, "The Riddles of Josephus," *HibJ* 53 (1954-55) 127-34. Dis-
       cusses the authenticity of the Testimonium Flavium and statements about
       Jesus in Slavonic Josephus; suspects that the Slavonic "additions" may de-
       rive from Josephus, but they are not necessarily historically well informed.

(e) Other Jewish Sources

There are relatively few certain references to Jesus in the Talmud. Most of the
references are of little historical value, for they usually represent nothing more
than vague acquaintance with the gospels or later polemic with Christians. A few
of the references, however, may represent fairly early, independent, and possibly
accurate tradition. The following passages, some of which are tannaitic (i.e., from
50 BCE to 200 CE), are accepted by most as referring to Jesus (see 1289,1292
[*t=Tosefta*; *b=Babylonian Talmud*; *Rab=Midrash Rabbah*; *Yal=Yalqut*]):

(1) On the parents and birth of Jesus:

> She who was the descendant of princes and governors [Mary], played the har-
> lot with carpenters [Joseph]. (*b. Sanh.* 106a, apparently an allusion to the
> virginal birth of Jesus)

> [The Angel of Death] said to his messenger, "Go, bring me Miriam [Mary] the
> Women's hairdresser!" He went and brought him Miriam. (*b. Hag.* 4b;
> "hairdresser" is *megaddela*, which probably refers to Mary Magdalene, who
> was sometimes confused with Mary the mother of Jesus)

(2) On the life of Jesus:

> When king Jannai [104-78 BCE] slew our rabbis, R. Joshua and Jesus fled to
> Alexandria of Egypt. On the resumption of peace...he arose, went, and found
> himself in a certain inn, where great honor was shown him. "How beautiful is
> this inkeeper!" Thereupon Jesus observed, "Rabbi, her eyes are narrow."
> "Wretch," he rebuked him, "do you engage yourself thus?" He sounded four
> hundred trumpets and excommunicated him. He [Jesus] came before him many

times pleading, "Receive me!" But he would pay no heed to him. One day he [R. Joshua] was reciting the Shema', when Jesus came before him. He intended to receive him and made a sign to him. He [Jesus] thinking that it was to repel him, went, put up a brick, and worshipped it. "Repent," said he [R. Joshua] to him. He replied, "I have thus learned from you: 'He who sins and causes others to sin is not afforded the means of repentance.'" (*b. Sanh.* 107b; cf. *b. Sota* 47a)

...not like Elisha who thrust Gehazi away with both his hands, and not like Joshua ben Perahiah who thrust away Jesus the Nazarene with both his hands. (*b. Sanh.* 107b; *b. Sota* 47a)

(3) On the ministry of Jesus:

Jesus had five disciples: Matthai, Nakai, Nezer, Buni, and Todah. (*b. Sanh.* 107b)

Jesus practiced magic and led Israel astray. (*b. Sanh.* 43a; see also *t. Shab.* 11:15; *b. Shab.* 104b)

And a master has said, "Jesus the Nazarene practiced magic and led Israel astray." (*b. Sanh.* 107b; cf. *b. Sota* 47a)

(4) On the teaching of Jesus:

One of the disciples of Jesus...told me, "Thus did Jesus the Nazarene teach me: 'For of the hire of a harlot has she gathered them, and to the hire of a harlot shall they return'." (*b. Abod. Zar.* 16b-17a; *t. Hul.* 2:24; cf. *Qoh Rab.* 1:8 § 3; *Yal. Shimeoni* on Micah 1 and Prov 5:8)

He [a judge] said to them, "I looked at the end of the book, in which it is written, 'I am not come to take away the Law of Moses and I am not come to add to the Law of Moses' [cf. Matt 5:17], and it is written, 'where there is a son, a daughter does not inherit.'" She said to him, "Let your light shine forth as a lamp" [cf. Matt 5:16]. R. Gamaliel said to her, "The ass came and kicked the lamp over." (*b. Shab.* 116b)

(5) On the crucifixion of Jesus:

On the eve of Passover they hanged Jesus the Nazarene. And a herald went out, in front of him, for forty days saying: "He is going to be stoned, because he practiced sorcery and enticed and led Israel astray. Anyone who knows anything in his favor, let him come and plead in his behalf." But, not having found anything in his favor, they hanged him on the eve of Passover. (*b. Sanh.* 43a)

(6) On the resurrection of Jesus:

> Woe to him who makes himself alive by the name of God. (*b. Sanh.* 106a, possibly an allusion to Jesus' resurrection)

> He then went and raised Jesus by incantation. (*b. Git.* 57a, MS. M)

(7) On healing in the name of Jesus:

> It once happened that ben Dama, the son R. Ishmael's sister, was bitten by a serpent; and Jacob [James?], a native of Kefar Sekaniah, came to him in the name of Jesus ben Pantera. But R. Ishmael did not permit him. (*t. Hul.* 2:22)

1286 G. H. Dalman, *Was sagt der Thalmud über Jesum?* (SIJB 11; Berlin: Reuther, 1891). Some of this material appears in Dalman, *Jesus Christ in the Talmud, Midrash, Zohar, and the Liturgy of the Synagogue* (with H. Laible; Cambridge: Deighton, Bell, 1893; repr. New York: Arno, 1973).

1287 H. Laible, *Jesus Christus im Thalmud* (SIJB 10; Leipzig: 1891; 2nd ed., 1900); ET: G. H. Dalman, *Jesus Christ in the Talmud, Midrash, Zohar, and the Liturgy of the Synagogue* (with H. Laible; Cambridge: Deighton, Bell, 1893; repr. New York: Arno, 1973). In the ET Laible's work has been translated and suppplemented by new work by Dalman. Although dated, an excellent survey; Talmudic passages are cited in the original language and are translated.

1288 G. H. Dalman, *Die Worte Jesu, mit Berücksichtigung des nachkanonischen jüdischen Schriftums und der aramäischen Sprache* (vol. 1; Leipzig: Hinrichs, 1898; 2nd ed., 1930); ET: Dalman, *The Words of Jesus: Considered in the Light of Post-Biblical Jewish Writings and the Aramaic language* (Edinburgh: T & T Clark, 1902).

1289 R. T. Herford, *Christianity in Talmud and Midrash* (London: Williams and Norgate, 1903; repr. New York: Ktav, 1975). A classic study; most of the examples cited above come from this work.

1290 H. L. Strack, *Jesus, die Häretiker und die Christen nach den ältesten jüdischen Angaben* (SIJB 37; Leipzig: Hinrich, 1910).

1291 H. Danby, *The Mishnah* (London: Oxford University, 1933).

1292 I. Epstein, ed., *The Babylonian Talmud* (34 vols.; London: Soncino, 1935-48).

1293 M. Goldstein, *Jesus in the Jewish Tradition* (New York: Macmillan, 1950).

1294 W. Ziffer, "Two Epithets for Jesus of Nazareth in Talmud and Midrash," *JBL* 85 (1966) 356-59. Suggests that the names Ben Stada and Ben Pandira, epithets sometimes applied to Jesus in the Talmud and midrashim, are really to be understood as Ben Satana and Ben Pandora.

1295 J. Neusner, *The Tosefta* (6 vols.; New York: Ktav, 1975-86).

1296 J. Maier, *Jesus von Nazareth in der talmudischen Überlieferung* (Erträge der Forschung 82; Darmstadt: Wissenschaftliche Buchgesellschaft, 1978).

(f) Roman Historians and Writers

There are only a few references to Jesus and early Christianity in the Roman historians and writers. They are as follows (see 1298, pp. 163-78):

(1) Tacitus (*Annals* 15.44, 110-120 CE):

> This name [i.e., "Christian"] originates from "Christus" who was sentenced to death by the procurator, Pontius Pilate, during the reign of Tiberius. This detestable superstitution, which had been suppressed for a while, spread anew not only in Judea where the evil had started, but also in Rome, where everything that is horrid and wicked in the world gathers and finds numerous followers.

(2) Seutonius (*Life of Emperor Claudius* 25.4, 50 CE):

> Claudius expelled the Jews from Rome who, instigated by Chrestus [sic], never ceased to cause unrest.

There are two basic interpretations of this passage. The "Jews" may really refer to Christians, who in the first century were viewed as no more than a sect within Judaism itself; or the designation may refer to Jews who quarreled with Christians (along the lines of what we see in Acts). "Chrestus" is probably an error arising from confusing the word *chrestus* with the title *Christus*, a title with which a Roman would not be familiar.

(3) Pliny the Younger (*Epistles* 10.96 [to Emperor Trajan], 110 CE):

> They [the Christians] assured me that the sum total of their guilt or their error consisted in the fact that they regularly assembled on a certain day before daybreak. They recited a hymn antiphonally to Christ as (their) God and bound themselves with an oath not to commit any crime, but to abstain from theft, robbery, adultery, breach of faith, and embezzlement of property entrusted to them. After this it was their custom to separate, and then to come together again to partake of a meal, but an ordinary and innocent one.

(4) Celsus, according to Origen, claimed that Jesus performed his miracles by the power of magic. He is quoted as having said (see 1297, pp. 10, 37, 65):

> ...it was by magic that he was able to do the miracles which he appeared to have done.... (*Against Celsus* 1.6)

> He was brought up in secret and hired himself out as a workman in Egypt, and after having tried his hand at certain magical powers he returned from there, and on account of those powers gave himself the title of God. (*Against Celsus* 1.38)

> These were the actions of one hated by God and of a wicked sorcerer. (*Against Celsus* 1.71; see also 1.68)

1297   H. Chadwick, *Origen: Contra Celsum* (Cambridge: University Press, 1953; repr. 1965).

1298   H. Conzelmann, *Geschichte des Urchristentums* (Göttingen: Vandenhoeck & Ruprecht, 1969); ET: *History of Primitive Christianity* (Nashville: Abingdon, 1973).

(g) Thallus and Mara bar Serapion

(1) Thallus the Samaritan Chronicler (*History* 3, 50 CE):

In reference to the darkness at the time of Jesus' crucifixion (see Mark 15:33), Julius Africanus (d. after 240 CE) reports (taken from fragment 18 of Africanus' 5 volume *Chronography*, preserved in Georgius Syncellus, *Chronology*; see 1299, vol. 6, p. 136):

> This darkness Thallus, in the third book of his *History*, calls, as appears to me without reason, an eclipse of the sun.

1299   A. Roberts and J. Donaldson, eds., *The Ante-Nicene Fathers* (10 vols.; Grand Rapids: Eerdmans, 1951).

(2) Mara bar Serapion (letter to his son, *ca.* 73 CE; see 1300, p. 73):

> For what advantage did...the Jews [gain] by the death of their wise king, because from that same time their kingdom was taken away?

1300   W. Cureton, *Spicilegium Syriacum* (London: Rivington, 1855). See also 1241, p. 27.

(h) The Qur'an

"Jesus son of Mary" (*Isa ibn Maryam*) is mentioned several times in the Qur'an (*ca.* 620). For a convenient assessment see Bruce (1242), pp. 167-77. The Arabic tradition appears to be dependent upon the New Testament Gospels, especially Luke (compare 3:37-41 with Luke 1:5-25, 57-79). Consider the following allusions (see 1302):

(1) On the birth and naming of Mary:

> When a woman of Imran said: "My Lord! Surely I vow to Thee what is in my womb, to be devoted (to Thy service). Accept therefore from me. Surely Thou art the Hearing, the Knowing." So when she brought forth, she said: "My Lord! Surely I have brought forth a female"—and Allah knew best what she brought forth—"and the male is not like the female, and I have named it Mary, and I commend her and her offspring into Thy protection from the accursed Satan." (3:35-36)

(2) On the virginal conception and birth of Jesus:

> And when the angels said: "O Mary! Surely Allah has chosen you and purified you and chosen you above the women of the world...." When the angels said: "O Mary, surely Allah gives you good news with a word from Him whose name

is the Messiah, Jesus son of Mary, worthy of regard in this world and the hereafter and of those who are made near (to Allah). And he shall speak to the people when in the cradle and when of old age, and (he shall be) one of the good ones." She said: "My Lord! When shall there be a son (born) to me, and man has not touched me?" He said: "Even so, Allah creates what He pleases; when He has decreed a matter, He only said to it, 'Be,' and it is. And He will teach him the Book and the wisdom and the Tavrat and the Injeel, and (make him) an apostle to the children of Israel, saying, 'I have come to you with a sign from your Lord, that I determine for you out of dust like the form of a bird, then I breathe into it and it become a bird with Allah's permission and I heal the blind and the leprous, and bring the dead to life with Allah's permission and I inform you of what you should eat and what you should store in your houses.'" (3:42, 45-49; see also 3:59; compare Luke 1:28-38, 42)

And mention Mary in the Book when she drew aside from her family to an eastern place, taking a veil (to screen herself) from them. Then We sent to her Our spirit, and there appeared to her a well-made man...She said: "When shall I have a boy and no mortal has yet touched me, nor have I been unchaste?"...So she conceived him; then withdrew herself with him to a remote place. And the throes (of childbirth) compelled her to betake herself to the trunk of a palm tree. She said: "Oh, would that I had died before this, and had been a thing quite forgotten!" Then (the child) called out to her from beneath her: "Grieve not...." (19:16-17, 20, 22-24; see also 66:12)

(3) The feeding of the five thousand:

When the disciples said: "O Jesus son of Mary, will your Lord consent to send down to us food from heaven?" He said: "Be careful of (your duty to) Allah, if you are believers." They said: "We desire that we should eat of it and that our hearts should be at rest, and that we may know that you have indeed spoken the truth to us that we may be of the witnesses to it." Jesus the son of Mary said: "O Allah, our Lord! Send down to us food from heaven which should be to us an ever-recurring happiness, to the first of us and to the last of us, and a sign from Thee, and grant us means of subsistence, and Thou art the best of the Providers." Allah said: "Surely I will send it down to you, but whoever shall disbelieve afterwards from among you, surely I will chastise him with a chastisement with which I shall not chastise anyone among the nations." (5:112-115; compare John 6:31-65)

(4) Jesus denies his divine sonship and denies the deity of his mother:

And when Allah will say: "O Jesus son of Mary! Did you say to men, 'Take me and my mother for two gods besides Allah'? He will say: 'Glory be to Thee, it did not befit me that I should say what I had no right to (say). If I had said it, Thou wouldst indeed have known it. Thou knowest what is in my mind, and I do not know what is in Thy mind. Surely Thou art the great Knower of the unseen things.'" (5:116; see also 5:71, 75; 4:171)

(5) The death and ascension of Jesus:

Allah set a seal upon them owing to their unbelief, so they shall not believe
except a few—for their saying: "Surely we have killed the Messiah, Jesus son
of Mary, the apostle of Allah." They did not kill him, nor did they crucify
him, but it appeared to them (like Jesus)...Nay! Allah took him up to Himself.
(4:155-158; a similar idea is credited to Basilides, according to Irenaeus,
Against Heresies 1.24.4: "He [Christ] appeared, then, on earth as a man, to
the nations of these powers, and wrought miracles. Wherefore he did not himself suffer death, but Simon, a certain man of Cyrene, being compelled, bore
the cross in his stead; so that this latter being transfigured by him, that he
might be thought to be Jesus, was crucified, through ignorance and error,
while Jesus himself received the form of Simon, and, standing by, laughed at
them." Trans. from A. Roberts, J. Donaldson, and A. C. Coxe, eds., *The Ante-
Nicene Fathers* [10 vols.; Grand Rapids: Eerdmans, 1951] 1.349)

1301 N. J. Dawood, *The Koran* (Harmondsworth: Penguin Classics, 1956). ET
of the Qur'an.

1302 M. H. Shakir, *Holy Qur'an* (Elmhurst, NY: Tahrike Tarsile Qur'an, 1983).
ET and Arabic text.

N.B.: Author's works are noted with bold numbers. Plain numbers indicate that the scholar is named somewhere in the bibliographical entry. Numbers in parentheses indicate page numbers, not bibliographical entries.

INDEX TO ANCIENT WRITINGS

NEW TESTAMENT TOOLS AND STUDIES

EDITED BY

Bruce M. Metzger, Ph.D., D.D., L.H.D., D.Theol., D.Litt.